THERAPEUTIC DISCOURSE AND

SOCRATIC DIALOGUE

Lying Down Together: Law, Metaphor, and Theology
Milner S. Ball

The Rhetoric of Economics
Donald N. McCloskey

Therapeutic Discourse and Socratic Dialogue
Tullio Maranhão

Heracles' Bow: Essays on the Rhetoric and Poetics of the Law
James Boyd White

Therapeutic Discourse and Socratic Dialogue

BY TULLIO MARANHÃO

THE UNIVERSITY OF WISCONSIN PRESS

Published 1986

The University of Wisconsin Press
114 North Murray Street
Madison, Wisconsin 53715

The University of Wisconsin Press, Ltd.
1 Gower Street
London WC1E 6HA, England

First printing

Printed in the United States of America

For LC CIP information see the colophon

ISBN 0-299-10920-8

For my students, colleagues, and teachers

CONTENTS

ACKNOWLEDGMENTS

I would like to acknowledge grants awarded to me by the Dean of Social Sciences and the Office of the President at Rice University, which allowed me to conclude the study on which this essay is based. I am thankful to Dr. Harold Goolishian and to the Faculty of the Galveston Family Institute for making therapeutic discourse available for my observation. I am grateful for Dr. Otto Kernberg's guidance and for Erika Loutsch's friendship. I am thankful to the members of Scientia at Rice University for giving me the opportunity to lecture on the topic of this book. I am equally thankful to my colleagues in the Rice Circle for accepting to discuss my project to study Socratic dialogue and therapeutic discourse during our seminar of 1983–84. My colleagues in the Department of Anthropology shared an increased burden of teaching and administrative activities during my leave of absence in the Fall of 1984. My deepest recognition to them. Finally, I am greatly indebted to the following people for a stimulating intellectual companionship during the preparation of the manuscript: Bradford P. Keeney, Eugene Holland, Gananath Obeyesekere, George E. Marcus, Ivan Karp, Konstantin Kolenda, Martha Tyler, Michael M. J. Fischer, Robert Lane Kauffmann, Stephen A. Tyler, and Vincent Crapanzano. My greatest debt is to my wife, Amanda M. Seel-Maranhão, for having joined me with unrelenting enthusiasm for the production of this book and sharing the work with me as if it were her own.

INTRODUCTION

Therapeutic discourse is represented here by psychoanalysis and family therapy. In recent times there has been a clamor to free psychoanalysis from tradition, abandoning the old Freudian sexualization of life and the outlook of clinical practice as a technical endeavor. The proponents of innovations want therapists to consider a wider range of motivations for behavior and to conduct the sessions of analysis in more personal and humanistic ways. Family therapy has hitherto presented itself as an antipsychoanalytic reaction. The therapists of this persuasion deny the determinism of intrapsychic forces and the transparency of symbols, treating meaningful actions as messages flowing through communicative channels. However, the community of family therapists has not rid itself of controversy. Some practitioners wish to aim their therapies at models of families, while others claim that the objects of their interventions are communicative matrices with the potential to interlace any groups of people, including the therapeutic system (family and therapist), or the members of a family. These are not the only disagreements in the therapeutic community, nor necessarily the most important ones, but only those which have flared up more glaringly in the two schools of therapy. The superficial and transient questions, nevertheless, reflect more complex issues whose difficulty has so far discouraged debate.

The crucial question to be asked about therapeutic discourse is: What is it that cures? Is it a science of the psyche or a rhetoric of communications? Since every school of therapy that bases treatment on verbal actions can claim a certain degree of success in "treating" its patients, it is delusive to acclaim one method to the exclusion of all others. It is now common practice to include all strategies for treatment under the rubric of "therapy," be it psychoanalysis, gestalt therapy, object relations, ego therapy, or family therapy, among many others. There must be something in the art that brings them all together under the same umbrella. In this essay, focusing on psychoanalysis and on family therapy, we will examine each in its own theory (system of knowledge), in its practice (repertoire of rhetorical maneuvers), and in the way it uses the power hierarchy of the therapeutic interaction.

Psychoanalysis and family therapy are naturally subspecialities in the field of mental health, but therapeutic discourse—that is, the complex of knowledge, power, and rhetoric wielded by the healing social institutions—is more than a profession or art, it is a cultural system invented in European and American societies, shaping the Westerners' worldview at all levels of life, and standing side by side, with its co-cultural systems, such as philosophy, religion, science, and politics. Within the Western cultural heritage these complexes of worldviews and principles for action are rent by similar tensions and puzzles, clearly revealing that they have unfolded in the course of a particular historical experience. Some of the dilemmas are, for instance: can a system of knowledge be imperishable? If not, should we cease to believe in those systems, or diminish the intensity of our beliefs? Are systems of knowledge free from power structures? Can the authority of knowledge defeat the authority of power? And, last but not least, is a refined rhetoric capable of making an unreliable system of knowledge prevail over a reliable one? These are some of the outstanding questions addressing the tottering struggle to integrate theory and practice in therapeutic discourse.

Ours are undeniably times inflamed by a crisis of confidence in discourse, be it religious, political, or therapeutic. The cultural criticism of this historical turning in the Western tradition is divided between those who want to preserve what they regard as the essence of this heritage, and those who are willing to give the coup de grace to what they see as a dying tradition. The former defend the products of modernity in philosophy, art, politics, science, and therapy, although accepting that some criticism and purge are in order; the latter cry out for an overall renewal, they are the proclaimers of postmodernity, who set out to shake up and whisk off old beliefs. Typical of these times of cultural transition is a staunch adherence to that which is under the threat of dissolution. Controversy within the therapeutic community is not a new fact under the sun; what is unusual is that the atmosphere of revisionism is now widespread, and may produce radical changes either towards revolutionary innovation or obdurate conservatism. Of course, it is also possible to steer away from both extremes.

Therapeutic discourse treats existential problems represented in verbal actions through verbal actions. Here we have a tearing dilemma: is the representation of reality in language reconcilable with the intervention over reality by means of language? We find three strategies trying to accomplish this integration: narrative memory, dialogical construction of reality, and textual congealing of knowledge. In the narrative memory—typical, for example, of the ancient epic poems—the world is what the storyteller remembers, and the authority of his tales resides in his memory and in his social recognition as a narrator. The dialogue construes reality through argument, and the picture of the world established as true is that which yields consensus among the discussants. The written text dispenses with memory and delays, at times even forbidding, the flow of dialogue. The cultural movements of philosophy, religion, science, politics, and therapy not only have tried to integrate representation with action, but have also incorporated, in their efforts, the three strategies or media of narrative, dialogue, and text. Therapeutic discourse is faced with all these challenges: the patient's narrative, the cure based on dialogue, and the importance of texts in training and furthering therapeutic knowledge; the meaning of what therapist and patient say versus the impact caused by the act of saying.

When Freud abandoned his "seduction theory" he also struck a blow against the truthfulness of narratives within therapeutic discourse. His alternative was not the dialogical mode, because treatment is not based on consensual conversations aiming at agreement. The therapist works with a blueprint of the psyche, or of the clinical interaction, or of the family, or of the communicative matrix, and these models are more akin to texts than to dialogues or narratives. Yet therapy continues to be a verbal art, poised, nevertheless, over this smoldering effervescence of the three conflicting media of discourse. What should therapists do? Should they adopt one mode of discourse to the exclusion of the others and attempt to integrate representation and action within it as Socrates did?

This is not a new dilemma in the Western heritage. It erupted in precisely these terms twenty-five centuries ago when the Sophist philosophers denounced truth and knowledge in the Attic culture, proposing a stronger rhetoric of persuasion as an alternative to the elusive representation of reality and controversial expression of opinions. Socrates agreed with their diagnostic of the times, but proposed a rather different solution. He claimed that although knowledge could not be encompassed by any system of representation (that is, by any mimetic copy of reality), it did indeed exist, deeply embedded in man's soul. His dialectic dialogues were the means to unravel this absolute virtue from the human soul, a virtue which, refractory to representation, was now knowledge *(sophia)*, now goodness *(agathon)*, both concepts remaining carefully farflung and undefined. The message of the Socratic testimony is that the solution to this dilemma cannot be sought through the elimination of either representation or action.

The Socratic riddle is dazzlingly similar to that of therapeutic discourse: the struggle to integrate knowledge, power, and rhetoric into a unity is as frustrating as the struggle to delete one or two members of this trinity and arrive at a consistent wholeness. Naturally, this is an epistemological puzzle, but its longstanding presence in the heritage beginning with the Greeks in classical times, and growing through the European and American societies, allied to the fact that it is not present in quite the same way in other equally old civilizations of the Middle East, Asia, and the Orient, makes it, on the whole, a product of the Western cultural tradition. The words here entrap us into the belief that the world is a collection of cultures each with its problems and puzzles. That, however, is not what I wish to imply. On the contrary, I would like this to be understood as a statement which cannot claim universality before it has reached a consensual basis.

This essay is divided into three parts. In the first, the problems of therapeutic discourse are discussed; in the second, I analyze Socratic dialogues, and the third part contains the conclusion. Chapter 1 presents Freud's metapsychology as the foundation of therapeutic practice based on the interpretation of symbols. In chapter 2, I examine recent suggestions for the reformulation of psychoanalysis, such as Merton Gill's proposal that psychoanalysts should devote more attention to the analysis of transference than to the interpretation of symbols deeply concealed in memory. Chapter 3 brings us to family therapy as practiced by Salvador Minuchin and his "structuralist" school, designing models of families and therapeutic procedures appropriate to dealing with them. The strategic and systemic therapists are those who envision therapy together with all other interaction situations, as communicative matrices, and develop approaches to dealing with their patients from this perspective. This is the subject matter of chapter 4. In chapter 5, I compare psychoanalysis and family therapy, characterizing the essence of therapeutic discourse as I see it, seizing cultural issues within the Western heritage. Chapter 6 introduces the second part devoted to the study of Socratic dialogues. We begin with the question of representation versus action, or mimesis (e.g., the copy of reality) and methexis (e.g., the reorganization of the categories with which we try to portray reality). In chapter 7, the discussion turns to the Sophist claim that rhetoric could resolve the wrenching controversy in which Attic culture was steeped, as well as to Socrates' reaction to the Sophists' educational program. In Plato's dialogues, Socrates is portrayed as the genuine educator, but his pedagogy combines philosophy, politics, education, and therapy. This is discussed in chapter 8. Chapter 9 addresses the main ingredient of the dialogues: consensus. It is through an unrelenting maintenance of a consensual basis that Socrates conducts what I am calling his "therapy for the soul," that is a dialogical questioning, destined to awaken enlightenment and to avoid antagonism. In chapter

10, I conclude my main discussion of Socrates' attempt to integrate representation and action with an analysis of two of the dialogues, the *Meno* and the *Parmenides*. Chapter 11 brings together Socratic dialogues and therapeutic discourse, focusing on the central issues of the argument, and chapter 12 concludes with the discussion of the theme cutting across all cultural movements in the Western heritage, the unity and fragmentation of knowledge, power, and rhetoric, which is examined in this essay from the point of view of Socratic dialogue and therapeutic discourse.

This is an essay on cultural criticism written from an anthropological point of view. Our experience of our own heritage has a numbing effect over our discriminatory capacities. We are too close, experiencing it as participants, and the preconceptual categories we use to filter the world are those of our own cultural milieu. The consequence of this lack of distance from our heritage and of prejudicial discriminations is that we learn to think about philosophy as a "science" of knowledge, and about therapy as a "science" of treatment, among other beliefs in our cosmology. The anthropological experience has the virtue of shaking up the unproblematic view of our own world. I do not expect that the philosopher or therapist reader will have sympathy for my casting of Socrates as a cultural character, and of the community of therapists, ethnographically speaking, as the tribe of my studies. Were I to compare the Vedas with Ayurvedic medicine, that reader would not be disquieted, since he would have no reason to resist the examination of those discourse traditions from without. But my aim is to arouse some discomfort, and look with strangeness at Socratic dialogue and therapeutic discourse, as something exotic.

PART ONE

THE RHETORIC OF INSIGHT:

INSIGHT OR ILLUSION?

1 THE PHYSIOLOGY OF INSIGHT

*Language disguises thought. So much so, that from the
outward form of the clothing it is impossible to infer the
form of the thought beneath it, because the outward form of
the clothing is not designed to reveal the form of the body,
but for entirely different purposes.*
L. Wittgenstein

*The transformation of the latent dream-thoughts into the
manifest dream-content deserves all our attention, since it
is the first instance known to us of psychical material being
changed over from one mode of expression to another, from
a mode of expression which is immediately intelligible to
us to another which we can only come to understand with
the help of guidance and effort, though it too must be
recognized as a function of our mental activity.*
S. Freud

It is difficult to overestimate the importance of psychotherapy in our present experience of the Western cultural tradition. We
like to trace our heritage back to the Greeks, see it Romanized, brought
to the New World by colonial Europe, and finally made into a commodity and transformed into a worldwide asset. Psychotherapy is a
Western rhetorical invention that blossomed precisely at the apogee of
the Euro-American domination of the world. For that reason it would be
natural to expect that it should be one of the most likely arts of suasion
to be exported by the West or used by it in its quest for domination, but it
is neither. This is in great part due to the nature of its rhetorical appeal,
which does not contain any claims for its widespread acceptance.
Psychotherapy is not the object of any organized propaganda effort by
the community of psychotherapists to expand their clientele, in sharp
contrast, for example, to religious or political communities. The psychotherapeutic is a community of professionals, but their craft, although a
technique like any other, is founded on an intellectual claim as ambitious as those of religion and politics.

For psychotherapists since Freud, the world cannot be divided into
the mentally or emotionally sick and the healthy, although this has been

a tempting view. Freud cast the frame of mind with which to regard psychopathology: every human being is the ontogenetic carrier of the seeds of the Oedipus complex, or of warped narcissistic formations sowed in his or her soul by phylogeny. The consequence of this stance is that the knowledge of what psychopathology is, and of how to deal with it, does not create a different rank for psychotherapists, does not divide mankind into two categories, the healthy and the unhealthy, those who know and those who do not, those who have faith and the unfaithful, or those who are conscious of the human drama of life and those who are alienated. This places psychotherapy in a very special position in relation to its co-cultural rhetorical systems: religion, philosophy, science, and politics. Refusing to have a division between insiders and outsiders, psychotherapy circumvents the tantalizing problems of the integration between theory and practice. The psychotherapeutic discourse does not move individuals from one sector of society to another, for there are no socially recognizable differences between those who were psychoanalyzed and those who were not. The therapeutic process is personal, amenable to acknowledgment only by the individual who underwent it and those who share his intimate life. It follows that the demands laid over practice cannot be too overbearing, because the practitioners are as fallible as those upon whom they practice, and the mastership of psychotherapeutic discourse does not make them any better human beings. The condition sine qua non for psychotherapy to work is that its discourse be hinged on a dialogical situation bringing face-to-face the therapist, who has some skills and is unrelated to the client, and the patient, who has the wish to do therapy and relates to the analyst as a professional. What this discourse does cannot be accomplished through a written text, or any other medium different from dialogues, which are verbal, immediate, and total to the exclusion of any subject matter: it cannot also take place in any context other than that of the relation between a professional and the client. It is no wonder that psychoanalysis has recently been invoked as a model of interpretation for hermeneutics by Ricoeur and Habermas.[1] Psychoanalysis would have overcome the Western split between theory and practice, between systems of knowledge and their application, interpretive strategies, and texts on the one hand and interpreters, and authors on the other, by welding these poles together with clearly identified beings: the analyst and the analysand, the theory of emotions and the emotional problems, the patient's narrative and the analyst's interpretation. The treatment or practice is a process of compromise between the analyst and his analytical framework, the analysand and his self-representation, and finally between these two actors and their representations. It proceeds by displacements, exploring the differences between selves and roles, persons and representational schemes. The analyst's approach can neither be foreclosed before the analysand's text is presented, nor can the latter be unravelled independently of the analyst's interpretation. Such a portrayal of psychoanalysis which serves so well as a springboard for hermeneutic reflection is, however, an ideal picture. After one hundred years of psychoanalysis, many interpretive schemas are foreclosed a long time beforehand and mechanically applied by the analysts, while the patients' discourse also suffers from the strictures of preformation.[2] On the other hand, because we have gathered and rendered explicit the foreclosing strictures of psychoanalytic discourse, we have enabled ourselves to probe new territories of spontaneity. This is precisely the case of the two landmarks of therapeutic discourse we will discuss in this essay: the analysis of transference and family therapy.

Philip Rieff has shown quite insightfully that Freud was intent on creating a rhetoric of persuasion alternative to Christianity. While the Christian preacher appealed to faith and tried to persuade through exemplary testimony, the psychoanalyst struck his interlocutor's consciousness with insight and worked toward dispelling any expectations developed toward him as a life witness. For Freud, the rhetoric of insight would be more attuned to the modern world of science and reason than the rhetoric of faith. He wanted a world without god and religion, because these beliefs stood for what man ignored and thus feared. The Freudian message was in sharper contrast with religion and, therefore, had a stronger appeal to an intellectual milieu whose underpinning religious morality had been washed away by the waves of evolutionism, science, and revolutionary politics. Morality had come to be regarded as a religious epiphenomenon which would have run its course. Naturally, in the beginning of the psychoanalytic movement, there was resistance to Freud's ideas, but these initial difficulties were relished in the complete triumph of the therapeutic.[3] In this substitution of psychoanalysis for religion, Freud's metapsychology replaced dogma, self-scrutiny replaced the belief in salvation, and the unconscious replaced mystery.

The impact of the therapeutic has become terribly decisive over our lives for three reasons. First, psychotherapy provides us with explanations about our lives at all levels, from the interior of subjectivity to the exterior of culture. Second, it introduced an institutionally established practice in which the critique of the individual's life does not have to be separated from society and from culture, and therefore every session of psychotherapy has the potential for being an act in social and cultural criticism. Third, the psychotherapeutic discourse enlarged our repertoire of maneuvers to transform states of affairs. The freeing of ourselves from the net of personality—in the postreligious and therapeutic world we are no longer the subdued objects of a personality type—added to the liberation arrived at in other quarters: that we could also free ourselves from language, society, and culture. Naturally, these different modes of discourse—therapeutic, linguistic, sociological, and anthropological—entertain the possibility of circumscribing their objects, and thereby create conditions for us to think about ourselves independently of the psyche, language, society, and culture. The reflection upon man's existence in these disciplines has two consequences: first, that man's self is perhaps a metaphysical entity; second, that the very existence of these specialized discourses bear witness to the fact that we are still entrapped. In facing these issues with regard to psychotherapeutic discourse, a series of questions hasten to mind: Is the therapeutic discourse related to others or unique? In other words, can the objective pursued by psychotherapy be achieved by other means? Is there a psychotherapeutic discourse capable of integrating all schools of therapy? What is the relationship of theory and practice in this type of discourse? And, finally: What is the influence of the therapeutic over our worldview? My answer is that these modes of discourse replicate a cultural theme endeared to us since the Greeks. I will show this link through Socrates' philosophy. Consequently, yes, they are related; yes, there is an umbrella psychotherapeutic discourse; and, finally, this discourse constitutes our worldview, insofar as it is an expression of a certain aspect of our cultural heritage which I will discuss through this essay, and particularly in chapters 11 and 12. The question of theory and practice will be the object of discussion in chapter 2 as we examine the analysis of transference. It will be discussed again in chapters 3 and 4 apropos of family therapy.

In Freud's own intellectual development, he first thought that the events narrated by the patients had actually taken place in their lives and the role of the analyst was to unveil the traumatic experiences covered by a thick layer of inhibitions. Later on he realized that the narrated events were not necessarily facts, or that whether they had or had not taken place did not matter, because their importance surfaced in fantasy and not in biography. From the concern with fantasy it was only a short leap to develop a theory of the mind. Side by side with these developments, Freud worked out a theory of symbol formation and of symbol interpretation. He found out that symbolization was not a process of representation alone, a mimetic copy of experiences of the mind, but that it fulfilled some methetic functions; that is, it organized those experiences in a certain way, and what is more, served as an alternative to the experiences themselves. In this early part of his writings, then, the same mechanism that creates the distorted symbols, the symbols of fantasy rather than the symbols of reality, creates the symbols of culture. Later, Freud grounded culture on a loftier bedrock, because like the ego it was not only a defensive response to the sexual and aggressive drives, the triggerers of everything, but it was itself a drive, a drive to self-preservation. Thus, culture earned ontological status in Freud's cosmology, although this refinement was only fully developed later on by followers such as Erik Erikson.[4]

What is interesting to us here is that culture, whether regarded as a dike against the overflowings of the id, or as a drive itself as atavistic as sex and aggression, is a permanent object for interpretation, and furthermore, once interpreted it can change. Freud's work comprises two major propositions: first, a metapsychology from which the hypotheses about the functioning of the mind, and the processes of symbol and culture formation are derived; second, a theory and technique of interpretation founded on the rhetoric of insight and also springing from the metapsychology. The symbol is a dummy replacing an affect that had its flow thwarted by censorship. The strong emotion which was repressed remains in a state of latency, and every time it is spurred by experience, the symbol is repeated. The patient camouflages the affect preventing it from becoming conscious and resisting any attempts to produce that result. Resistance takes the form of rationalization through metasymbolization. Suppose a patient represses the feeling of "hatred towards the father," replacing it by the symbol "hostility against every form of authority." His analyst denounces the maneuver, leading the patient through defense mechanisms to rationalize his hostility against authority at a higher level of symbolization, transforming it into a discourse against domination. The analyst uses technique to make the patient expose his symbols, and then, combining insight with the theory of the psyche, interprets the symbol establishing its connection with the suspected affect encapsulated in an unpleasant experience. The analyst knows when he is right because the correct insight leads the patient to release affects related to the interpreted fact. The problem naturally is how do we identify these affects, because they are always clad in experience.

Freud's rhetoric of insight fulfills its goal of persuasion by having the therapist lead the patient to realize something about his history which was lost from consciousness. The therapist does not argue or reason with the patient, as Socrates would with his interlocutors, nor does he enjoin and preach as a Christian missionary would. But, similarly to these two other rhetorical traditions, the object of persuasion is already inside the interlocutor. For Socrates the truth lay in every man's soul, and for the Christians faith is potentially in the heart of every man. For

Freud every symbol is amenable to reaching consciousness. The great difference between psychoanalysis on one hand and Socratic dialogue or Christian preaching on the other, is that in the rhetoric of insight the therapist argues with the patient from the point of view of the latter's discourse, while the Christian and the philosopher have a predetermined repertoire of subject matters for discussion, and act in an outwardly persuasive manner. These two other rhetorical traditions also experimented with indirect modes of persuasion, like psychoanalysis, through examples and testimony, the narration of myths and parables, but they made the coherence between word and deed into a major pillar of their suasive appeal, and as a consequence developed enhanced discursive practices aiming more at resolving the contradictions between the speaker's words and deeds than at persuading the interlocutors. The next inevitable consequences were that they became self-reflexive, and while philosophy remained contented with its withdrawal from the world, Christianity, in addition to the self-justificatory discourse about coherence between words and deeds, also developed enjoining types of discourse like sermons and other forms of passionate oratory. Psychoanalysis is remarkable because of the paucity of means it employs to persuade its interlocutors.[5] The secret of Freud's success in developing such an economical rhetoric of persuasion lies in his theory of symbols which he worked out side by side with the notion of insight.

Today Freud's theory of neurotic symbols is regarded with skepticism and advances in psychoanalysis usually mean departures from it, but somehow we continue to pay tribute to it and treat it with intellectual curiosity. This may be in great part due to the fact that Freud's indelible legacy, that is, the treatment of patients with existential problems through a discursive and dialogical practice, was generated in the womb of his theory of symbols. Before we understand how the therapeutic discourse of a psychoanalyst can be efficacious we have to turn to Freud's ideas about the origin and function of symbols in the human mind.[6]

Freud interprets the meaning of signs by means of an explanation about how they are transformed from the denotative, e.g., "hat" meaning the piece of garment used to cover the head, into the connotative, e.g., "hat" meaning penis. He proceeds with a strategy that opposes that of hermeneutic philosophers, who establish their interpretive viewpoint outside and in front of the text or system of meaningful action. Freud places himself behind the meaningful actions and, instead of interpreting their signification, employs them as heuristic devices illustrating his theory of psychological conduct. (Paul Ricoeur calls this interpretive stance a hermeneutics of suspicion.)[7] Such a procedure inevitably leads Freud into a classification of actions and representations as normal and pathological. Thus, he uses the word "symbol" in the sense of a "disguised representation of latent thoughts."[8] Hats are symbols of the male genitals; being run over by a car is a symbol of sexual intercourse; buildings, stairs, and shafts are additional masks for the genitals; people themselves represent male genitals; while landscapes stand for the female organ, he suggests.[9] In his discussion of cases, however, the idea of a dictionary of neurotic symbols proves to be nonviable, because the patients' use of signs is flexible and often even creative. On the other hand, there are obvious limitations imposed by culture upon the choice and use of actions and representations as neurotic symbols,[10] although individuals can always criticize cultural symbols, draw on private symbols, and even lead symbolic revolutions within culture. Freud is always more interested in the mechanism of symbol use than in the intrinsic meaning of symbols. He explains, for example, that the reluctance of the obsessive neurotic patients to lift their hats to greet acquaintances in the street, although related to the concern with initiating the salutation and thereby taking an inferior position, is ultimately founded on the fear of castration. The consequence of this potential multiplicity of meanings for symbols is that there cannot be a one-to-one relation between the denotative and connotative meanings of the conduct.[11] Freud provides lists of symbols with their respective meanings, but nevertheless cautions his readers: "Interpretation based on a knowledge of symbols is not a technique which can replace or compete with the associative one."[12]

The interpretive stance of psychoanalysis, however, does not dissolve the fact that there are chains of meaningful action which cannot be explained by the economy of desire and repression. Therefore, if on one hand genetic interpretations encroach on the formation of symbols, on the other hand hermeneutic interpretations, that is, those carried out from an exterior vantage ground, emphasize the speaker's address and reception of the interlocutor's symbols. Freud circumvents the exterior side of texts (systems of meaningful action), and casts his lot in the mechanics of the psyche. It is, however, inevitable that the dialectic between desire and repression produces cultural symbols, amenable to hermeneutic interpretation as well as to psychoanalytic scrutiny. In the brief description which will follow, I take Freud's ideas about symptoms one step further, and treat them as sketches of a theory of symbol formation.

In the early phase of his writing (1894–1896) Freud cast his psychology as a psychopathology, that is, as a science of neurotic as opposed to healthy symbols. But after *The Interpretation of Dreams* (1900) his theory became a psychology of everyday life in which all symbols were amenable to analysis. Towards the end of his writing career he even developed an effort to ground his theory of symbols on the wider foundations of culture.[13]

The symbol formation processes in Freud's writings can be classified in five categories. (1) Some events remain in memory as a potential for symbolization. In some cases the experience of these events will be separated from the affects (intensification of the emotions) which become congealed, occupying the place of a symbol as a behavioral symptom. A second possibility is that in which the experience itself becomes the symbol. In a third possibility a symbol emerges by displacement, a symbol deprived of evident links with either the experience or the affect. (2) The second category of symbol formation is that of drives (impetuses to do things), which for Freud were of two kinds: sexual and aggressive. Drives run into the barrier of defenses and as a result what should have been behaviorally acted out is repressed and thereby becomes a symbol. (3) Another source of repression against drives leading to symbol formation is that represented by reality constraints (the wishes which are impossible from a realistic point of view). (4) Self-censure is another type of constraint curbing drives and producing symbols. (5) The final constraint exercised against drives stems from the social pressure inherent in every cultural environment. We will examine each of these formative processes along the chronological perspective in which they were formulated in Freud's writings, in the order listed above.

The Early Beginnings: A Detective's Search and a Talking Cure

Freud's patients came from the bourgeoisie of Vienna at the turning of the century, and the cultural cast of their existential plight influenced the initial shaping of psychoanalysis. These patients were diagnosed as hysterical, phobic, obsessive, and paranoid. Many were women who had suffered sexual molestation in their childhood. Freud explained that the traumatizing event had been so painful that its intellectual representation became suppressed. Only the affects had remained and were acted out in the form of hysterical symptoms: unjustified crying, sudden and convulsive changes in facial expression, excessively low or high voice, among other features. These, in turn, were acts blocking the true expression of the traumatic affects. Symptoms with this genesis were stereotypes, that is, dispositions to act which do not find any conscious representation. We cannot talk about these dispositions as being part of a memory because they have no intellectual content or linguistic expression. They are like behavioral leanings, covered from the intellect, flowing in the psyche without being represented in the mind. With the obsessive-compulsive patients the painful memory of the traumatic event again had been suppressed, but the affect had become symbolized by displacement or transposition. These patients revealed extreme and exacting concern and were meticulous about the finicky tasks of everyday life. The obsession for precision was the symbol through which the anxiety effects of the traumatic experience were played out. The paranoid patients had interrupted the continuity of both the experience and the affect and developed a symbol at odds with the facts of their biography. It is interesting to notice that in the recent developments of psychoanalytic theory there are no absolute biographies, and the patient's history is a compromise between drives, experiences, and the shaping forces of ego, the superego, and of reality of which the interaction between the analyst and the analysand is a fundamental part. Freud, in his early groping for psychoanalytic theory, was looking for a classification of the causes of neurosis and symptoms, and trying to correlate both domains through a comprehensive explanation.

In this initial stage Freud believed that his patients had suffered a concrete trauma of sexual molestation and thus therapy consisted in searching for this fact, much like a detective, through the person's blurred memory. The way to pursue this treatment consisted in making the patient talk by asking questions. One of the first and most famous patients in the psychoanalytic literature, Anna O., called the method a "talking cure," as she realized that being able to talk about her painful experiences allayed her condition and made her feel better. Joseph Breuer, Freud's teacher and later collaborator, had begun to hypnotize his patients and lead them to talk about their painful experiences, and had noticed that after each session the symptoms were reduced. Freud realized the importance of talking as a healing process, but preferred conscious speech to reports induced by hypnosis. He encouraged his patients to talk about anything that came to their minds in the same way that a passenger in a carriage describes the landscape he sees through the window. In this practice there was an irrefutable element of confession as the neurotic, like the sinner, by virtue of talking about the facts afflicting him, freed himself from their spell.

Sex and Symbolic Narratives

Having learned that the seductive episodes were not true, Freud came to the conclusion that they could only be fantasies standing for something that could not be accounted for by the individual's experiences, but which must come from a more general psychological mechanism common to all. He also started to do self-analysis and apply to the cases he was observing in others the intuitions about his own experience as testing hypotheses. He wrote that, "If hysterical subjects trace back their symptoms to traumas that are fictitious, then the new fact [new for him at the time] which emerges is precisely that they create such scenes in *phantasy*, and this psychical reality requires to be taken into account alongside practical reality."[14]

While in Freud's earlier assumption the victim of the trauma made an effort to forget the event, in this new formulation a psychological force, the drive, became blocked by a repressing move, thus the physiology of neurosis happened in the inner psyche, not in the external world. In addition, the patient did not have to be necessarily the victim anymore, but could be the victimizer in fantasy, producing the same symptomatic behavior. The drive was basically sexual, not genital but erotic along very broad lines. The patient, however, needed to have had an actual sexual experience which triggered the already repressed drive creating an unpleasant feeling. The sexual experience could be, for example, body playing among children, singled out by the patient as a bad thing, although not yet represented as such. That child had experienced the pangs of pain, but had not learned why or what the meaning of his impressions was. There was, then, an originally repressed sexual drive, an experience bringing that psychic event to the realm of feelings, and the formation of a symbol, ambiguous in nature because it had been forged to express something it could not mean, and therefore meant something else. A stereotype could also be formed and remain as such evolving as inadequate behavior or be converted into a symbol. Both stereotypes and symbols, however much belying the true experience, fulfilled an alleviating function by decathecting (letting pressure out) the tabooed representation. The decathecting function, however, was not sufficient to eliminate the problem because it did not remove the stopgap constituted by repression. It was only an escape valve. At this point in the development of his theory, Freud used interchangeably the words "repression" and "defense" in referring to the operation of suppression of an experience's representation.

An interesting consequence of this aspect of his theory of symbol formation is that the unconscious emanations can only be known because they crystallize in symbols to which consciousness has access. Freud writes that "the physician cannot learn of these unconscious processes until they have produced some effect upon consciousness which can be communicated or observed."[15] But since these two processes, the conscious and the unconscious, are totally different, and the symbol furthermore is not an index of the unconscious fact, but a disguise of it, Freud maintains that the analyst must "proceed by *inference*."[16] The psychoanalytic interpretation, then, does not proceed through reasoned argument in the Socratic sense, but through *inferences*, a word probably used to characterize a mode of knowledge different from the science of Freud's day, although it means deduction in the scientific sense, because the subject matter under study, products of the unconscious, has a reality very different from that researched by the natural sciences. Thus, consciousness for the psychoanalyst is a scaffolding not to be mistaken for the building represented by the unconscious. The link between the two that the physician and the patient pursue together is the insight.

There are two important consequences, for our essay, to be derived from this move from the detective's search of actual facts of seduction to the consideration of these facts as fantasies. First, what remained unaltered in the move was the fact that the present is explained by resort to the past. Second, the patient's discourse gained a different relevance, it was no longer a "talking cure" but a window into consciousness through which the unconscious could be inferred. Both consequences converge to emphasizing the patient's narrative in the psychoanalytic process, because it is a form of past reconstruction and a picture of the patient's consciousness.

Dream Narratives

After the study of symptomatic symbols Freud turned to dreams because they have a texture very similar to that of the neurotic symbols, but he suspected that they probably worked differently. Dreams, for example, are noted to be illogical and incoherent, with the same character becoming different people in the same sequence of the dream, or with objects being transformed into people and other paradoxes of the kind. Dreams also convey a very strong sense of reality because of their stressed visual aspect striking consciousness in repose. They seem contemporaneous and create the feeling that the events dreamt about are truly experienced. Furthermore, dreams transform exterior stimuli into dream sensations, for example, when the actual discomfort of being on the edge of the bed enters the dream as the fright of being about to fall from a cliff. Finally, the materials of a dream are events of everyday life, mostly recent, but also remotely past.

The surrealistic aspect of dreams is derived from the fact that they are gagged on both ends of conscious and unconscious (a description of the topography of the mind follows in the next section). On the side of the unconscious, the "manifest dream" is only a symbol of something else which Freud called "latent dream thoughts." On the side of the conscious, when we wake up our dreams have generally been forgotten, or we only remember fragments, and when we try to put them into speech it feels as if we were imparting to them a coherence they lacked. At this end of the mind, dreams are censored by defenses protecting the ego. What is left of a dream is naturally not very encouraging for the exercise of interpretation. Freud, however, used this limitation to strengthen his approach to interpret dreams. Instead of trying to reconstruct dreams following the logic of verbal narratives, he chose to look at the nature of the fragments, what was remembered and what was left out but could still be retrieved, what were the dominant themes in a series of dreams, where their sequences were broken, and what kinds of bizarre transformations of reality they produced. He looked at dreams as having their own narrative structure. In addition, he maintained that the interpretation of dreams should be linked to the person's biography. This set of propositions for the study of dreams today seems straightforward and uninspiring, but probably because of the influence of Freud's approach which shaped our view of dreams. The first chapter of _The Interpretation of Dreams_ is devoted to a review of the current (1900) literature on the subject matter, and shows that had those notions prevailed, we would have a rather different idea of dreams, but today the then embattled claims of Freud seem to be common sense.

Dreams are like symptomatic symbols. They represent an experience submitted to the restraints of defense such as an unsatisfied wish. But unlike symptomatic symbols their representation is vivid and more faithful to the represented material because it takes place within the safe confines of consciousness at rest. Like symbols, they also function as an escape valve by dispelling the excitation cathected by the experience and thereby allowing the person to sleep. But again, like symbols, they do not overcome defenses, their effect is only palliative.

Freud began on the track of pursuing actual episodes of seduction, then shifted his research to the fantasies contained in the patients' narratives and, then, looking at dreams, he developed a technique of interpretation which was to be largely applied in psychoanalysis to all symbols and stereotypes. This technique consisted in looking for clues and fragments in the patient's discourse that could produce a new understanding of the situation in relation to that explanation the patient had held. The new understanding could enlist at least two powerful appeals in its rhetoric of persuasion: the impact of the unexpected interpretation and its solid grounding on a plausible reorganization of the patient's life history.

The Topography of the Mind

As we have seen so far, two components have remained constant in Freud's theory throughout its successive modifications: the importance of the process of symbol formation, and their sexual motivation. Now we will turn to a third component of his metapsychology introduced in chapter 7 of *The Interpretation of Dreams:* the topographic picture of the mind. To stay within Freud's own metaphor, let us suppose that the mind is like a telescope with each of its parts being a lens. At the end receiving the images, there is a perceptual apparatus composed of the sensory activities; at the other end is the motor outlet. Next to the perceptual end come the lenses of memory of which there are several, since we have differential capacities and degrees of storing that which penetrates our perceptions. The association of ideas consists in the movement of a trace from one memory compartment to another, where it becomes linked to an item in that storage area. Now suppose that the ideas flowing through the telescope are of three different qualities: conscious, preconscious, and unconscious.[17] The unconscious ideas cannot become conscious before they are preconscious. There are two kinds of preconscious ideas, those that cannot be immediately retrieved, such as the name of a person or a telephone number because they are encumbered behind a clutter of memories, and those whose inaccessibility is protected by defenses. Symbols flow through this system towards the motor end, and have potential to be transformed from preconscious into conscious ideas. Dreams flow in the opposite direction, and are eliminated through the perceptual end as dream sensations, leaving the person's sleep unperturbed. The reason invoked by Freud to support this claim is that dreams do not operate as ideas, but more as hallucinations. The symbols flowing from the memories forward in the direction of the motor outlet have potential to change from unconscious to preconscious, and then to conscious. In wakening life, traces of symbols like dreams may move backwards in what is characterized as regression, but unlike dreams they are not hallucinatory. "During the day there is a continuous current from the Pcpt [perceptual end] system flowing in the direction of motor activity,"[18] writes Freud, a process absent at night when the flow takes the opposite direction.

The status of symbols may be changed according to the energy that may enter them as "attention cathexis," for example, giving them dynamism to progress towards consciousness. They may also be decathected and released as motor behavior without reflection. Wishes are the main source of cathexis for symbols traversing the mind. Repression is the obstacle in their path. The peculiarity of the mind's topography resides in that it does not harbor symbols which stay put. Every experience and every wish has to surface, either by being remembered and made conscious, or by being spelled out and repeated. Wishes and experiences can only vanquish if they are made conscious in a complete way, or fully acted out. But they stumble on repression, are then represented by symptoms, and therefore yield to the unrelenting drive to be expressed through repetition. The patient repeats the neurotic symptoms. The function of the therapist is to place himself in a position trustworthy enough for the patient to repeat toward him. He has an expert knowledge of the patient's life acquired in a careful and informed listening which places him on a very special position among the patient's other relations in the world. The treatment's strategy consists in culling the drive or the experience out of the repetitive behavior (generally verbal) from the patient's reconstructed biography. This process is known as transference, in the sense that the patient is encouraged to transfer the symptoms to the therapist. What triggers the entire process is the shocking encounter between the patient's internal reality, which needs to be brought to fruition, and the reality of the external world. The psychoanalytic treatment, as envisioned by Freud, is an adaptation between the two. It can begin at any stage of integration and can also end at any point.

Freud defines transference as "an intense emotional relationship between the patient and the analyst which is not to be accounted for by the actual situation,"[19] arising in every analytic treatment and inevitably substituting for the patient's desire to be cured. He compares it to the "suggestibility" developed in hypnosis, and attributes it to the special "rapport" emerging in a close relationship such as the psychoanalytic. This relationship, nevertheless, is characterized by an effort on the part of the analyst to lead the analysand to replace the experience of the interaction as intimacy by a rational representation of his biography. In Freud's writings, most references to transference focus on therapeutic technique rather than on psychological mechanisms of the ego. Transference is almost always regarded either as an obstacle to analysis when associated to resistance, or as a facilitating process, the very staple upon which psychoanalysis feeds itself. The affection developed by the patient towards his analyst prompts him to eagerly seek to associate ideas, an endeavor which will eventually make him aware of his difficulties, thereby curing him.

In summing up the history of the psychoanalytic movement, Freud writes that initially the physician's task was to "discover the unconscious material" and interpret it for the patient. Interpretation, however, was not enough to accomplish the cure. Thus analysts realized that they must lead their patients "to confirm the analyst's construction" with recollections of their own memory. Even this was not enough, because some memories were irretrievable, and since the patient could not remember, "He was obliged to *repeat* the repressed material as a contemporary experience instead of, as the physician would prefer to see, *remembering* it as something belonging to the past."[20] The history of the psychoanalytic movement, therefore, according to Freud, was a passage from the conception of symbols as meaningful texts to symbols as meaningful actions. If the first stage opened the procedure to the interpretation of a narrative focusing on the past, the second presented psychoanalysis at least as an interpretation of the present (repetition), and perhaps as a dialogical or multivoiced exchange, aiming not as much at the interpretation of symbols as at the resolution of a conflict expressed in the here and now of the therapeutic interaction. The latter phase of psychoanalysis pointed to the analysis of transference. But Freud regarded transference, as I contended in the foregoing discussion, in rather ambiguous terms, either as the venue of treatment, or as an ancillary force of resistance, an ally of repression which helped keep the deeply concealed meanings of action beyond the reach of consciousness. The analysis of transference for him could not become a goal in and of itself, it was a complementary procedure within the analyst's struggle against resistance. The psychoanalytic treatment, however much contaminated by the "present-ness" of the interaction, was indeed an excavation of the past only rendered more difficult by the patient's compulsive repetition towards the analyst. Cure was not to be obtained by means of rhetorical maneuvers, by means of the actions relating to the here and now of the analytic interaction, but through consciousness, that is, the rational knowledge of the past. Cure was reflection, not action.

We have briefly reviewed three items in Freud's metapsychology: the sexual motivation of behavior and of symbols, the centrality of symbols in the human psyche, and the topography of the mind. In addition, we discussed two steps in the process of symbol formation: the struggle between memory and events and between drives and defenses. Now we turn to a fourth important component in Freud's metapsychology, the theory of drives, which will also shed light on the process of symbol formation, as drives run into ego defenses, superego's self-reproach, and reality constraints.

Drives and the Persuasiveness of Insight

It was seen in the preceding section that two entities flow through the mind, traces of memory or symbols and dreams. Now, there is a third entity in that traffic, the wishes. There are wishes that can be promptly recalled into consciousness, such as the wish that a certain day were sunny for an outing that did not materialize, wishes which are repressed remaining preconscious, such as the self-censored wish for hostility against one's parents, and finally wishes deeply seated in the unconscious, those of a sexual or aggressive nature. As it can be noticed, a wish is only recognized as such when it is frustrated, for if it is satisfied, it can no longer be classified as a wish. If the child attacks the parent, or the sexual desire is satisfied, the wish is dispelled. Wishes are then forces generated within the psyche independently of external inputs.

The explanation of human behavior grounded exclusively on sexual and aggressive drives was limiting because it failed to account for different attitudes such as aesthetic contemplation and political action, for example, reducing them to the more "physical" drives and thereby overlooking their abstract creative power. These other elaborate behavioral constructions could not be credited to the work of repression alone, and thus Freud proposed a third type of drive, the instinct of self-preservation.[21] The functioning of the mind is presided over by the pleasure principle. This creates an enormous tension of psychical energy, since the two drives seeking satisfaction (pleasure) are sex and aggressiveness. The sexual choices may not match, while a release of aggressivity may not find any complement in its human object. The ego's drive for self-preservation enters to remedy the situation by replacing the pleasure principle with the reality principle which transforms the negative effects of constraints into positive drives towards construction.[22] An example of how sexual and aggressive drives combine with self-preservation can be found in the Oedipus complex. The sexual drive in infants attracts boys to mothers and girls to fathers, at the same time creating aggressive tensions for the child with the parent of the same sex. As the sexual drive becomes more genital, the unleashed tensions are curbed by defense and repression. Traces of the trauma may pass through the surveillance system and become symbols such as the fantasies of incest that Freud found among his earlier patients. But it is not these symbols which create culture, art, politics, and philosophy. The child is not left with a curtailed sexual wish and a thwarted aggressive impulse. It also experiences intimacy with the mother whom it wanted to transform into a sexual object, but who, by virtue of being real, and not only a creation of the child's fantasy, continues to love the child and be loved by it. Also the father is not only a threatening figure and an object of hatred. The child loves the father, is loved by him, and experiences intimacy with him. The result of the Oedipal stage cannot be frustration and rage alone, for the child learns about the persistence of love together with sentiments opposite to it and develops not only defenses but also accepts ego ideals.[23]

The drive theory has a most interesting consequence for our essay, for it provides an answer to the question, "How can the therapist be sure that he is on the right track and having the correct insights?" The patient could agree with a certain interpretation just because he is influenced by the therapist and not because it is relevant within the context of his biography. In Freud's theory the rightness of the analyst is not a matter of chance or of gratuitous consensus. The psychoanalyst's insights are confirmed when he picks the right symbol, or fragment, or stereotype, which then becomes cathected into consciousness releasing intense affects. The therapist may reach an intellectual understanding of what afflicts the patient much earlier than he can bring it to the patient's attention in effective ways, that is, with cathected affects.

Psychoanalysts can count on a powerful theory to guide their practice as well as to evaluate and correct their performances. Freud's apostolate covered a wide range of possibilities couched in explanations strictly derived from his metapsychology. For example, it was obvious that although painful, some symbols also brought about a certain satisfaction in the patient, because they allowed the repressed wish to let off steam, partially releasing the tension created by the repressed drive. Freud called these effects "primary gains." There were also cases in which in addition to the primary gain the patient experienced a secondary gain. Holzman illustrates the idea of secondary gain with the example of a patient whose "neurotic sexual impotence may elicit from his sexually uninterested wife a gratifying display of pity, compassion, and tender nurturing, which the patient, when potent had been unable to elicit from her."[24] Secondary gains naturally pose a difficulty for psychoanalytic treatment because they reinforce resistance providing good reasons for the patient not to want to change. But they also represent an outstanding theoretical expansion preserving the metapsychology in face of difficult empirical situations which otherwise could challenge Freud's schema of symbol interpretation.

The Study of the Ego and Structural Psychology

In the 1920s, Freud went through a new and major change in the formulation of his metapsychology; he abandoned the functionalist model of the psyche and introduced a structural theory centered on an ego which filtered the drives from the id and raised defenses against external stimuli.[25] The ego was the focus of memory, perception, anticipation, and concept formation. The ego was the abode of reason in this new tripartition of the mind. It was conceived as a mesh of dikes preserving the integrity of personhood against the id's disruptive drives, and defending it from the onslaughts of the external world.

The ego is the product of the encounter of the id's drives (the pleasure principle) with the external reality (related to the reality principle) which calls for defensive moves capable of preserving the self and of intervening maneuvers destined to adapt the self to reality. Two processes secure the ego's defense and adaptation: identification with influential others, and progressive decenterings allowing the ego to experience itself as dissimilar to itself, and therefore to grow through self-reflection.

The ego grows through progressive stages of autonomy in which the self becomes different from other experiences characterized by dependence. But the ego defenses do not let the self endlessly decenter, it keeps the process within certain limits by means of guilt and self-reproach. Social and cultural pressures and the superego also play a role in limiting the ego's expansion and self-differentiation. Guilt, self-reproach, and censorship, however, are mitigated by the love of others which boosts self-esteem. In the Oedipal phase of ego formation, in order for the infant to develop a sexual interest for his mother, he must have achieved a certain degree of differentiation from her, so that as an autonomous self he can desire sexual gratification. The obstacle represented by the father stands for social censorship and forms the superego as long as the infant yields to the force he sees in it. At the same time, the father is also a love object with which the child experiences intimacy, that helps him accept the father's prerogatives over the mother. In the end, the child identifies himself with the mother, the object of his desire which he had to give up, thus experiencing loss. Loss leads to identification because this is the means the ego has to preserve something from the lost object. We readily see, in this sense, the ego is by and large a symbolic complex of identifications constituted by bits and pieces of lost objects. But identification does not only take place in the wake of loss, it also occurs with positive and gratifying experiences. The infant derives negative identifications with the father through hatred, and with the mother through loss, as well as positive identifications with both through love. These decentering experiences teach the self loss, fear and autonomy, dependence, the threat of death, and survival. Enriched by this knowledge, the self experiences itself as an entity at the same time subject to those states and independent of them. These states become symbolized and are stored in the memory. The self builds ego defenses against the threatening experiences at the same time that it realizes its potentiality to grow in the sense of having a continuity which surpasses the complete set of experiences.

The task of psychoanalysis is to reconstruct the symbolic congeries of the ego's experiences, a process in which the analysand frees himself from those complexes of symbols in which his self became mired, precluding him from a complete engagement in the reality of life here and now. Notice that psychoanalysis does not create a new state for the self, but restores its transparency, its agility to realize that it is bigger than the sum total of its experiences. The fact remains, however, that this outcome is itself an experience, and therefore it is also acceptable to claim that psychoanalysis attaches a new experience to the patient's biography. Freud is not unaware of the latter possibility, because for him, there is not a present self completely different from all past experiences and beyond the symbolic complexes. The self is always a history of the integration between the past and the reality-laden present, although it cannot be reduced to just any narrative collection of facts. Psychoanalysis is part of the present rearrangement of the past. The consequence of this outlook is that psychoanalysis can neither be regarded as symbol interpretation alone, nor as interaction or negotiation pure and simple.

The shift from the functionalist (unconscious, preconscious, and conscious) to the structuralist (id, ego, and superego) picture of the mind was not followed by changes in the practice of psychoanalysis. The functionalist view of treatment relied on the notion of *insight*. Its underlying assumption was that by bringing the repressed symbols from the unconscious to the conscious, the patient dissolved them under the irresistible light of consciousness. Nevertheless, many patients with consciousness of their problems still suffered from intense malaise. Freud himself seemed to be aware of the issues in his psyche and was disenchanted; his self-analysis played a role in the denouement of analytic thinking, as he registered that in the interpretive failures either the insight was wrong or consciousness was not enough to dispel the symptoms. In his later writings on technique Freud becomes ever more pessimistic about the suasive accomplishments in psychoanalysis. Quoting his psychoanalyst friend Mitscherlich in an interview, Habermas aptly captures the tone in which Freud bequeathed us his psychoanalytic project, by saying: "therapy often achieves 'no more than the transformation of illness into suffering, but into a suffering which enhances the status of *homo sapiens*, because it does not extinguish his freedom.'"[26] Freud was not very interested in the development of clinical rhetoric itself, and preferred to regard the breakdowns of insight as cases of obstinate resistance, accounted for more by the ego mechanisms of defense than by the strength of the analytic rhetoric of persuasion. In addition, at this stage in his career[27] more occupied with lecturing, writing, and struggling amid the politics of the psychoanalytic movement, Freud had less time for clinical practice. The new advance in theory proceeded without major changes in treatment. The ego, however, was a far more complex entity than the function of consciousness, that which was the object of analysis based on insight. It performed some of the functions previously attributed to the unconscious, encompassed part of the preconscious and embodied the entire realm of the conscious. Endowed with self-reproach, it had to defend itself from adverse impulses and pursue the ego ideals tailored in the superego.

Looking back through the history of psychoanalysis from today's vantage point, we can see that analysts needed a different repertoire of therapeutic maneuvers other than insightful interpretations, but they were not to obtain it until much later. It was only with the school of object relations that analysts began to exercise their patients in a ritual cure which took time to mature. The patient's awareness of his problem was no guarantee that it would eventually be resolved. The treatment unfolded gradually, the patient had not only to develop a consciousness of the problem, that which was still obtained through the rhetoric of insight, but also needed to emotionally outgrow the causes of neurosis. Treatment had become, to a certain extent, a species of training, training in being healthy. The analyst, turned into a transitional object, served the patient by leading him to use this therapeutic object until he had exhausted his symptoms and diffused the compulsion to repeat. Donald Winnicott, one of the founders of object relations, argued that the subject first experiences the object as an omnipotent projection of his own. Then he tries to destroy the object in a counterphobic echoing of the fear or loss. The object, however, whenever underscored by a real person aware of the maneuver, resists destruction, the backlash of the subject's attempt leads him to a critique of his destructive impulse, bringing the projective fantasy out in the clear. This was the role of the analyst: to let himself become part of the object of the omnipotent fantasy; furthermore, to live on within that cloud of the patient's psyche until he was ready to dispel it, and then struggle to survive as a real object in sharp contrast to the fantasized one.[28] There we have in a nutshell the updating of clinical work to theory, carried out by the analysts of object relations.

From Psychodynamic to Communicative Symbols

Freud maintained that it would be simple if everything ego related could be attributed to conscious processes, and all the rest to the unconscious, and that this must be the case among the animals. "But in man there is an added complication through which internal processes in the ego may also acquire the quality of consciousness. [Freud is referring to the preconscious quality of ideas.] This is the work of the function of speech, which brings material within the ego into a firm connection with mnemic residues of visual, but more particularly auditory, perception."[29] This "function of speech" performs the "reality testing" of what is going on inside the ego, and thus accomplishes the two goals of establishing consciousness and thereby facilitating pleasure. That is not the only duty of the ego, which also has to filter sexual and aggressive drives from the id, transforming them into suitable actions in the external world, as well as coming to grips with the constraints imposed by the superego. But undoubtedly, this language mediated raising of objects to consciousness and adapting them to reality indicates that, for Freud, communications with others were among the most fundamental of the ego's faculties.

This was not always the case in his theory, however, because in its early formulations verbal interaction had virtually no role to play vis-à-vis the all-powerful game between memory and events or drives and defenses. It was only with the structural theory of the ego that the importance of communication was brought to the foreground of Freud's reflection, and this happened relatively late in his writing career and it remained only roughly enunciated. The upshot of Freud's theory of symbols in its complete version—that is, the symbols resulting from reality constraints and ego defenses against drives, from the ego's defensive and adaptive self-reproach, from the superego's constraints, and, finally, from the surrounding social pressure in whose centripetal force the ego ideal emerges, carving its figure in the avoidance of shame—is that every human being is a "symbol's crucible" and has a history of defense and adaptation amenable to analysis. At this point in his theory it becomes difficult to sustain a classification of psychopathology. Freud sums up, the neuroses "shade off by easy transitions into what is described as the normal; and, on the other hand, there is scarcely any state recognized as normal in which indications of neurotic traits could not be pointed out."[30]

In our sketch of Freud's original formulation for psychoanalysis, we saw that the backbone of his conceptual system is constituted by two theories of symbol formation and mind functioning that are strung together. In the earlier part of his writings, before 1900, symbols resulted from intrapsychic struggles, and events in the external world had a direct influence over the "symbol's crucible." From the time of *The Interpretation of Dreams* (1900) until the writings of the twenties, Freud introduced a theory of the mind, refined his hypotheses about symbol formation, and completed a sketch of the ego, cast in structural terms.

Freud's symbols are transparent and refract the past. The goal of the psychoanalytic treatment, however, is not an exhaustive reconstruction of the past, capable of revealing it in its full history. The analyst looks for indices in symbols, stereotypes, and fragments, permitting an archeological reconstruction, not of the sequence of experiences entertained by the patient, but of the psychical process which unfolded in the core of those experiences. The symbols are disguises of these psychical processes. Freud studies how they camouflage our psyche. On the other hand, there would be no psycho-logical life in the absence of symbols.

The corollary of such propositions is that the self is not the exclusive product of intrapsychic forces. Two other elements are equally decisive in the shaping of the person: the external world and the communicative actions which bring together psyche and reality. Both the external world and the intrapsychic dynamics gain more autonomy in his later writings. The inevitable consequence is the swelling of the importance of communication, but Freud did not have time to develop this prong of his theory.

Nevertheless, communications do not have any degree of autonomy to be sought out in Freud's writings. It does not create anything that was not already there in the patient's psyche or in the world. Communications are not supposed to do anything unforeseen by the psychoanalytic theory. The treatment consists in insights about key elements whose truthfulness is not an object of persuasion or of conversion. The analyst restores or awakens the truth in the analysand. If he does so through communications, it is not in the sense of entreating, but in that of manipulating transference. Psychoanalysis, as conceived by Freud, is a theory of the dynamics of the psyche and of the mind, which has a tendency to complete its course, but which can be facilitated by the aid of a transitional object, the analyst.

As the epigraphs indicate, language and appearances are misguiding indices to the substance of conduct. There are two alternative venues: communicative actions or speech and theories of the psyche. Freud dealt with the first alternative through his insights about transference; he also provided us with an iridescent description of the second and tried to integrate the two in his clinical practice as it transpires from his case reports. He failed on all three endeavors in the sense that none were satisfactorily brought to completion. I believe it is in this failure that his great success resides, as he managed to reenact foundational aporias of the Western heritage without falling into the temptation to resolve or ignore them, which would have placed him outside our cultural tradition. His effort of culture reproduction continues within therapeutic discourse, carried on in psychoanalysis by an enormous variety of schools and approaches, and in therapy, in general, by an even greater variety of practices. In the following three chapters I discuss two opposing varieties of therapy, the analysis of transference and family therapy. The first endeavors to carry on Freud's project, undertaking to integrate the communicative aspect of therapy with the theory of the psyche. Its proponents straddle the two horses of symbols in their complex referentiality and even more complex pragmatic usage. The second, family therapy, ignores the transparence of symbols, and tries to develop approaches based on the assumption that the meaning of that which is said is opaque. As a consequence, the clinic of these therapists attempts to restrict itself to communicative actions.

2

PERSUASION IN

PSYCHOANALYSIS

It seems to be characteristic of the thriving systems of knowledge, power, and rhetoric to keep alive the flame lit by their forefathers. This is true about every major tradition of the Western heritage: philosophy with Socrates and Plato, Christianity with Jesus' preaching in the gospels of Matthew, Mark, Luke, and John, science with Descartes and Leibniz, and Marxism with Marx and Engels. The more vigorous the cultural subsystem is, the greater the number of interpretations of its founding scriptures, resulting in a permanent freshness imparted to the canon's touchstone. The meanings attributed to the founding texts enter different spheres of our literate life and we go on thinking through these widespread categories of knowledge, even if we have never read the original proponents of those ideas. This is clearly the case of Freud and psychoanalysis. Furthermore, once the subcultural tradition becomes established on solid grounds, every exercise of interpretation or critique looks minuscule, because it confronts a continuity stretched back to a founding father, which is consequently gigantic and ordained to ever grow. Every interpretation or correction is irremediably attracted by the magnetism of the whole, and sooner or later adds to its massive size. The work of the founding father begins to look ever more open-ended, capable of shedding new light over every turning of life. We must keep this in mind, as we plunge into the intellectual traditions initiated by Plato and by Freud, in order to avoid the cult of heroes, and do justice to the cultural workings which in point of fact created these awesome complexes of knowledge, power, and rhetoric.

The psychotherapeutic imagination has indeed penetrated all spheres of life in our cultural heritage. It is an all pervasive mode of discourse in popular and elite culture: it enters the media and literature; it concerns philosophy and science, and challenges politics and religion; it establishes a new ethics without asking permission to do so by forming in clinical practice a normative corpus of principles about how we should lead our lives. We can say, without fear of exaggeration, that we live in a

Freudianized world, a culture of the therapeutic on which an ever-growing gamut of existential problems are dealt with by professional psychotherapists. This, however, does not mean that the therapeutic became established without problems. The main dilemma seems to be the divorce between theory and practice, because if on one hand the clinical practice flourishes incessantly, on the other hand we can neither say that we are leaning towards the adoption of a morality couched in psychoanalytic theory, nor that psychoanalysis has invented a new form of discourse. The questions introduced in chapter 1 come back to mind: How can therapeutic practice defined by the psychological theory become divorced from its own theory? What impact does this ever-growing practice have over our lives? Now that there are so many competing schools of psychotherapy there is also great temptation to debunk Freud's metapsychology, but we still regard the many practices as species of the genus psychotherapy. Moreover, no school of treatment has risen to the heights of knowledge achieved by the Freudian tradition. Freud's launching of the analytic movement continues to be the best system of knowledge, fabric of social power, and smithy of rhetorical maneuvers informing the practice of psychotherapy. Nonetheless, many practitioners closely identified with the Freudian doctrine have been revealing restlessness within the theory and the practice of psychoanalysis, but this is not new in the history of the psychoanalytic movement. Furthermore, now that the founding father is dead, innovators do not have to become dissidents. No living psychoanalyst can claim to be as central to the movement as Freud once was, and as a consequence there is less cohesion among the defenders of the canon.

The pressure for change is applied over theory and practice. On the first front, reformers claim that Freud's exacting construction of the ego should be loosened up, a tendency started long ago with the proponents of ego psychology, such as Heinz Hartmann and Erik Erikson, and pushed on by others. Some of the most immediate consequences of this reform are the diminution of the role of the id and of the superego and a tempering of internalization, to the extent that some facts and behaviors would have merely external reality. On the other front, it is requested that therapy become more "humanistic," that is, that it be regarded more as a relationship between two persons than as a technical procedure between a professional and a patient. This later claim is not new and has in its favor the fact that in spite of all the precision in technique, no two practitioners apply exactly the same interventions over identical problems, nor does the same therapist treat any two of his patients in quite the same way.[1]

Psychoanalytic Discourse as Narrative Discourse

Roy Schafer proposes that the psychoanalytic session be regarded as a negotiation between two different narrative structures of analyst and analysand.[2] He argues that the patient's narrative does not have an absolute meaning and that its signification results from the compromise between the interpretive scheme of a certain analytic tradition and the patient's own leanings. The analyst also has his narrative, or a narrative structure which he borrows from Freud. The story is evolutionary and tells the tale of man on a phylogenetic scale, evolving from the wild id into the tamed ego, building sociocultural scaffoldings around his desires in order to conquer the territory of the unknown which so threatens him, and to expand that which is familiar. The plight unfolds between the quest for pleasure and the injunctions of repression which lead to renunciation. First, man acts by killing the father to possess the mother; then, he ontogenetically expiates the guilt of his action, tethered to this psychological exorcism. Some of his actions to circumscribe pleasure become painful, some of the actions to procure pleasure become remorseful. Little by little man's story written by nature unfolds into the building of culture. Thus goes the Freudian mythical narrative. The analysand's story, once shuffled with Freud's, becomes a tale of castration complex in a hurt and angry son who displays aggressivity against the father, or of overgrown narcissism which once protected the infant from feelings of rejection and loneliness, but now prevents the adult from developing meaningful attachments to others.

The telescoping of the psychoanalytic with the patient's narrative can only occur if the two interactants adapt the narrative genre to the dialogical situation. Narratives dispense with challenges because the coherence of the plot takes precedence over the consistency or verifiability of each narrated event. The listener is induced into a passive attitude, while the speaker can ward off questioning by taking refuge within the narrative structure. Freud suggests that the patient's narrative must be shaken either by the analyst's interpretation or by silence, which unsettles the speaker's narrative confidence, or still by recommendations destined to crack open the analysand's narrative. He advises patients, for example, that while in usual narratives they "try to keep the thread of [their] story together and to exclude all intruding associations and side-issues, so as not to wander too far from the point,"[3] in the psychoanalytic situation preference should be given to those associations that break the flow of the plot spreading the narrative sidewise. This naturally makes it easier for the therapist to wedge his interventions in the patient's narrative, retelling it in the psychoanalytic narrative.

Indeed, both the representation and the experience of life can be thought of as narratives. After we shuffle our collection of narratives and wring them dry of too much detail, we arrive at a narrative structure which looks to us like a much better knowledge of matters than that one provided by the original narratives. This is at least what we have been taught by science to be the progress of reason. Freud's intellect grew in the age of modernity, when the scientific view of the world was hegemonic, and thus he learned to bow to science and conceived of the human mind as a machine fuelled by drives and symbols. Had he done only that, the psychoanalytic project would have died in the womb, or have found another bearer. The imprint of his genius resides in that he also invoked the mythological narrative about the evolution of mankind, a tale expunged of the sophistication of narrative structures derived from stories told and retold. Freud took up one of these stories and combined it with his scientific machine mind. In doing this he bridged the modern and the romantic ages and rose above his time.

Freud's epistemology contains a grave antinomy: how can this machinelike picture of self and mind à la Descartes reconcile with the evolutionary story? If the story is true, it is just a story; therefore, it must admit to other stories and cannot be confined by the straitjacket of the mechanical mind and self. Otherwise, to put it in different terms, how can Freud's metapsychology stay outside of the representations of life and in addition be a method to analyze those representations, if the entire story of life is itself a representation? Take for example the theory of drives. Why should we accept that drives transcend all other facts of life? The introspective tapping of drives depends on the person's feeling that he is "being driven" to do something by a force external to his will. Rather than showing that drives are external to representation, however, this places them in a narrative explanation according to which drives are a metaphor for the conversion of a passive self into a wishing self.[4]

Psychoanalytic discourse creates the impression of a psyche beyond narrative precisely by deconstructing narrative structures in powerful ways. This is not the opportunity for us to treat the subject in great detail: it will suffice to discuss a few features of the psychoanalytic deconstruction. First, similarly to the structuralists who de-chronologize narratives, psychoanalysts un-plot them by linking the events which constitute the mark of the story to events lying outside the story. A woman's irritation against her employer, for example, becomes the female's atavistic penis envy, as we shall see in our forthcoming discussion of a psychoanalytic session. Notice however, that this deconstruction of the plot is achieved by means of another narrative structure, the psychoanalyst's. Second, the patient's narratives are constantly centered around his self, his reports of others' reactions to him are translated in terms of his feelings. For example, when he says that his father thinks he is incompetent, the analyst rephrases it as his own thinking that he is incompetent, which further leads him to think that his father thinks he is incompetent. When the self is given such a power over narrative structures, it can only become omnipotent, and as such be perceived as independent of the narratives. Third, narratives are by definition the establishment of a relation between the past and the present. Even in the analysis of transference, directed to the here-and-now of the therapy session, the underlying motive is a resistance, or a neurosis harking back to the past in the psychoanalytic narrative. Narratives, thus, are made to cover the entire spectrum of time, and a self and mind with absolute control over them tend to be thought of as standing outside time. Fourth, psychoanalysis stimulates a rationalized discourse, that is, a talking-about-something as opposed to a talking-for-doing-something. Naturally, the intimacy of the face-to-face interaction between analyst and analysand creates a context propitious for direct verbal action, but the psychoanalytic discourse controls this possibility by means of its rational discourse about experiences. In an illustration, a patient who has sexual fantasies about his therapist projects them over the therapist himself. The therapist does not say "yes" or "no," but talks about the patient's fantasies. The patient follows his lead, and what started off as a fantasy dangerously pressing for action becomes neutralized in a discourse about fantasy. The heat brought about by the imminence of action is removed from the situation. This leads us to the fifth characteristic of the psychoanalytic narrative deconstruction: the referential convention. In oral discourse, the reference is ostensive and can be pointed out by an indexical gesture, with the speaker pointing with his finger to the object he is talking about. The convention about reference in the written discourse loses this indexical potential, because the text cannot point to anything. The psychoanalytic discourse, although oral in form, abides by the referential conventions of written discourse. The patient's sexual impulses towards the analyst are transformed into thoughts and talked about rather than acted out. If the telescoping of past and present blasts time, the separation between speech and action and words and objects blasts space. The psychoanalytic discourse is chronotopic in the sense that it coalesces time and space under narrative structures which are now taken for the self, now brought under control by an omnipotent self who stands outside the stories.

A discourse so empowered can either lead to domination or isolate itself from the audiences who oppose resistance to it in order to preserve their freedom. Psychoanalysts such as Roy Schafer and Merton Gill regard the psychoanalytic project as only half unfolded as long as it prepared itself to deal with neurosis but left the question of transference dormant. They are struggling to bring this project to its complete fruition.

Transference is the process by which a patient, unable to distinguish the external autonomy of the analyst, projects his fantasies onto him. There is a positive transference, which Freud called "unobjectionable," and a transference serving the purpose of resistance to treatment. While the former is characterized by the constructive hope that the analyst will cure the patient, the latter unfolds grievances and reservations to the analyst. Transference may be direct, that is, patient and analyst may realize transferential feelings and directly talk about them, or it may be indirect, with the patient, for instance, projecting criticisms to the analyst over a scapegoat figure, and the analyst remaining unaware that the villain is he and not the person being talked about. Naturally, the indirectness of transference underscores the vitality of resistance.

The question of transference cannot be treated, as most analysts do, outside its historical framework. In the early days of psychoanalysis, or during the introduction of psychoanalysis to a population unfamiliar with it, the treatment entails a different commitment on the part of the analyst, who has to establish procedural rules and explain to the patient how analysis works.[5] The analysands, likewise, in these unschooled contexts, are more prone to fall into transference. The contemporary sophisticated patient, who lives in a large metropolitan center and is well informed about the procedures of psychoanalysis, may find it harder to identify his transference or his resistance, burying both attitudes under many layers of rationalization, which may render it extremely difficult, even for the experienced analyst, to unearth them. After one hundred years of psychoanalysis and the unquestionable triumph of the therapeutic in a number of subcultural pockets in society, the population of patients no longer looks withdrawn and hysterical, afflicted by fantasies that it does not dare discuss, as, we are led to believe by reading the psychoanalytic vignettes, were the Viennese bourgeoisie of the turning of the century. Psychoanalysis helped bring about a different attitude in relation to feelings and emotions: first by encouraging their representation in thought, and second by making the discourse about them public. The publicness of the analytic discourse about feelings is what led Philip Rieff to acknowledge the triumph of the therapeutic, and Christopher Lasch to diagnose society as narcissistic, overconcerned with its discourse about the self to the detriment of community issues.[6]

The Analysis of Transference in Earnest

The recent suggestion by Merton Gill that the emphasis of analysis be placed on the process of transference rather than on the genetic interpretation of neurosis,[7] in addition to being a much-needed development in the history of psychoanalysis, may well reflect changes occurring in the population of patients. After the patients became "virtuosi of the self,"[8] they also developed stronger links to resistance. The new patient knows that analysis stimulates transference and that he is bound to project his fantasies onto his analyst. So, it makes sense that the analyst pay more attention to this process rather than to the old resistance which protects neurosis from interpretation. For many analysts, however, with the support of Freud's writings, transference is the first and foremost of the tactics of resistance. As long as the patient conjures up displaced fantasies about the analyst, his relevant fantasies remain undiscussed, protected by a smokescreen of transference. But for Freud neuroses were not unrelated, consequently the transferential resistance is obviously an extension of the genetic neurosis. Gill enlists this strong argument, stemming from Freud's theory of the psyche as a whole, in order to back his claim that the centrality of transference in the psychoanalytic process was already envisioned by Freud.

I will introduce the discussion of the analysis of transference through two lines of reasoning. In one, the argument is about whether psychoanalysis is a technical procedure typical of a personal relationship. In the other, the nature of the psychoanalyst's intervention is examined.The discussion will be completed with excerpts from one session of psychoanalysis transcribed in Gill's book, in which he and Irwin Hoffman point out instances in which the analysis of transference could have been successfully carried out.[9] The session, as well as Gill and Hoffman's comments, provides us with an excellent opportunity to reflect upon the rhetoric of insight and discuss its relation to the psychoanalytic system of knowledge and uses of power.

The question is: must analysis be regarded as a technical relationship in which the analyst allows no personal bonds to develop between him and the analysand? The question has historical depth in the psychoanalytic movement since Breuer, who was Freud's earliest partner, became so entangled in the transferential fantasies of his patient Anna O. that he had to withdraw hastily from her treatment and pass her on to Freud. At the same time that Freud outlined the technique of psychoanalysis, shaping it after the impersonal model of the relation between doctor and patient, he engaged in friendly and warm relationships with his patients, asking them extra-analytic questions, offering them food, or talking about himself. In the wake of such an ambiguous beginning, psychoanalysis developed as a technical relationship which brought together a rational professional, whose task it is to hide any personal feelings behind his technical skills, and a neurotic patient, who cannot acknowledge the difference between his transferential construction of his analyst and the autonomy the therapist has outside the analysand's fantasy world. The client develops expectations about the analyst that cannot be fulfilled, as well as anger against deeds the therapist only performed in the patient's own imagination, and against the fact that he remains an object of his fantasies, incapable of responding.[10]

For Freud, repetition was always transferential.[11] As a consequence, the non-neurotic relationships were rational and real, in the sense that they were original and heeded the reality of another completely autonomous from self. The question is begged: can a neurotic patient behave in a non-neurotic manner? Freud's line of reasoning seems to indicate that his answer is "No." Gill claims that those who overlook the distinction between real and transferential relationships may be perceived as taking flight from the challenges of human relations behind the walls of technique, while those others who emphasize the distinction may be perceived "as betraying a softhearted inability to maintain an appropriate neutrality in the face of patients' demands or importunities."[12] The issue, to me, seems to be power and not technique. The proponents of the distinction must admit that sometimes the analyst will be wrong and the analysand right, while those others who downplay the difference must assume that the patient is always wrong, because he is always relating to the analyst through transferential bonds.

The fact of the matter is that we cannot separate real from transferential relationships, neurotic from non-neurotic behavior in absolute terms. The psychoanalytic distinction is heuristic and instrumentally useful in treatment, but cannot by any means serve as a springboard for a moral classification of relationships. The closing of the psychoanalytic universe within a technical relationship obfuscates the power asymmetries and games that take place between analyst and analysand, enthroning the former in unquestionable power superiority.[13] In order to experience the relationship as real, too, the analyst has to heed the question of power, and decide when to use it for therapeutic purposes, and when to concede. At both ends, the technical and the real, the therapist will find himself now in a subordinate position, now in a superordinate position. Sometimes he may choose to change the balance for therapeutic reasons, other times in the name of fairness.

Gill places himself in the mainstream of the Freudian heritage in assuming that the insight, with its effect of bringing the repressed into consciousness, whenever correct, should produce the resolution of the neurosis. This is not tantamount to saying that a single statement may dissolve the symptom, because often the neurotic symbol only becomes completely uncovered after lengthy conversations, which in the case of some treatments may take years. There is a resistance to the awareness of transference, which Gill proposes to break with the candid establishment of the appropriate connection, as illustrated by the following intervention: "The episode you told me about your wife is an allusion to something similar which you feel is going on between us but which you are reluctant to mention."[14] There is also a resistance to the resolution of the transference, which Gill equally proposes to break with insightful interventions, establishing the appropriate connections between the transferential material and the patient's genetic neurosis, for defenses to the here-and-now of the analytic session. This is all very Freudian as long as the system of neurotic symbols is considered as a whole, and the correct interventions are confirmed by the analysand's correlative release of affects.

Transference is resistance to an interpersonal relation as much as defense is resistance to intrapsychic interactions. From this platform, Gill launches his program for an analysis of transference, since what the analyst will almost always have access to is resistance and not defense. The interpretation of transference, however, may lead into more transference, for talking elicits talking, and the patient's resistance may find it useful to perpetuate transference thus rendering the analysis interminable. This, of course, will only constitute a problem when the analyst embarks too readily in mechanical interpretations. Normally, the analyst can always back up and reassess the difference of opinion between the patient and him as a failure on his part to grasp all the necessary information. This is crucially important for the psychoanalytic strategy of preparing interventions, and perhaps it constitutes a good reason for neither Freud nor Gill to propose rhetorical maneuvers too powerful to break resistance. The weight of the intervention must be borne by the correctness of the insight, and not by the persuasive power of the rhetoric. The simple attitude of interpreting carries the connotation that what the patient is saying is symptomatic and may therefore trigger his resistance in the most unexpected ways. The danger is that the analyst's reluctance to interpret may be perceived as a lack of understanding or interest. From an ethical point of view such a discursive philosophy is irreproachable. The analyst does not keep a hidden hand behind his back; the ultimate ground to decide about the correctness of the intentions is the patient's acquiescence. Notice, however, that the patient's acquiescence is not the same thing as release of affects. The former depends on a consensus of reason, the latter on the impact of the insight. The first one speaks to the intellectual faculty, the second to the emotions. They are obviously different, but psychoanalysts have systematically overlooked the difference and assumed that the arrival of emotions in consciousness is equivalent to rationality. The reason why the therapist ultimately looks for rational consensus resides in the fact that psychoanalysis is dialogical, and any attitude shorter than consensus would break the dialogical basis of the interaction which, I claim, bears at least as great a responsibility for treatment as Freud's metapsychology. Having laid out this argument, we should now go back to Gill's proposal of an analysis of transference, examining excerpts from a therapy session annotated by him. In the second volume of *Analysis of Transference*, written in collaboration with Irwin Hoffman, Gill presents nine sessions of psychoanalysis with different patients and therapists, and discusses where the analysts aptly use the analysis of transference and where they fail to do so.

The session I choose to analyze presents a therapist dealing with resistance and thereby establishes a sharp contrast with Gill's suggestions. The therapist addresses the question of transference, but overlooks a great deal of nontransferential material, regarding as symptomatic what the patient presents as real. The patient reacts against the interpretations, the analyst considers her reaction as resistance, and further interprets it along the same lines. This is the 95th session of a treatment, and begins with the patient saying:

P: I remember that you mentioned it and then I didn't get it. [Unclear reference.]
We're rehearsing today. And I love to rehearse. And, uh, it doesn't seem unreasonable to me to leave two and a half hours. But I'm getting a lot of static [inaudible] from J [boss]. He seems to use two things when he wants, when he wants to get at me. We had a huge fight last night. Such a, such a big fight, that I ended up screaming at him. And G [boyfriend] was there, and H [woman] and J's wife, L. But the crying finally got him. I didn't really do it on purpose. I just was very

overwrought. But every time I'd get in an argument with him, he smirks and says, "Are you having your period?" That and my coming up here are the two things that he waves at me. Like when I left today, I mean, I told him all day, that I was, you know. Yesterday, he calls up in the middle of the afternoon yesterday, and he decided that G's volunteering to help was an arch-insult and that it's just full of shit. And that he didn't want to have anything to do with it and so he was going to come over and work with me. And then we were going to rehearse today. And I said, "O.K. That's fine." I said, "Well, you know I'll be leaving for a couple of hours in the afternoon." He said, "Why, where do you have to go?" And I said, "I have to go to the shrink." And then he said, "Oh my God." He's always going on like that. And it was interesting, when he called to tell me that, that he decided that uh, G's offer was, uh, an insult and a putdown. The first thing he said [inaudible]—he called while I was gone, while I was here yesterday and when I got back I got the message. And I called him up and he says, "Hello," and I say, "Hello" and he said, "Well, how is the shrink? [voice raised] I just can't understand what it is, tell me what it is that compels you to go up there four times a week, like going to the movies. Think how many movies I would see. Now tell me what it is it does for you." He had a long speech like that. And, uh, then launched right into the thing about how he decided that it was all bullshit. So, M was here today too. I don't know that she knew where I was going. And she probably thought it was a little odd that I left [inaudible]. You know, I was thinking about it, feeling shitty about it on the train, because J was probably giving her a big number about how much time I spend coming and going. And he said yesterday, "You don't even, you don't have time to do anything. How can you spend all that time?" [sigh] [inaudible] He's just so gross about it. Like he's always yelling and screaming and embarrassing me.

At this point Gill and Hoffman speculate whether the patient is not putting in her boss's mouth her own misgivings about analysis, but ponder that it is too early in the session to carry out an interpretation of transference lest the analyst had evidence from previous sessions. The patient goes on complaining that her boss, a stage director, kept pushing her in her job without giving reasons. She was being treated by him in a mechanical way. The analyst continues to listen to her and to elicit further information which leads Gill and Hoffman to wonder whether his restraint does not stress the patient's identification of her boss with him. She proceeds:

P: And the first thing that pissed me off was his, his insisting that I change my attitude. And he said, "What's, you know, what's the matter with you?" And he said, "You're, you know you're not acting the way you've always acted." And I said, well you know, "I'm not in a particularly jolly mood. And sometimes people's moods just don't fit in with the way you want them to be." And I said, "You just have to accept that." And he said, "that's a lot of shit." And I said, well, "Come on, let's you know, let's keep doing this." And the other thing that [chuckle] he sort of looked a little embarrassed about and laughed at was that he was saying he didn't like my attitude. And I said, "Yes, I'm not acting like I love you every minute." And he said, "No, no it's just that we've been working so well before and I don't understand, you know, I don't understand why you're behaving this way. And, you know, why you act the way you did before. You know, we're going to keep a pleasant working relationship." I said, "Yeah, the only way that it's pleasant is for me to act the way I, as if I love you all the time." So anyway, so today everything was fine, you know. Until I said I was going to leave, like, and I warned him ahead of time. And I said, you know, "Let's do this." And H was working with him. It's not like I left him by himself. And H knows how everything is supposed to be done and where everything is and all that. And, uh, the thing, another thing that pissed me off was he made it like, he made it look like I was leaving for all afternoon, you know, while P [woman] was there and I said. . . .

Her grievances against her boss seem to be quite reasonable, and his reaction to her, in her narration, imparts reality to her experience of the situation. She proceeds in her complaints after the analyst asks for clarification about a few more details of her clashes with her boss on the previous day.

P: Oh, like this morning I—when we're doing the scene with the teacher and the little kid, we've been using a blackboard. But because we don't have our sets yet, somebody has to hold it up all the time. So we had been talking about temporarily getting a device where we can, like, put it up and lean it, like, on or against something, so that we didn't have to have a person standing there holding the thing all the time. So [inaudible] we were down there getting ready to do the scene, and I said, ah, "Are we going to have to go through this holding the blackboard trip again?" And he said, "Oh God!" I said, "What's the matter? I just asked." And he said, "I hear G talking there. That's G talking, that's not you." I said, "Gee J, if you just forget about G for a few minutes you'd probably be a lot more comfortable." You know, it's a combination of, I have a feeling on one hand he thinks I'm mindless and on the other hand, you know—and, and mindless and, and, uh, driven by G's every whim. And on the other he, he thinks that I'm much too strong-minded. I'm giving him a lot of trouble you know; it's got to such a point now where even, even when we say we like each other, I don't feel that we do. You know, I'm just so, so very sensitive to being picked on in little ways I just, it just doesn't roll off my back very well. [inaudible] He's the sort of person where if he knows you're sensitive about something, he'll rub it in your face, rub your nose in it—salt in the wound—instead of trying to be nice about it, you know, I mean, he, he just thinks he can decide how everybody is to behave.

Gill and Hoffman comment that she probably is feeling that her analyst sees her just like her boss J, as "mindless" and "strong-minded," always "giving him a lot of trouble." Rubbing salt in the wound may also be what the analyst does. The session continues with the analyst saying the following:

A: So what about salt?
P: What?
A: I said, "What about salt in the wound?"
P: Ah yes, the great aching wounds. Also rubbing your nose in it, which is what I don't, I remember talking about, um. . . .
A: Because you take his comments about you having to go to the shrink four times a week, as, as if he were saying, "Boy there must be plenty wrong with you that you have to do that."

Gill and Hoffman inform us that the "salt in the wound" metaphor refers to material covered in previous sessions and stands for "the female genital conceived as a wound."[15] It is obvious that she is construing herself as victim, and her boss as villain and the analyst's comments shift the responsibility for her pain from her boss's shoulders to hers.

Her reply above already shows signs of irritation with the analyst's interpretation.

P: Yes, sort of, except I—I know that. I think one thing that he resents about it is that he knows I'm talking to somebody else instead of talking to him. And the reason I think that is because he likes to know what everybody's up to and he likes to, you know, know where they're at. And I think he considers it like a threat to him. Just the way he considers, you know, my talking to G about things a threat. Anytime anybody makes, you know, yells at the top of their lungs about my seeing a shrink, I don't mean it's not something I'm particularly proud of, you know, it's cool but—or with people that I feel comfortable with I guess is a better thing. And I guess what it is, is people that I think are going to stick with me till I get fixed, you see. I remember the thing I didn't like about T saying it was that it's like I assumed that everybody else would say, "Oh, we wouldn't, we're not going to have to pay attention to her, you know. Poor crazy girl."

A: She doesn't have anything worth paying attention to.

P: Allright, if you want to put it that way. Or did I already put it that way? You know, I'm getting sick of this. Every time we come back to the same thing and then [inaudible] just stops there. Mental block. Done this routine many times before. I'm thinking of knocking all the books off the wall again. So what about it?

For Gill and Hoffman this passage confirms that the dictatorial man she complains about in the figure of her boss refers to the analyst. The analyst's interpretation, "She doesn't have anything worth paying attention to" refers to her devaluation of the female genital. She is tired of that interpretation—based on sexual motives—which leaves her in the dark and fails to address her complaints. That kind of interpretation is bookish and mechanical, consequently she feels like knocking the books off the wall.

I would like to draw the reader's attention to a different possible understanding of this passage. I would say that even if her complaints against her boss are transference of her feelings towards the analyst, therefore negative transference, there is also positive transference in the fact that she invokes the analyst as the opposite of her boss J, someone she is talking to, who makes J jealous, and may well constitute an alternative to her recent painful experiences in life. The analyst overlooks this positive aspect, and by emphasizing the negative one infuriates her. Her desire for privacy about going to psychoanalysis seems quite reasonable, and I do not see how it could be subsumed under her self-devaluing feelings. The analyst may be right in his interpretation, but I doubt that the patient is wrong in the sense that all the things she talks about are transferences or resistance to dealing with the neurosis and consequently lack reality. The analyst's interpretation leads her to feel precisely that he is denying the reality of what she is saying.

> A: What about knocking all the books off there?
> P: It's, I'm getting mad. I'm lying here getting mad and I'm afraid to move because I'm mad. I mean, what it seems like—and I know it's worked—but what it seems like is that you're always, no matter what I say, you're always bringing it back to this, you know—my thing about something wrong with me. And then we just get to that and then nothing fucking happens. We just end up saying "Well, you think there's something wrong with you." So big fucking deal. What about it? You know, when are we going to get away from illness and onto the cure? [sigh] Huh? [phone rings] [several inaudible words].
> [. . .]
> A: [inaudible]—I take the idea about knocking all the books off the wall as if you wanted to knock my penis off.

This interpretation of resistance is singled out by Gill and Hoffman in order to establish a sharp contrast with their proposal of analysis of transference. The analyst threshes the theme of penis envy harping on the sexual motive: the patient devalues her genital because she envies the male genital and that is what her complaints against men stem from. The analyst is interpreting resistance against this genetic diagnostic of the situation, while Gill and Hoffman suggest that he should rather address the patient's dissatisfaction with his interpretation. Notice that insofar as the Freudian system of knowledge is concerned, there are no disagreements between Gill and Hoffman on one hand and the analyst on the other, for all agree with the sexual motivation of neurotic behavior surfacing either through resistance or transference. Gill and Hoffman's suggestion is, therefore, that by addressing the analytic situation rather than the resistance, the analyst would loosen up his power domination of the patient, and water down the rhetoric of his intervention resulting in its greater persuasiveness.

> P: You do?
> A: Yes, I do.

P: [laugh]

A: That your reaction to my saying it is to want to do that.

P: Is to want to be [inaudible]—what?

A: Is to want to do that.

P: Well, if that's what getting mad is.

A: It wasn't just getting mad. It was also knocking all the books off the wall.

P: But why, but why are books a penis now? [sigh] Huh? Yeah, I think I always thought they were. That's why I read so much. I'm serious and I'm saying it sarcastically, but think back about trying to be smart.

A: Yeah, I know.

P: [inaudible]—O.K. Well, I'm admitting it ruefully, but I'm admitting it pissed-offedly. [inaudible] If I can't have one, you can't have one either? And you won't give me one, then you can't have yours. But it's still the same question. And it's still the same feeling. Take that lamp, for example.

At this point in the session, Gill and Hoffman see the patient in partial agreement with the analyst, and write that her dilemma resides in her puzzled recognition of the plausibility of the interpretation. Though she accepts that the analyst is right, she does not want to see her dissatis-faction with him lumped together with her annoyance at the boss. I believe it is quite clear now that there is a power struggle between analyst and analysand. The analysis of resistance regards this tug-of-war as an offspring of symbol distortion, and claims that such conflicts must be resolved by the authority of knowledge, that is, the correct interpretation based on the metapsychology. A different position is that of Gill and Hoffman who, without disagreeing with the diagnostic about the cause of the problems, suggest a more flexible attitude for dealing with them. There is still at third possibility which I would like to invite the reader to consider, based on the disassociation of the interventions from the system of knowledge: the patient's complaints against her boss may be real and not ruses of resistance or projections of transference. This being the case, the analyst would have to choose when to act as technician (analyst), and when to act as person in a conversation. The obvious problem with this third position is that people do not seek psychoanalysis in order to find conversation partners; they look for healers. The patient's question in the passage before last illustrates the point: "When are we going to get away from the illness and onto the cure?" However, if the reason to avoid conversation with the patient is the need to trigger and interpret transference, and if patients want to be analyzed in order to improve their existential experience of life, the excessive conversing on the part of the analyst would sooner or later trigger the patient's dissatisfaction and transferential reaction, and therefore it does not have to be avoided.

A: But at the moment J is a convenient target, I would think.

P: Yes, he's a convenient target because he really is a prick.

A: Yeah, he lords it over you.

P: That's right.

A: And he's very easy to get mad at.

P: That's true. Yeah, I feel like, you know, what you're saying is that I'm mad at J when I'm really mad at you. And that you want me to be mad at you, really, and admit that I'm really mad at you, and that if I won't admit it, then I'm, you know, denying you that, which is mean.

The authors suggest that the patient may be hearing her analyst as encouraging her to act out the transference by feeling mad at him instead of her boss. They argue that the analyst could have addressed the issue of transference without robbing the reality of her anger against J, by stressing that her experiences with the boss could bear resemblance with her experiences with him, although she was reluctant to address the latter. They suggest that the analyst should then link her experience of him with her attitude toward the analytic situation. I think that the patient is progressively moving toward a nonpsychoanalytic conversation. She is surprised at her understanding that the analyst wants her to be mad at him, because this certainly does not count as therapeutic. Actually, she has just voiced her anger by threatening to knock the books off the wall. Would the analyst, uncomfortable with her acting out of this, have made the suggestion of her wanting to knock his penis off in order to make her believe that her outbursts do not threaten him, so much so that he even encourages her anger? In addition, she reasons, if she refuses to feel that anger, the analyst will not consider her attitude as neurotic, which would be a technical classification of behavior, but as mean, which is a moral judgment.

P: [sigh] Do you really think this is all about penises? Or do you just think it because you're a man and, and a Freudian? You know, I mean, I wonder sometimes. You never said you were a Freudian; I assume that you are. Always showing me those dirty pictures [several inaudible words]. Maybe this is all because of the couple of days when I decided you were so brilliant and I knew I would have to get into combat again. So I was just going to say, "I don't think you like me," and that what I, what I was thinking before was that after all this time, I still don't like you. I thought I didn't like you first.

This passage supports my interpretation, for she separates the analyst from the man. The analyst is hopeless, he believes that books are penises, he is a Freudian (with negative connotation). She admired him a couple of days ago (it is not clear who: the analyst or the man?), but she does not like him, and does not think he likes her either. She did not think that analysis had to be "combat"; she tries to talk to him outside the analytic situation, but he is a die-hard analyst and does not concede an inch; she began with that impression and did not like him then, now she confirms her initial impression.

Gill and Hoffman argue that her "masochistic surrender" (her admiration of his "brilliance") is overshadowed by her singling out of "interpretation as a sadistic assault."[16]

A: No, I think you're afraid that, you know when we started to talk about this that you—what comes up is how angry you feel at [inaudible]. . . .

P: Yes, at you?

A: Men. And you are frightened that you won't be liked.
[. . .]

P: I never was. "When you get to college, dear, boys will like you," my mother said. I don't think she said "boys will like you"—that's what I, that's what I felt it really meant. But she said that you'll find boys that you like, that you have more in common with. You see, [inaudible] be based on common interest and good healthy things like that couldn't be based on [raises voice] fucking and sex—[inaudible] to be something nice. It had to be a real relationship, not just sex. Shit.
[. . .]

P: You know, I feel like I'm going to be released from this room and that I'm going to be raging, in a raging fury, and nobody will know why. [laugh] [inaudible] I just walk along, you know, nice and straight. If I get angry enough all at once, then would I get over it? Primal scream. I can't imagine, you know, feeling really, feeling like there isn't anything wrong with me. I was thinking about that the other day. What would it be like, you know to feel that you really just, you know, you were where you ought to be, and everything is just really full?
[. . .]

P: [pause] Just thought of my brother again. I don't think

anything in particular. I just thought of [inaudible].

A: Well what about him?

P: His existence. I was thinking about men. I was wondering whether or not, you know, whether it really—first I was thinking, well, "Is this sort of a chauvinistic position to decide that, you know, women really want to be like men, and they're pissed-off that they don't have cocks?" And what I was thinking about [yawn]—whether that was really true or whether you know what the story really is. And I was thinking about—because, you know, I don't feel that I've ever been particularly dumped on. And I was thinking of men that I knew. [inaudible] Thought of my brother, because we talked about him before. It's weird, because I never really thought of my brother very much until, you know—I mean, when we were kids I did. But I never really thought of him as a figure in my life, an influence. I always thought that I was the stronger personality. But I think the reason I thought that is because I had to think that. [pause]

The patient abandons the power struggle and behaves like a good patient, free associating and looking for analogies in her memory that can illustrate the points made by the analyst: penis envy and hatred against men. Gill and Hoffman write that she is enacting a submission to the analyst. I would say that she just gives up on a struggle that seems totally unrewarding. She is going to analysis because she feels the need for help. She knows the theories of penis envy and hatred against men thrown at her in inappropriate contexts will not help her, and she rises against them by calling for a break in the analytic discourse and a renegotiation of the procedures. The analyst, however, does not allow them to talk outside of the analytic situation, as defined by him, and proceeds to treat her for resistance. She is probably desperate for help, and in a cogent shift makes an effort to go along with the analyst's mentality, and see if psychoanalysis can work for her after all. The shift is so sudden that it catches the analyst unaware as his next question illustrates.

A: You mean: as if to deny that you envy him anything.
[. . .]

P: Right. And I started doing that so early that I never even really thought of it, you know, never entered my mind, probably never left my mind. Ha. The meaning of the madness. So, you know, I mean, what I'm thinking is that I don't even have the balls to be mad. You know, I wonder what that means. And it is, you know, in the realm of events, like it is conceivable that I can rise up off this couch and rip a couple of shelves off the wall. But I just would never do it, I don't think. I want. But I just really couldn't do it. Why couldn't I really do it? It's either I'd feel like an ass, or either I would feel—ah, yes, great deal of anger had built up in me and it would certainly justify to rip down the shelves on the wall. And I'd have to think that you thought that. You know—what a good healthy act. And that just seemed like bullshit to think that.

[. . .]

P: Snap up the couch like a folding bed—me in it.

A: I'm not clear about that image about the couch. I would snap up. . . .

P: No, I would make it snap up so I could disappear.

A: Snap up how?

P: Like those folding beds [makes noise], like that. Snap it into a jelly roll. Jelly rolls, black blues music, a synonym for pussy.

A: Yes, I know.

P: You know a lot. Well, I just want to tell you in case you didn't know. [pause] [sigh] What's folding bed mean? Back to the womb?

Gill and Hoffman note that she feels so vanquished that she wants to disappear into the folding bed. She sarcastically out-Freuds her analyst by throwing at him another cliché interpretation: folding couch meaning womb. At this point it seems to me that she has given up on him. She is disillusioned in the realization that he cannot help her. Even when she yields to his terms the effort is unrewarding. At this conclusion she should give up and look for another analyst. But, ironically, she is in analysis precisely to resolve her ambiguity about choosing which shelves she should tear down, and the analysis becomes just another situation steeped in indecision.

A: And also it sounds like some image of using the vagina in such a way as to snap something out.

P: Back to the womb?

A: [several inaudible words]—since it's jelly roll that comes to your mind.

P: [laugh] Well, at least then I think that I have one. Yeah, but what does that mean using that as my weapon? What does all this mean in terms of real life? I know it's real life. It just seems, it seems that nothing is what it seems.

[. . .]

P: The think I liked so much about all the stuff in [inaudible] house was that none of it was what it was, it was all like, you know, trains made out of, uh, apple wood and little granny dolls with fruit faces and all kinds of things like that. You know everything was transformed—a little, a little lighter [yawn] that was a gun. The other things they were all bigger or smaller and weird. Uh, trudge, trudge. [inaudible] Climbing up the hill to Golgotha carrying a cross on my shoulders. [chuckle] Actually I was first thinking of trudging out of the room.

A: [several inaudible words]—you have to get out of here. [. . .]

P: Sure, I would like to. You know, I mean, I say that I know you're not, you know—first I say that you're making up all of these things. And then I, I mean, I know you're not. But I don't, I haven't the faintest idea of what to do about any of it, you know, so I say that. You know, I don't know what it really means. [pause] I wonder if it's good or bad, though. I feel because of this job that I can't really have it out with J. You know, I can't even decide. I mean, sometimes he seems so nice, other times he—I just can't stand him. [pause] Like you, I guess. It's weird to like or not like somebody you never look at.

Note here that, along the line of interpretation I am suggesting, she arrives at a perfect understanding of her predicament. She probably needs her job, but has to deal with J. She needs therapy, but has to deal with her analyst. Would trudging away from her job and the therapy relieve her angst, or should she put up with both, because another job and another analysis are hard to come by, and after all the other boss and the other analyst may be as bad as the present ones? Indecision may be her stereotypical impasse in life which she wants to break and change. The analysis of resistance based on the interpretation of neurosis as linked to a sexual genesis can certainly lead analyst and analysand to a satisfactory outcome. The analysis of transference, likewise, can be successful, and in the present case, as Gill and Hoffman claim, it would have been a more suitable path to take. But it is hard to believe that the analysis of transference would be the best choice in every case. My claim is that a conversation focusing on the central problem of this patient's existential ordeal, her ambiguity to make decisions, could also lead to a satisfactory result. As a consequence, what seems to me to determine the best line of analysis to pursue is the agreement between analyst and analysand upon the conceptual interests they wish to discuss, even if the consensual platform is just a temporary basis from which the dialogical disagreement will unfold.

In a last effort to get something out of analysis, the patient drops her critical approach and behaves as an apprentice to the language of psychoanalysis, in the hope that by learning this form of knowledge, she will eventually be cured. The following excerpt from the session reveals the patient's new role as a disciple of the analyst.

P: [silence] Hmm. I was thinking about a lot of things. And I was thinking I didn't want to tell you any of them, because I wanted to just, you know, deliberately keep it all from you. I was just thinking about whether or not I really hated men. And I was thinking of ones that I don't hate, and I either, either I—if I really like them a lot [yawn] then I feel nervous if I'm around them; if I feel sort of neutral, neutral and positive, toward positive, then that's cool. But there aren't a lot that I really hate. Except I don't know if that's really true. I only hate them some of the times. Like, it's only some things they do that I hate, it's not their whole, whole selves. Every attempt fails. I really want you just to cure me, so I can walk out, you know. I don't want to cure myself, because I don't think I can cure myself.
     [. . .]
A: And what do you think your idea of a cure is?
P: To not want the cock. To be happy not having one, because I don't have one. And I'm not ever going to have one.
     [. . .]
A: But you thought of a cure as being, getting one. Being given one. Finding out how to get one.
P: Did I say that? Probably did. Well, either one. It's worse to be left sitting between two stools. Yeah. I guess I really want one and that I'd be—you know, it's like being given Soma, figuring how to live with your infirmity. Just take dope till you die. I guess the real cure would be to figure why I feel I got to have one.
A: Yes.

The patient abandons the idea that cure means to learn how to decide without ambiguity. She adopts the belief without much conviction that she will become cured when she frees herself from penis envy. The analyst pushes the interpretation further along these lines, "satisfied that she has seen the light," as Gill and Hoffman ironically conclude.[17] For them, during this session neurosis was enacted, and not analyzed.

The Rhetoric of Insight

The three possible approaches to interpret this session of psycho-analysis—here outlined as the analysis of resistance based on the sexual motivation of the symptomatic behavior, the analysis of transference focusing on the actual interaction without losing sight of the sexual causes, and the pragmatic discussion of what common sense indicates as the problem (the patient's ambiguity)—are not exclusive among themselves. They are not the only possible interpretations either. And it is impossible to decide on the merits and shortcomings of each outside of an actual conversational context, I do not mean that one of the transcription, but the one of the real interaction when it took place. Had the patient accepted the analyst's interpretation, Gill and Hoffman could still claim that there were transferential projections, and that although they had not been dealt with directly, they were ultimately resolved in the patient's realization that she had always hated men, because she envied their penises and felt downtrodden for not having one. Her animosity against the analyst would have been one instance of such a hatred. If, in turn, either Gill or Hoffman were the analyst, her anger could have also been successfully diffused by the therapist's analysis of the frustration she was experiencing towards him, developed side by side with his acknowledgment of the painful situation in which she was involved with her boss. As for the causes of such a discomfort, they did not need to be sought after in atavistic sexual frustrations, but if causes were demanded, they could be imputed to the patient's anxiety to get cured, or on any other thing retrievable from the interaction and less exotic than penis envy. Finally, the patient's indecision could have also been made into the central topic of therapy without excluding the possibility of being translated either as the repressed sexuality lurking under resistance, or as the transference to the analyst disguised as irritation with her boss.

The question, therefore, does not seem to be theoretical, for different systems of knowledge could have worked, if only analyst and analysand could agree upon their choice. The question seems to be one of rhetoric: the analyst, operating along the Freudian classical line of shaking the patient with insight, goes through the travails of irony, sarcasm, and outright exhortation in order to elicit a response from the analysand. In Gill and Hoffman's analysis of transference, the interpretations would probably be less sensational, they would be couched in the dialogical situation and, therefore, unfold out of a certain consensus between analyst and analysand: the former accepting that the anger against J is real, the latter agreeing that it also constituted a good symbol for the anger against the therapist. The recognition by the patient that the underlying problem was indecision, repressed fantasies about the analyst, or hatred against men does not have to be followed by cathartic emotions. It can be rationally recognized without much turmoil, and consequently we are in a position to challenge the Freudian assumption that what proves the therapist right is the release of affects in the patient, and propose that the correctness of the approach can be evaluated by the level of consensus between analyst and analysand. Naturally, the analyst in the transcribed session could easily defend himself, by arguing that this is just one session out of ninety-five, and that he was only able to stretch the limits of the patient's tolerance that far on the basis of previously developed consensus. Still, the question is rhetorical, because in the end all that mattered was the move from the patient's discourse to some underlying motives, which could be any within certain limits of acceptability for analyst and analysand as long as agreed upon by both. What seems to cure is not the right interpretation, but just any interpretation plausible for the two interactants, and the great therapeutic move resides in the deconstruction of the analysand's narrative, that is, in picking out underlying themes.

The issue of power is not explicitly addressed either by the analyst or by Gill and Hoffman, although there is a genuine power struggle between therapist and patient during the first half of the session. The analyst plays doggedly in the pursuit of his interpretive schemes without conceding an inch to the patient. He sighs with relief when, towards the end of the session, the patient becomes more accepting of his doctrines revealing disposition to cooperate with him, although she does not do that wholeheartedly. She challenges him, but ends by giving up, because defeating her own analyst is naturally not in her best interest since she hopes that he will eventually cure her. Gill and Hoffman's analysis of transference overlooks the question of power and has the consequence of allaying the struggle that otherwise may arise in the analysis of resistance. By discussing the issues of the here-and-now the analyst diffuses the dominant position in which he finds himself in that asymmetrical power relation, but circumventing the question of power is not necessarily the best therapeutic strategy since power dominance is one of the healing gifts as we so well know in our cultural heritage. Remember the healing power of the royal touch for scrofula in the Middle Ages as well as all the saintly Christian miracles carried out by those who, placing themselves outside of the secular structure of power, became themselves endowed with the awesome power to cure.

We turn now to a form of therapeutic discourse which moved to the opposite extreme of psychoanalysis: family therapy. These therapists give primacy to power in their strategies for treatment, but use it in both subordinate and superordinate positions, depending on the inclinations

The Rhetoric of Insight

of different schools or even on the suitability to each situation of different power constellations. They assumed that the divorce between system of knowledge and therapeutic interventions is complete and designed a form of therapy centered on rhetoric and power alone. In family therapy, the theory is the practice and the practice is the theory.

FAMILY AND THERAPY

AS POWER STRUCTURES

*To try to understand linguistically the power of linguistic
manifestations, to search within language for the principle
of the logic and efficacy of the* language of institution, *is to
forget that authority comes to language from without.*
Pierre Bourdieu

Can saying make it so?
John L. Austin

In the past two decades numerous forms of therapy
have arisen in America, many, and maybe most, owing their inspirational fountainhead to Freudian psychoanalysis, either by drawing
directly on it, or by criticizing it, and thereby unveiling new possibilities
for therapeutic discourse. Family therapy branched off from psychoanalysis by taking both approaches, but it also shaped its practice after
intellectual traditions rather alien to psychoanalysis. It looked for its
founding stones in the works of Gregory Bateson, an anthropologist,
philosopher of science, ecologist, and free thinker, as well as in biology,
cybernetics, and systems theory, hoping to find a formal language to
formulate a theory or describe the clinical practice. Simultaneously with
this intellectual search, the practice of family therapy burst forth, ignited
by a social constellation of factors such as the trend of the late sixties and
early seventies to enhance social welfare. It was more economical to
"treat" families rather than individuals. In addition, the professional
therapeutic establishment had become highly inflated, and the infusion
of the new army of professional therapists, predominantly recruited
among social workers, also helped bring down the cost of therapy,
making it accessible to a wider segment of the population. The first
practitioners, however, were not only social workers, but also psychol-
ogists and psychiatrists who had turned their backs on Freudian ideas
and were beginning to regard the patients' complaints (or the symptoms) as communicative acts, meaningful only within the communicative matrix in which they arose as responses to other acts. Among

51

these early family therapists were Theodore Liz, Nathan Ackerman, Murray Bowen, Salvador Minuchin, and Braulio Montalvo, as well as those already associated with Bateson such as Don Jackson, Jay Haley, Paul Watzlawick, John Weakland, and Virginia Satir.

For these new therapists, "psychological problems" did not stem from the struggle of intrapsychic forces. They were neither psychological nor individual. The complaints brought up by the clients were problems of family communication. Even illnesses with a potentially physical basis, such as anorexia nervosa, alcoholism, and schizophrenia, could have their onset in the family situation and be thereafter supported by the family's communicative matrix. An anorectic girl, for example, would be keeping the family together by playing out her refusal to eat and thereby diverting her parents' and siblings' attention from another problem they all feared might split the family. This other problem could perhaps be tensions between the parents, or a structurally potential clash between a parent and another child. Her anorexia was then a secret pact, established without awareness by the family, in their communicative practices, as the lesser of two evils. As long as the medical and psychiatric establishment treated the disease as the girl's problem, her refusal to eat was reinforced and the symptom aggravated. Normally she kept the whole family mobilized around the duty of feeding her. When the therapeutic establishment joined in with the family, she had to increase her resistance against food and her physical state could only be worsened. The family therapists started to deal with problems such as this by gradually removing the burden from the girl's shoulder, and by facilitating conversations bringing into light different issues of relevance for the family. One tactic often used was to create an alliance with the girl, generally very solitary in her existential plight, by supporting her refusal to eat. The therapist could say, for example, that he did not want the girl to make any efforts to eat in the first weeks of treatment, because if she did, the usual picture of the situation could be altered, raising a barrier against his understanding of the problem. In order not to lose the parents, the therapist could invoke his professional competence and expert judgment. In other words, the therapist would be sending the following message to the girl: "Don't eat now, don't give in to any pressures, you can find people like me, ready to side with you even in your self-destructive struggle." At the same time, the therapist would be enlisting the parents in his effort to save the girl, through a tactic of his own, his expert judgment about what should be done, and not of theirs, which consisted in applying pressure for the girl to eat. This, of course, called for great communicative talents, and family therapy not only placed its diagnostics at the level of communications, but also developed forms of treatment entirely dependent on discursive abilities.

Family therapists reject any concepts of psychodynamics. In connection with their claim that the problems presented by clients are not the product of intrapsychic conflicts, but communicative patterns developed by the group in the course of a history of interactions, they advocate a "treatment" consisting in joining in the family's communicative matrix and helping its members steer their negotiations from within. For these clinicians the word "treatment" is becoming progressively inadequate, but they have not provided us yet with clear phrases describing what they do. They "coach" family communicative rituals, assuming that the communicative matrices are cybernetic models with self-regulating processes and are constantly evolving. The therapist does not change the group from stage "A" to stage "B" like a *deus ex machina*, but becomes a member of the group. His major responsibility is to participate with full awareness in the process of change in operation, helping the family members to steer it. The results are not always the expected ones, sometimes they are not even previously thought of, nor is the therapist's awareness of what is going on always correct, but if the outcome is satisfactory, there is no reason for him not to go along with it. This clinical approach naturally moves family therapists in a direction opposite to psychoanalysis, for the analysts' métier consists in adjusting the clinical interaction with their explanatory schemes of psyche and treatment.

Family therapy, like most fields in clinical practice, is subdivided into many rival schools laying strong claims for the uniqueness of the principles of each which would be irreducible and irreconcilable with the principles of the others. Looking at this speciality of therapeutic discourse from the point of view of a cultural critique, it is inevitable to conclude that these schools have a great deal more in common than the noise of their disputation permits us to believe. My description of their mode of therapeutic discourse aims to capture common trends and is not intended to do justice to any particular school. I do recognize, however, a grand division among family therapists: those who conceive of families as structures or systems of psychosocial roles, and those who regard their groups of clients as people who join in certain communicative matrices. We will begin our discussion, in this chapter, with the therapists who regard families as psychostructures.

Suppose that a family is a group of people classified in psychosocial roles such as father, husband, daughter, sister, and so on. Each role is defined within a cultural tradition, recognized in a society or community, and psychologically carried by each person. The roles are defined, not in isolation, but vis-à-vis other roles, into complexes of rights and duties that link together the dyads of husband-wife and mother-son, the triad of parents-child, and all other possible constellations. This would be a portrayal in cultural, social, and psychological fiction, because although categories such as roles with rights and duties do exist, they are not defined with precision (except by those who regard them as natural entities), and the reality of life is not the enactment of those roles, but their transformation in creative ways whose principles, once written down and made mandatory, would crush that very creativity. This constant process of role transformation is a great deal more a part of reality than the existence of static categories. Structural family therapists are well aware of this and do not regard families as lattices of roles, but, instead, as constellations in a permanent dynamism. In such a realm of metaphor, it follows that family problems are matters of overacceleration, clogs in the wheel, or hindrances of the flow of relations in family life. However, we must temporarily abandon this domain of metaphors, because it is more akin to the systemic family therapists, those who are more interested in communicative matrices than in families. Indeed, the structural therapists do find selves who play roles, but whose lives consist in drawing the boundaries of self. This is naturally not a simple undertaking since it involves a deep-seated cultural heritage, a system of social recognition, and the personal needs of the self. The members of the family carry out this task in their everyday negotiations of boundaries, of closeness and distance, and rights and duties. This is intimacy. Intimacy undoubtedly varies from one cultural tradition to the next, but culture is not its sole underpinning, as some family therapists, bewildered with the cultural variety of their patients, have been led to believe. The workings of intimacy are by and large the task of persons and their "selves." We may define, for example, a sense of intimacy for Japanese culture, and find Japanese families who do not fall within it. Later on, after checking our models to exhaustion, we may realize with surprise that no families entirely fell within it. The conclusion is that it is pointless to draw portrayals of cultural stereotypes of individuals and groups. This statement, however, is never sufficiently emphasized, particularly because the popular view of the social sciences is that these disciplines aim precisely at drawing such static portrayals, a view espoused by many social scientists themselves. But a large number of family therapists learned through their clinical practice to mistrust fixed pictures. What is more, they realized that even the pictures brought in by a particular family must not be taken as an ersatz for reality. As a consequence, the negotiation of boundaries, in the exercise of intimacy, does not fall within any set of parameters that the therapist can know before he has spent some time with the family, and learned what the contours of intimacy are for that group of people.

The structural therapists find two ideal-type poles in the family's exercise of intimacy: disengagement and enmeshment. Either a member of the family may become disengaged, or enmeshed with another, or entire subsystems—such as alliances of siblings, father and son, and others—may move towards these extremes. Salvador Minuchin, one of the foremost family therapists identified as a structuralist, warns us that although these extremes cannot be readily equated with dysfunctional patterns of family interactions, they "indicate areas of possible pathology."[1] Actually, since there are no fixed parameters against which one could plot the degrees of disengagement/enmeshment, it would be inconsistent to assume that any of these states of interaction between persons could be functional or dysfunctional before the therapist finds out which goals they are fulfilling in the family. A suballiance may have been formed between mother and children with a high degree of enmeshment in dealing with a disengaged father who is dying of cancer. On the side of culture, it is generally assumed, for example, that white Anglo-Saxon Protestants tend to enjoy greater distance and clearer boundaries among people than Muslim Arabs, to counterpoint our example. Precisely because of that cultural stereotype, the former group, when perceiving their situation in family life as that described by the stereotype, will define their agenda for transformation through the pursuance of the opposite tendencies; likewise, the latter group will try to counter whatever discomforts they experience in family life by doing the opposite of what they perceived as the root of their problems. These labels have no value whatsoever, either for the social sciences or for family therapy.[2] Consequently the therapist has to find out how the family is organized and how its organization is affecting its present life. The criterion, again, is not a general conception of how families should lead their lives, but what the presented problem is.

Families have sought therapy for all kinds of reasons, from the coercive intervention of a government agency trying to compel a truant to go back to school, to families in which the adults are experiencing marital difficulties. One thing that became clear over these almost forty years of family therapy is that parents tend to detour their problems through their children, or more specifically, through one child whom they choose, or who offers himself, as a volunteer to embody the difficulties of the group. This child begins to behave outrageously by becoming an anorectic, by becoming sexually promiscuous, by failing in school, or revealing all kinds of antisocial behaviors. The parents (more often the mother) decide to seek professional help and go to therapy assuming that there is something wrong with that child. (Many centers of family therapy have developed around child guidance agencies.) The presented problem, then, is what the parents regard as the child's abnormal behavior, which becomes a diagnostic that the therapist will rearrange through a series of rhetorical maneuvers. The most immediate and natural goal will be to shift attention from the scapegoat child, the identified patient, to the parents.

In relinquishing notions of normal and pathological, or theories of family functionality, family therapy is forced to deal with the patient's diagnostic. However, despite the fact that they have not forwarded theories explaining why parents play their differences out through one of their children, or why family constellations come to depend on the efforts of a single member (should the optimum rule be an equal distribution of the burden?), family therapists have agreed on many principles of family life which constitute the bedrock of their clinical practice. Thus they do agree that there are some states of affairs which become uncomfortable for the family, and that in those cases a change is in order. However lacking in theory about family life, the understanding of the process of change is no problem for structural family therapists. They "restructure" families, restore boundaries where they are wanting, or render these boundaries clearer or more diffuse, more or less rigid. They undo alliances and form new ones, engage and disengage family members,[3] all in the name of the problem originally presented by the clients, which in the therapist's churning evolves in different directions, gaining new meanings. In these therapists' explanations, it is this modification of meaning which constitutes change, a process which is always lurking underneath the family communications, and not induced by the clinician. Change thus conceived does not derive from any a priori notions, but becomes defined in the patient and therapist discourse as a rule of thumb which these clinicians discovered after years of experience with families, and intensive teaching and training, as well as publishing transcripts of sessions of therapy with families. Books of family therapy usually present transcriptions of sessions with patients followed by explanations about what the therapist was doing, not explanations of the patients' discourse. We do not find in these books theories and hypotheses illustrated by clinical cases, but only reported sessions with reconstructions of the clinician's interventions which are presented in an ad hoc manner, although fitting the described situation in plausible ways. In two extreme interpretations of this clinical approach, some therapists claim that every step in the session is calculated and every result planned, while others argue that they are improvisors and that everything in a session of family therapy is unexpected. In summary, there are no explanations as to why families operate in a certain way which lead therapists in turn to treat them with the interventions they do. It is all practical knowledge forged in the heat of experience. This, of course, does not render family therapy better or worse as a therapy, but simply rather unusual.

Structural therapists are those who come closer to the formulation of a theory of the family. Some of them, like Murray Bowen for example, operating out of a psychoanalytic matrix, developed notions of growth within the family, transgenerational genesis of behavior and family dynamics.[4] The key concept among the therapists of this persuasion is "self-differentiation." From the moment of birth, the self of the infant develops through progressive stages of differentiation from the mother's self. In this growth it is fundamental that each new leap into the unknown be buttressed by the love of a nurturing adult, whose responsibility is to release control over those parts which need no longer be manipulated, but who at the same time has to continue to support those other parts which still need support. This narrative of structural family therapy would be identical to the Freudian Oedipus saga if it were not for the fact that while Freud plunged this story deep in to the id, the family therapists assigned it to the perceptible surface of family history, as do ego analysts. Minuchin does not deal with genetic processes of self-differentiation, but his concept of enmeshment is equivalent to nondifferentiated selves in the here-and-now, while the narcissistic self of psychodynamic theory resembles Minuchin's disengaged member of the family.

If a theory of the family is lacking among the structuralists, they at least sketch one, while systemic family therapists deliberately turned their backs on theorizing about family life. They preferred instead to reflect about the ad hoc procedures of therapy and of the family's presentation of problems, fused both discourses into one, and proposed a theory of that discourse, as we will see in the following chapter. However, the structuralists' writings about clinical practice are few, although books and videotapes of sessions of therapy are abundant. They have not integrated their methods, which consequently remain, by and large, the product of the therapist's personal talents. Minuchin, for example, who is a wizard in the ballet of family therapy, employs all kinds of intuitions in his clinical practice, to the point that, insofar as his technique is concerned, it becomes meaningless to call him a structuralist or a systemic therapist. As Lynn Hoffman points out, it is extremely difficult to teach his approach, but while she attributes this to peculiarities inherent in the structuralist method,[5] the difficulties stem indeed from the absence of method and its replacement with creative communicative abilities of such a talented therapist as Minuchin.

Since the clinical techniques of family therapy are largely improvisational we will be better assisted in understanding it further by looking into an actual session, unravelling the key concepts with the vivid illustrations from the family and the therapist. This is the first interview of a treatment conducted by Minuchin of a family with an anorectic daughter. But before we plunge into the data, one further consideration is in order. If on one hand Minuchin does not provide his reader with a full-fledged theory of family pathology, on the other hand his specialization with families that have an identified patient suffering from an outstanding illness—such as anorexia nervosa, asthma, or diabetes—camouflages that lack by characterizing the family as pathological, if not because of its way of living, at least because of the fact that it has one member severely ill. Later on, in chapter 4, we will discuss the concepts of systemic therapists who rebelled against the classification of patients into normal and pathological.

This is one of Minuchin's "psychosomatic families."[6] It is composed of Margherita and Carlo, two Sicilian immigrants in their mid-forties, the husband a laborer, and the mother a housewife. They sought therapy for their anorectic daughter Loretta, who was at the time of this first interview sixteen years old. The other children are Sophia (fifteen), Maria (thirteen), and two younger siblings not present at the session. Loretta's narrative about anorexia began two years earlier when she was admitted to a hospital for the first time because of intense abdominal pains. At that time the doctors concluded that there was nothing wrong with her health and suggested that she should look for a psychiatrist, which she refused to do. There followed a history of hospitalizations, and Loretta's weight dropped as low as 75 pounds. The session begins with Minuchin eliciting the story.

Excerpt 1

MINUCHIN: First, I want to understand what has been happening.
            I understand that Loretta has been losing weight for
            the last three years. Is that correct?
LORETTA: Right.
FATHER: Two years.
MINUCHIN: When did it start, Loretta?
FATHER: Two years.
MOTHER: It started at the beginning of Lent. I take her to St.
            Francis Hospital because Loretta, she don't feel too

MINUCHIN: good. She got pain all over. So they want to take picture inside Loretta's stomach, but I say "no." "I take my daughter home."

MINUCHIN: Do you remember that Loretta? (*Loretta nods.*)

MOTHER: So I take Loretta home because I don't want nobody to touch my daughter. So I take her home, and next day Loretta throws up. She cries. She has a pain. So I call the car service, put Loretta in the car, and take her to Dr. Smith. He calls Tenafly Hospital, and from there we go straight to Tenafly Hospital. Loretta stay in bed two weeks there in the hospital.

MINUCHIN: I would like to know from your point of view, Loretta. What was it that you were having?

Minuchin explains that families present their "public" image in first interviews, and that only after having witnessed several "family scenarios" can the therapist form a congruent picture of the problem. However, as experienced as he is with these psychosomatic families, he already knows that her symptoms will decrease as soon as she gains the autonomy necessary for a sixteen-year-old. It is interesting to observe that this initial exchange in the session contains for Minuchin all the ingredients that will compose his diagnostic scenario. The parents speak for Loretta, indicating that she is incompetent to narrate the facts of her illness. Minuchin perceives the mother as claiming to be a good parent and sees the picture of enmeshment with two sides: on one, the mother's overzealous control, on the other, Loretta's hopeless dependence. The session proceeds.

Excerpt 2

LORETTA: The first night that I went to St. Francis Hospital was because I was having strong pains in my abdomen and my back and they found it was a kidney infection and they gave me intravenous since the pain was so great.

MINUCHIN: Okay, so you went then for something very, very specific. And when you went to the Tenafly Hospital, was it a continuation of the same issue?

LORETTA: I don't know. I mean, they never actually said anything there.

MINUCHIN: Since Mother is the memory of the family she will tell, but you will need to check it, because it is your life that she is describing. Okay?

MOTHER: So I take her to Tenafly to my doctor. For two weeks they check Loretta. Loretta, she doesn't eat enough, and the doctor told me, "Take your daughter home and take her to a psychiatrist."

Knowing that Loretta's symptom is interlocked with the mother's concern, Minuchin has to deal with both simultaneously, and so, at the same time that he insists he wants to hear the story from Loretta, he praises the mother as "the memory of the family." He already indicates that he will lead the conversation. He immediately perceives the mother as the more powerful member of the family, and starts from the beginning to introduce the theme of Loretta's autonomy. Notice that all this knowledge he has can hardly be inferred from those initial exchanges; it springs out of his own experience.

Excerpt 3

MINUCHIN: Hold it a moment, because I want to check something. Loretta, when you were in the hospital, you did not eat anything?

LORETTA: For a while, they put a sign up on my bed that said I wasn't supposed to eat anything because they didn't know what was causing the pain. And then I didn't have any appetite. So I had the IV's from the first time until I went home.

MINUCHIN: Okay. Do you know that this happens to many people? If they are two or three days without eating, they lose the appetite. It was at this point that you stopped eating, and this was when? Two years ago?

LORETTA: Right.

MOTHER: So, I stay two weeks with Loretta in the hospital.

MINUCHIN: You stayed in the hospital with her?

FATHER: Yes, she spent many nights with her.

MINUCHIN: But, Mr. Menotti, didn't you miss her?

FATHER: Well, I did miss her, but we managed to go on, you know—

MINUCHIN: What about the little ones? Who handled Giuseppi and Enrico?

SOPHIA AND
MARIA: *(in unison)* Both of us.

MINUCHIN: Both of you? I have the feeling that you, Maria, are a manager. Who is the one who takes responsibility when Mama is away?

MARIA: We share it.

MINUCHIN: Does Sophia try sometimes to boss you around a little bit?

MARIA: Yeah.

He has already decided that the mother is the adversary he will have to conjure with. She tries to resume the thread of the narrative, but he wards her off, first by talking to the father and then to the two other girls.

Excerpt 4

MINUCHIN: That's wonderful. Okay, and Mother stayed two weeks in the hospital. My goodness. That's an Italian heart for you.

MOTHER: One day, my husband told me to come home to see the kids and, "If you still want to go tomorrow, I'll take you in there." So, I said I would see what I can do. So we go home. When I go home, I got a funny feeling. Loretta, she doesn't feel good, so I say to my husband, "You better take me back to the hospital. I have a funny feeling about Loretta." He say, "Oh, no, you stay here." I say, "You take me or I go." So my husband take me there. When I go back, I find Loretta all black and blue. She has pains. She's screaming. I say, "We will call the doctor." So they say nothing is wrong with Loretta. And I say, "What do you mean nothing is wrong with Loretta? She's all black and blue." "That's all right, don't get nervous." So they give her needle, and Loretta, she sleep all night.

MINUCHIN: That means you had the feeling—

MOTHER: Loretta could die.

MINUCHIN: Do you have the same sense about Maria?

MOTHER: Yes, with everybody. All my kids.

MINUCHIN: I don't think Maria sends vibes. I think she is a very self-sufficient kind of girl. If Maria has a pain, I bet you don't know.

MOTHER: If I kiss her I do.

MINUCHIN: What do you think, Maria? If you have a pain, do you think she knows?

MARIA: Yes.

MINUCHIN: She does! What about Father? That's a special gift. Does Daddy have that?

MARIA: Yeah.

MINUCHIN: Is that so, Carlo? Can you experience the pain of your kids as your wife does?

FATHER: Well, I can see by just taking a look at them. If they don't look good, then I assume there is something wrong, you know.

MINUCHIN: That must be just the kind of thing that happens when a family is concerned with children. You look at them a lot.

FATHER: Right.

MINUCHIN: But Margherita says she can hear vibrations from the hospital.

FATHER: I brought her back from the hospital, right? The minute that we were home, she says, "I want to go back." When she got back, Loretta was in bad shape.

Minuchin already sees himself challenging the notion that Loretta is the sick member of the family. He wonders how difficult his task will be to challenge the enmeshment of that "Sicilian Mama" with her daughter. Her claim to know what goes on with her children is "magical" and indicates a pattern of "overinvolvement" which Minuchin tries to challenge by probing an apparently nonenmeshed sibling, but is promptly disqualified by Maria's agreement with her mother.

Excerpt 5

MINUCHIN: I'll tell you something, that feeling is very, very important when the kids are young. That's essential. Let me ask you a little bit, Loretta. You are sixteen now?

LORETTA: Yeah.

MINUCHIN: That kind of sensitivity that Mom and Dad have toward you is very helpful because if you have a problem or a care, then they respond, but when you begin to be a little bit grown up, as you and Sophia are, does it sometimes bother you that Mother still is so sensitive to you?

LORETTA: Sometimes.

MINUCHIN: What about you, Maria? Do you feel sometimes that Mother doesn't know that you are thirteen, that she still thinks you are twelve or eleven?

MARIA: *(sighing)* I don't know. No-o-o.

MINUCHIN: Sophia, what's your feeling? Sometimes she forgets

	that you are fifteen. She treats you as if you are younger?
SOPHIA:	Yeah.
MINUCHIN:	This always happens. When you are very sensitive to the pains of the younger kids, there is then a problem of how to become the mother of older children. A good mother of younger children sometimes becomes a difficult mother for older children. So, you are still a very good mother for Maria, Giuseppi, and Enrico, but I think there is some problem with Sophia and Loretta. I think that you are too much for them.
MOTHER:	No. *(Father laughs)* How?

Minuchin is careful not to deny the mother in her role, but makes sure to convey to her his disagreement with her overprotectiveness. He reflects at this point in the session and states the goal of therapy for this family: to replace the family's view that "we are a normal family with an anorectic child and helpful parents" by the therapeutic teaching according to which "you are a family that got stuck in your development and must grow up to adjust to the growth of your adolescent children." And, he concludes: "The family and I will build this alternative with material carefully culled from their own language and transactions, so that they can feel they are still dealing with the familiar."[7] In the very elicitation of the story he is already doing therapy and his probing is destined more to find the right language than to find out what is going on.

Excerpt 6

LORETTA:	You always have arguments with me and Sophia. Always.
MINUCHIN:	Carlo, help the two girls to talk, because Mama is too strong and they are in the hot spot. Help them to say how they would like Mama to be sometimes.
FATHER:	Why don't you express yourselves about what the doctor is saying? At fifteen, you should know how to say a few words by yourself, huh?
SOPHIA:	I don't have too many fights with Mom.
FATHER:	We are talking about how you wish Mom treats you from now on, since you have become fifteen.
SOPHIA:	I don't know. She doesn't treat me bad.
FATHER:	Do you think Mom needs to be changed to somehow make you feel better?

The Rhetoric of Insight

LORETTA:	I think that's not the point, Dad. It's not the point of changing.
FATHER:	What is the point?
LORETTA:	Dad, you really can't change. Once you are the person you are, you have to try and then compromise a little.
FATHER:	But you wish that Mom could change toward you somehow.
LORETTA:	I am not saying change totally. I'd rather have her worry less.
MINUCHIN:	What you are saying, Loretta, is that it's not total change, but you would like your mother to be less worried about you and the other kids.
LORETTA:	M-hum.

In the last excerpt, Loretta follows the therapist and challenges her mother. Minuchin tries to enlist the father as "co-therapist," beginning to form a "father/daughter coalition against mother,"[8] but his success is not immediate: Sophia backs out, the father only reluctantly accepts the task, and Loretta challenges his ability to lead the family. Loretta brings out an interesting reflection about the concept of "change," and Minuchin glosses it over in terms of his therapeutic goals.

Excerpt 7

MINUCHIN:	Do you think that Mama has too big a heart and that sometimes that makes her worry more than is necessary?
FATHER:	Well, what I've seen, Mama does herself much of the things that the girls could do by themselves. She makes it too easy for them. Now they find it a little hard to begin to manage by themselves and try out this situation.
MINUCHIN:	That's a very interesting and very sensitive view. Can you say it again, because I think Margherita is deaf in this ear? [*touches her ear*]
FATHER:	I am sure Margherita understood already what I'm talking about.
MINUCHIN:	Do you understand what he says? What do you think about that?
MOTHER:	Why do I have to think? I am a mother. The things they can't do, I do.
MINUCHIN:	If the kids say do something, you do.
MOTHER:	What am I to do—let the kids down?

MINUCHIN: Now, what about what Carlo says, that you do more than what they need?

FATHER: You've been doing, and you don't mind doing anything for them, right?

MOTHER: I don't. I help my kids all the time in all ways. That's what I do for my kids, then, all the time.

The overall picture of this family is rather clear to Minuchin: everybody challenges everybody else. In the end the only strength surviving the constantly eroding disqualification is the mother's control, but this proves to be an inadequate model for this family which now has adolescent daughters. The therapeutic strategy is clearly defined as a redressing of power. Loretta needs to feel stronger, but the therapist cannot boost her autonomy without increasing the level of conflict between mother and daughter. This may turn out to be the only alternative to change the power balance, but Minuchin tries a smoother path by bringing the father in to confront the mother, thereby creating a space for the girls in which to gain independence with little aggravation towards the mother.

Excerpt 8

MINUCHIN: I think that you still do not hear clearly what your husband has said, and what Loretta said. Loretta also said something which you did not hear. So say it again, Loretta, so that Margherita can hear it.

LORETTA: That you worry too much. And you've got to try to worry less, because I am sixteen and she is fifteen and she is thirteen and you worry too much, as if we were ten and not sixteen, or fifteen. And let us try to do some things by ourselves. Because if we want to try something, you say, "No, let me do it. It's better if I do it."

MOTHER: Wait a minute, Loretta, I give you the chance—

LORETTA: In certain things that are easy to do. But in other things, you don't dare give us a chance.

MOTHER: Well, sometimes it has to be no.

LORETTA: But it's no to the things that are new to you. To things that you already know about, everything is yes. But to things that are new to you, it's always no. You don't want to hear about it.

MOTHER: When it have to be no, it have to be no.

LORETTA: But, you don't care to listen about it either. You say no

	and that's that. You don't want to talk about it or nothing. You just say no and that's final.
MINUCHIN:	Loretta, I just want to congratulate you. I think you are very good. Sophia, do you help her sometimes?
SOPHIA:	In what?
MINUCHIN:	Do you help Loretta? Because she took the leadership position to defend all three of you. Do you sometimes join her?
SOPHIA:	No.
MINUCHIN:	So, Loretta, you are the only fighter?
LORETTA:	Yes.
MINUCHIN:	Carlo, you have a lovely wife. Your children have a lovely mother. But I think that she can become a problem for the children that are growing up.
FATHER:	Yeah, I thought that, too. In the situation of these two girls, now that they wish to do things but they are not really prepared to do, just because—
MINUCHIN:	They didn't have any experience. Yes.

In formulating general principles, family therapists have concluded that these identified patients who bear the brunt of the symptoms of family problems have no capacity to react differently than behaving symptomatically. It is interesting, though, to compare Minuchin's comments on the case in his book of 1978, with those in the book of 1984. In the later book he concludes that Loretta can challenge her mother "in the area not related to food,"[9] and consequently the hypothesis of the hegemony of the symptom falls through. In the earlier book, however, the discrepancy between symptomatic and asymptomatic behavior is at best puzzling. This is the comment for the same passage: "Loretta's challenge seems effective and appropriate. Therapist feels impressed by its quality and wonders why Loretta is involved in anorectic behavior, since she does not shun interpersonal conflict in other areas."[10] The two slightly different assessments of the situation can become problematic if one expects that these explanations of therapy sessions are theories of therapeutic discourse, but if one assumes that no sphere of discourse can be foregone by a priori explanations and that a posteriori explanations are capricious reconstructions, then these explanatory incongruities become irrelevant.

In the previous excerpt, Minuchin introduces the notion of a power struggle in the family by asking if Loretta fights alone. He prevents the father from sliding back into solidarity with the mother against the daughters, as he rephrases Carlo's statement that the girls "are not really prepared to do" by "they didn't have any experience."

Excerpt 9

FATHER: You don't understand. You'd worry if they went out
            and weren't back on time.
MOTHER: I don't know what kind of boys she meets afterward,
            but with the school boys, they don't bother me. I'm a
            mother, right? So I say, "You have to watch yourself
            and at ten o'clock you have to be home." What's
            wrong with that?
MINUCHIN: I don't know that anything is wrong.

Commenting on this passage, in 1978, Minuchin wrote that he found
himself lost, wondering whether he had not been unfair with the
mother. He writes that the common transaction pattern in this family is
to make challengers feel disqualified and guilty, and that he falls into
this trap.[11] In 1984, the same passage leads him to ponder that "as a
father I recognize and respect the parent's fear."[12] These different
nuances in the evaluation of the session tell us that the reconstruction of
the situation is open-ended, and that these descriptions of sessions of
therapy cannot serve the purpose of underlying theoretical principles, as
much as they could not already in the comments on the session of
psychoanalysis in chapter 2.

Minuchin introduced the notion of "triangulation" according to which
parents' disagreements are effaced by the reframing of the problem in
terms of the "bad" behavior of the child. These actions regarded as "bad"
bring the parents together in their effort to make the child change. The
identified patient, in turn, persists in the behavior as long as he perceives
it as fulfilling that role of averting conflict between his parents. The
parents come together in opposition to the child in what Minuchin calls
the "detouring-attacking," or in support of the child in the "detouring-
supportive."[13] The triangulation, in addition to buttressing the family's
view of itself, also serves the purpose of diffusing conflict in actual
exchanges when a confrontation between two members is detoured by
the intervention of a third member who starts a symptomatic behavior
in order to distract the attention of the two fighting relatives, or start a
fight of his own. This idea naturally draws heavily on some notion of
unconscious, or unawareness, because neither the child nor his parents
are aware of what is going on, but family therapists do not explain to us
in what part of thought these underlying meanings of behavior stand.

Excerpt 10

MINUCHIN: You feel defeated. Carlo and Margherita, talk with
            Loretta about that, because that is a very important

	issue–the issue of how to help each other. And I think that since you are from the old country and they are from the new country, they have different ideas. And I think that they don't know how to talk with you.
MOTHER:	They know how to talk to me. I am of the old country, but I grew up over here, too.
MINUCHIN:	The girls feel that you are too strong for them.
MOTHER:	No.
MINUCHIN:	I said yes.
MOTHER:	With Sophia, there are no problems. She never asked me thing do I have to say yes or no. We have a little problem with Loretta.
MINUCHIN:	Margherita, you are not hearing.
LORETTA:	I would like to interrupt for a minute. It is a big problem with my parents coming from the old country and us being raised and educated and born here, because we use certain words, but they don't understand them.
MOTHER:	Oh, Loretta.
LORETTA:	Like, right now, you're getting kind of angry because I'm saying this, but it's true. We use certain words and you don't understand them. You know your own meanings for them and you misunderstand what one of us is trying to say to you, and when we explain to you what the real thing is, you don't want to hear about it and won't unless it was the way you said it.
MOTHER:	Well, this is—Loretta—
LORETTA:	Even now it's happening. You don't understand sometimes what Daddy's saying or the doctor is saying or even what I am saying now. You're getting angry at me.
MOTHER:	No, I don't get get angry with you. I want to know when I disappoint you.
LORETTA:	I am not saying you disappoint me, Mom, but it's time you let loose a little bit.
MOTHER:	I lose all the time. You win all the time in the house. Not your sister, not the other sister, not your brother, not your father. You win, Loretta.
LORETTA:	You know why? Because I'm the only one who fights back. The others just sit back and take—
MOTHER:	Why do you fight back then? Why do you fight back and you stop eating?

LORETTA: That's another thing. You are always bringing up
             eating. That's what makes me even sicker.

Excerpt 10 provides us with an illustration of Minuchin falling within
the trap of triangulation. Loretta then takes over the fight from
Minuchin, as she steps in, begging her pardon to "interrupt for a
minute." In this part of the session we come full circle from Loretta's
assertiveness on issues different than food, such as her mother's inability to understand the values of the young, to the mother's final move
which equates Loretta's forays into independence with rebellion and
anorexia. In the cases of two other psychosomatic families previously
presented in the book, the identification of the anorectic patient's refusal
to eat with rebellion is considered a therapeutic move destined to thwart
the symptom. In this family, on the contrary, Minuchin is culling the
rebellious behavior out of the symptom and trying to preserve it. In
Loretta's family, the efficacity of the equation of anorexia with rebellion
has lost its impact, because the mother herself uses this diagnostic as one
of her weapons to subdue her daughter. As it can be inferred, no
behavior is pinned down into a definite meaning; every move or communicative action is a strategic maneuver in a game of power. Whatever
is said means exclusively what it entails as a power claim. The restruc-
turing of the family is a redistribution of power in which the therapist is
the arbiter and main player, forming and undoing alliances without
alienating those whose power is being diminished. The verbal skills
called upon to accomplish such a task fall nothing short of Minuchin's
favorite metaphor for therapy: ballet.

Excerpt 11

MOTHER: That's why we're here. I told you this morning—
LORETTA: Mom, I am the subject in this case, and that's why I'm
             scared.
MINUCHIN: Loretta, you are wrong. You are not the subject, the
             family is the subject.
LORETTA: Yeah, but none of us would be here if it wasn't on
             account of me.
FATHER: She thought she was the focal point, and that's why—
MINUCHIN: I am interested in the family.
LORETTA: I realize that.
MINUCHIN: To me, it is very important what's happening now.
             That the girls are growing up and don't know how to
             grow up.
FATHER: Right.

MINUCHIN:	Carlo, you think that Margherita is too easy and that it's not helpful to the girls. They are fifteen and sixteen and Mama needs to change a bit.
MOTHER:	Tell me something. Why am I to change?
MINUCHIN:	Carlo will—
MOTHER:	Come on, say it.
FATHER:	Well, really, I didn't know the ways she needs to change.
MINUCHIN:	The things that you were saying. That she is too easy—
FATHER:	You see, I have a problem. There is a misunderstanding between me and my wife and Loretta.
MINUCHIN:	M-hum.
FATHER:	Loretta was assuming that I was the odd father—the one who said no all the time. If I see a situation in which she wanted to do something, I would let her do it. My wife blames me that I was going to say no even when I didn't know anything about the situation.
MINUCHIN:	Let me understand. Sometimes you feel that Margherita and Loretta are together in something and that you are the bad guy.
FATHER:	In their own mind, they assume that I want to stop whatever they are planning to do, you know.
MINUCHIN:	Do you know what your father is talking about?
LORETTA:	I know what he's saying, but that's another misunderstood situation.
MINUCHIN:	Do you know what Carlo is saying, Margherita?
MOTHER:	What about, Carlo?
FATHER:	What about? Just about everything. When she wanted to go out, you assumed I was going to say no, right?
MOTHER:	Wait. When Loretta was asking me, "Ma, I want to go out," I say to Loretta, "Yes."
FATHER:	You say, "Loretta, yes," before telling me, then?
MOTHER:	Yes. I say, "You go out, Loretta. I tell Daddy." When you came home, you asked, "Where is Loretta." I say, "Out" "Where?" "With a boy." "Who?" you say. I say, "I know the boy. I know the mother. Don't worry about it. She's okay." I gave Loretta until ten o'clock to go out because Loretta stay one month at the hospital and the doctor say, "You have to give freedom to your daughter." I do what the doctor say.

FATHER:	But this is not the point.
MOTHER:	That's the point, Loretta went out.
FATHER:	The point is that you two undermine me.
MOTHER:	I'm sorry because you say one day, "If Loretta go out with a boy, I'll break her neck because she is too young."
FATHER:	That was when? When she was ten years old or eleven years old.
MOTHER:	No, thirteen. She tells me, "I'm afraid to tell Daddy because I will go out with a boy and Daddy don't want me to go out!" And I say, "Forget about it, don't worry about it." Loretta wants to go out with a boy, I say yes. I told you, Carlo, please don't work in the nighttime no more. I want you in the daytime. I want you at the table with the family because I told you I'm tired to take care of seven people, go shopping, go for the bills. I'm tired.
FATHER:	Let's come to my point, right? She claimed that I was going to stop her and all of the things that you have been planning to do. Assuming I was going to stop her. And I don't understand why you wanted it that way.
MOTHER:	Loretta told her mother because you told Loretta if she goes out, you break her legs.
FATHER:	Loretta should tell me—
MOTHER:	No, Carlo, because you're her father. She comes to her mother.
FATHER:	No, what you did was wrong. You taught her wrong about me.

In excerpt 10, is Minuchin trying to "detriangulate" Loretta by taking her place in the confrontation with the mother, or is he falling into a trap? It does not matter. Now, in excerpt 11, he coaches the father into the role of mother's sparring partner. Carlo is reluctant to accept Minuchin's encouragement and walk on thin ice. He glosses the situation over by calling it "a misunderstanding between me and my wife and Loretta," thus warding the therapist off, but soon his exchanges with his wife escalate to a confrontation in which Margherita accuses him of being the true tyrant in the family, the one who refuses to give freedom to the girls, while he counteraccuses her of imparting this "wrong" image of him to the daughters.

Minuchin leads the family in the enactment of their drama. The tension underlying these rough exchanges is probably different from the tension present in similar situations at home. In Minuchin's office they talk about the problems at the therapist's request. Furthermore, they enact their difficulties under the therapist's direction. No single scene evolves freely; Minuchin controls every move. The metaphor of ballet is absolutely appropriate because even if they do not dance, they are definitely on stage, representing.

Excerpt 12

MINUCHIN: I want to talk with both of you, Loretta and Sophia, because your father says that you two don't know him. That if you would talk with him, you would find that he is a person who can understand and can compromise. And he is saying that you don't know him because you go and talk with Mother about him instead of talking directly with him.

For Minuchin, the two therapeutic moves par excellence, are "blocking" and encouraging operations which the therapist carries out in a forthright manner as he does in excerpt 12, putting an end to the bickering between husband and wife.

The strategy of his therapy with psychosomatic families consists in challenging their *reality*, that is, their representation of the family situation, their *enmeshment*, their *overprotectiveness* and their deep-seated patterns of *conflict avoidance.* He leads the family to perceive that they are not a normal family with a "sick" or "bad" child; that the autonomy of each member is not a threat to the integrity of the group, a fact which in the case of these families often translates as: the children can be given more freedom; that, as a consequence, the children can do many more things by themselves than the parents expect; and finally, that disagreement does not have to lead into unending conflict which threatens to jeopardize the family welfare, but which is necessary in the process of negotiation of boundaries and in the experiencing of intimacy in family life.

The session proceeds with Loretta assuming her usual role as the family fighter. She attacks her father, and when the situation gets too tense for her, she lets off steam by presenting herself as the great victim of the family insofar as only she fights her parents' unfairness, speaking for her siblings who are ungrateful. Minuchin supports the argument trying to change its meaning from conflict and dead end to negotiation and beginning.

Excerpt 13

MINUCHIN: These arguments are good. Loretta needs to be able to express her mind to you, and you need to be able to tell her what you have in mind. What your father said about Sophia and Maria are true. He said that Mother does that with you, and now he is saying that you do that with them. He has an eye for the process of growing. He knows that to grow up, one needs to struggle. And he says when you take the job of fighting for Maria, she is not growing up.

LORETTA: I know, but I'm not struggling for her. I'm doing it for myself, is what I'm saying.

MINUCHIN: Loretta, your father says that if you say to him, "Father, I am sixteen years old and I have a date and I want to go out," he'll say, "Yes." Carlo, talk with Loretta. Because she needs to know you, and she needs to know how much power she has.

In the treatment of anorectic families the first session is long, sometimes lasting many hours. The first part is devoted to what Minuchin calls "forming the therapeutic system," a process in which the therapist "joins in" with the family system and assumes its leadership. In the first exchanges of this session he shows us a little bit of everything that is to happen throughout the treatment. He supports the family system as it is, but also challenges it; he agrees with their view of matters and proposes alternative views; he acquiesces with the positions of strength and weakness of different members or subgroups, but introduces imbalances in these hierarchies by boosting the weak and restraining the strong. In the second part of the session, he eats a meal with the family. When the food is brought in, Loretta starts to cry and leaves the room. Minuchin follows her and talks to her in the hallway. He tells her that she does not have to eat. They make a pact: her eating problems will be private, she will eat alone. She writes her present weight on a paper napkin and passes it over to Minuchin. Only the two of them will know if she is gaining or losing weight. For now, Minuchin informs her that her task will be to keep her weight stable. With this move he attempts to dissociate the family conflicts from Loretta's eating habits. He wants Loretta to realize that she can fight her parents and win without having to hold her body hostage in her blackmail maneuvers to keep them at bay.

Excerpt 14

MINUCHIN: Loretta, how old does your mother think you are?

LORETTA: I don't know. Apparently not sixteen.

MINUCHIN: I absolutely agree with you. If you are not sixteen, you will not begin to eat. Because Loretta is fighting a battle for winning. She is fighting in the area of food and she says, in this area, "I will win."

MOTHER: She wins me all the time, my daughter. Do you know by what? Because I say something, "Loretta, we have to do this." "Oh no, Mama, we have to do this." I say, "No." Loretta then she stop eating, because we have to do it Loretta's way all the time. If we don't do it Loretta's way, we have to put our hands in the air; we have to stop everybody. I have to stop Sophia. I have to stop my husband. I have to stop the phone ring. I can't talk to nobody because Loretta, she nervous. She do anything to send me, my husband, her sister, her brother, any way she wants. We say, "Yes, Loretta." We have to do anything you want and everything will be okay. If we do something we don't have to do, forget about it. Loretta, she say, "No."

MINUCHIN: Can you answer your mother, Loretta? Carlo, let Mama sit near Loretta. Loretta, talk with Mother, because she says that you are controlling the house.

LORETTA: I am not controlling nobody, Mama.

MOTHER: You're controlling your father, you're controlling me, Sophia, Enrico, Maria, Giuseppe. Why, Loretta?

LORETTA: I'm not controlling nobody. It's just that somebody has to do something.

MOTHER: No, you do not. That's me and your father's job. You have to do something by yourself. You are not to interfere with Sophia, Maria—

LORETTA: I want to stand by myself and you are stopping me.

MOTHER: No, Loretta, Mama never stopped you.

LORETTA: Yes, Mama. You may not realize this sometimes, but you're doing it anyway.

MOTHER: But sometimes, Loretta, you put us in the world in a way that we can't do nothing. We have to agree with you. We have to do what you want. But sometimes we can't. And if we don't get what you want, you start crying.

LORETTA: No, I'm not saying that, Ma.
MOTHER: Screaming. Pulling the chair. Pulling anything the
           way you want.
LORETTA: No, Mama.
MINUCHIN: Does she do things like that?
MOTHER: Yeah. I'm sorry to have to—
LORETTA: Pull the chair?
MOTHER: She gets nervous so forgets about anything that she
           does. She pulls the chair, she throws her shoes, her
           clothes, everything—
LORETTA: Since when?
MINUCHIN: She has temper tantrums? Like little children?
MOTHER: Oh, she got the temper, Loretta. I'm sorry—
MINUCHIN: Like little children, she does?

Minuchin warns his readers that working with anorectic families can be very frustrating, because if on one hand they show ready acceptance to the therapist's interventions, on the other hand they undercut every move in their endless recursive exchanges. The passage above illustrates the pattern as Loretta and her mother compete for the role of loser in the family; on other occasions they compete for the role of winner. Nobody ever loses or wins. Minuchin culls out of the exchange the image that Loretta is childish, a view that he will insist upon as a substitute for "sick" or "bad." Loretta reacts to her mother's accusations.

Excerpt 15

LORETTA: That is not the truth. You're making me sound like a
           bad person.
MOTHER: You're not a bad person. You're—
LORETTA: Well, that's exactly what you're doing.
MINUCHIN: She is saying that you have temper tantrums. She is
           saying that you are childish.
LORETTA: I am not childish.
MINUCHIN: That's what she's saying.

The exchange continues as Minuchin draws progressively more heavily on the image of childishness at the same time that he monitors the conflict between mother and daughter.

Excerpt 16

MOTHER: Sophia tells me, "Don't do these things. You're killing
           yourself." Now you, Loretta, you tell me this, see?

How many aspirin? I'll get them for you, because
when you get nervous, you stop eating. Right away,
no food. Not get up from the bed. You don't want to
see nobody. You don't want to talk to nobody. And
Mama cries.

MINUCHIN: Is your mother saying that you are blackmailing
them? That your not eating is a way of controlling
them?

LORETTA: That's not—

MINUCHIN: That's what she's saying. She's saying that you are
controlling her by having temper tantrums and not
eating.

LORETTA: I don't have temper tantrums.

MINUCHIN: That's what she's saying.

LORETTA: Well, she's wrong, because it's not true.

MOTHER: Why you do the same thing to the hospital? You
blackmail the doctor. You don't want to eat. You don't
want the tube out. The doctor told me, "Your daughter
say she eat. I'm sorry, Mrs. Menotti your daughter, she
don't eat." So then I have to tell the doctor the truth.

LORETTA: I don't blackmail nobody.

MOTHER: That's what they told me. You don't eat. They bring
food in and you give it to somebody else.

The confrontation momentarily recedes into enmeshment, a situation
in which the mother experiences Loretta's self-destruction as her own,
and Loretta, in turn, experiences her mother's unhappiness as the cause
of her own misfortune.

Excerpt 17

MOTHER: I lose a daughter if you do that way.

LORETTA: Well, you have to be compromising, too. If you're
losing her, it's because of you too. It's not because—

MOTHER: No, Loretta, I want you. I want all my kids healthy.

LORETTA: Well, then help. Then don't insist—

Minuchin intervenes again in order to break the vicious circle of the
pattern of confrontation which keeps the issues simmering, never
escalating into open conflict nor being resolved, but every time he tries,
he himself becomes trapped in the whirlpool of bickering that per-
petuates that family's stalemate. He tries to break that balance by
making Loretta's behavior complementary to her mother's, which is an

attempt to proceed with a certain degree of enmeshment. Excerpt 18 illustrates the point.

Excerpt 18

MINUCHIN: I think that Loretta feels a loser in your family. You say that Loretta is a winner. I think she is a loser.

MOTHER: No, she's a winner.

MINUCHIN: I saw, just now, that she was a loser.

MOTHER: Because she cries?

MINUCHIN: Because she feels absolutely helpless to defend herself. I don't know. You are very powerful. Do you know that?

MOTHER: Might be because my daughter lose weight. Everyday I told her she have to eat.

MINUCHIN: The issue is not eating. Loretta will begin to eat when she is sixteen and when you treat her as if she is sixteen.

MOTHER: You see, I can't do anything with Loretta. Loretta, she say, "You don't love me because you don't want to get this." I have to do what Loretta say. If I don't do what Loretta say, what I have to do? Loretta talk.

MINUCHIN: I know that she feels that you are very powerful. I don't think that you let her feel that she is sixteen.

MOTHER: No, she is the winner. Loretta, Mommy don't tell you you are sixteen?

LORETTA: Yeah, you tell me, but you don't treat me like sixteen. You treat me like I was two years old.

MOTHER: No, Loretta.

LORETTA: Yes, Mama.

MINUCHIN: Margherita, you do so many things for your daughter that she becomes an extremely childish, incompetent person.

He insists on this point and later on in the session takes Loretta's hands and arms and moves them as if he were handling a puppet, in an illustration of what the mother does to her daughter. He enacts the descriptive metaphors with which he redefines the family situation, as well as the old images that the family share, with the objective of making them see with clarity, see from outside, instead of acting out. He makes them feel as if they had written a play without being aware of it. They write it by enacting it in their everyday lives. So he makes them enact it one more time and brings them simultaneously off the stage, to sit in the audience and watch the drama.

Excerpt 19

LORETTA: With all of you.

MINUCHIN: Carlo, she said something that was nice. She said she is looking for a job because she wants to be out of the house. And this is important for a young person. You want that, also. Why are you making that an argument? Answer her without making it an argument.

FATHER: If it is possible, can you tell me what kind of a job you are looking for?

LORETTA: Anything that I'm able to do.

FATHER: Anything, like what?

LORETTA: Office work or help around the office. Straighten papers and what not. Nothing so difficult that I won't be able to do it.

FATHER: That will make you happy if you find something to do like that?

LORETTA: Yes, it would.

MINUCHIN: Could you help her? Could you help her with that?

FATHER: She never asked me before. If it's possible, why not?

MINUCHIN: Could you talk with her about some of the ways in which you could help her?

FATHER: Well, if she had told me exactly why—

MINUCHIN: She is telling you now. Don't make an argument out of it.

FATHER: You want me to help you find a job?

LORETTA: Yes, I'd like that.

MINUCHIN: Okay. It's possible, but it is difficult. You have been involved in many fights. And I think you need to fight, Loretta, but with arguments suited to teenagers. I think that you should not start eating with the family until you are sixteen. How old are you now?

LORETTA: Sixteen.

MINUCHIN: When was your birthday?

LORETTA: Last week.

MINUCHIN: Last week, but you are not sixteen yet. I would say to avoid fighting about food. And since Loretta will not start eating until she is sixteen, I want Loretta to eat alone. At the point in which she begins to eat, she will be exactly sixteen. Then, she will come back because then you will not fight with her about food. I think, Loretta that you should not put too much weight on because your face looks rather nice long. But you need to gain probably ten pounds. But, this is for you to decide. Because at sixteen, you will need to do things on your own. At home, I want you, Carlo, to talk with your wife, and then talk with Loretta, about what rights does a sixteen-year-old have and what obligations. Can you help your wife to think like that? That a sixteen-year-old has obligations?

FATHER: I will try.

MINUCHIN: Can she hear?

FATHER: Margherita, did you hear what I said?

MOTHER: I hear good.

FATHER: Do you think you need the doctor to tell you?

MOTHER: I think so.

MINUCHIN: Okay. Carlo, you will need to talk with Margherita. I think she has run the house for too long alone, you know. You will need to talk with your father about jobs, Loretta. Maybe he can help you with this and other things. Carlo, can you begin to let Loretta know you—

FATHER: What I want for Loretta—excuse me for interrupting you—is to think different about me. She has to think about me not as an obstacle course.

LORETTA: Well, I can't think it, Dad, unless you show it.

FATHER: I have to show you before you will believe me, huh?

LORETTA: Well, so far you haven't proved anything to show me that you are any different. You say it here, but when we go outside, it's no different.

MINUCHIN: For this week, before you return again, I want you, Loretta, to talk to your father twice for a half an hour. Carlo, you will select two evenings to talk with your daughter. Today is what? Friday? Talk with him during the weekend one time and talk with him next week, Loretta. If she doesn't do that, you make a time, Carlo, and you say, "I want you to know me." And you talk no more than half an hour.

FATHER: Okay.

MINUCHIN: No more than half an hour and twice during this

> week, Loretta. I want you to talk with your father.
> Maybe the first time you tell him something about
> you. Okay? So that he will know you. The second
> time, I want you to tell her something about yourself,
> Carlo. I think she needs to know you and that will be a
> help. Carlo will take over more of helping Loretta.
> Will that be a help, Margherita? Loretta, when your
> parents argue, you do not enter. Okay? Margherita,
> she will start eating at the point in which she is
> sixteen, and she will not die of that. If she loses
> weight, then we will think differently. If she
> maintains the weight which she has now, it's safe for
> the moment. So, you don't worry about that.

He concludes this long session with each actor, leading them to perform the roles present in his own script of a new life for that family. The problem is no longer anorexia, but that Loretta wants to find a job. Loretta is no longer going to deal with her domineering mother, but with her weak father made strong. The father drifts towards the usual bickering (". . . if she had told me exactly why"), but Minuchin shores him up: "She is telling you now. Don't make an argument out of it." The closing remarks are optimistic and present an entirely new portrayal of the situation. Loretta is sixteen, but has not grown up to that age. Her mother is loving, but also smothering. She must be kept out. The father should be brought in.

The treatment went on for four months. Loretta stabilized her weight around 105 pounds. In a follow-up one and a half years later, she had found a job which she had kept for six months, and had reenrolled in high school. Her relationship with her mother continued to be stormy.

In the description of the session in the book of 1978, the procedures are described exactly as they are, ad hoc, and the whole picture emerges step-by-step as a direct reflex of the immediate consequences of the participants' verbal interventions. In that account there is a pressure to illustrate the techniques and principles outlined in the beginning of the book. In 1984, Minuchin presents an edited transcription of the session, discussing his therapeutic moves from a deductive point of view, that is, as an illustration of his general assumption about families and therapy. The account is more relaxed and without denying the earlier interpretation of the session, it provides a more integrated picture. In a postscriptum between an imaginary reader and himself, Minuchin explains that the road with that family was "long and meandering," that what triggered the crisis in the family was the emergence of Loretta and

Sophia into adolescence, a change which challenged the family's hier-archy. He writes: "Now—and this is an interesting paradox—Loretta developed a symptom of rebellion that also contained increased close-ness. It was change without changing, since her illness elicited a concern and overcontrol common in this family, while her rebellion was con-fined to food. It's what systems analysts call a first-order change: the individual changes in a way that maintains the system's patterns."[14] He changes the family's view of the situation, however, his target is not really their system of knowledge, but their power structure which he changes by freeing Loretta, if not completely, at least from the imme-diate grip that made her feel so helpless. At this point, Minuchin's imaginary reader asks if that is enough, if the family should not have been led to understand where they were coming from, what was being done to them. Minuchin's answer is this: "If I say yes, I will dilute my message. If I say no, I will dilute my message. I can't go on."[15] The answer, however, is not as riddled as he makes it seem, and can be found in the other book where he originally presented the case and where he writes, "Issues of ethics and morality are important, but they must not undercut the healing process."[16] Healing is made into an issue bigger than morality, an assumption quite common in therapeutic dis-course, from psychoanalysis to family therapy. In addition, the process of healing is regarded as a change in power relations and therapy, as a rhetoric capable of effecting such a change. The therapist does not have to explain his procedures to the patient. Since explanation is only the other side of interpretation in understanding,[17] the therapist also is released from interpreting. Therapy becomes improvisation in the here-and-now of the session, and therapeutic knowledge is the reconstruc-tion of these improvisational maneuvers. The consequence of this view is that knowledge is regarded as the grist for the mills of power and rhetoric; however, it remains undeniable that the therapist leans to-wards some solutions rather than towards others, and this is a form of knowledge.

In the following chapter we turn to systemic family therapy and its view that healing is not necessarily change, because power relations are in constant flow. In certain circumstances the role of the therapist may be that of a mere witness of a process of change that inexorably breaks forth. And not only that, but power itself is a metaphor of knowledge and, therefore, equally an object for manipulation. The therapists who espouse this view retreat to the last trench lines of the Western heritage: rhetoric.

4 SYSTEMIC AND

COMMUNICATIVE MATRICES

Novelty is a quality which does not depend on the use-value of the commodity. It is the source of the illusion which belongs inalienably to the images which the collective unconsciousness engenders. It is the quintessence of false consciousness, of which fashion is the tireless agent. This illusion of novelty is reflected, like one mirror in another, in the illusion of infinite sameness.
Walter Benjamin

As we discussed in the preceding chapter, the family therapists have yet to fully spell out their ideas about families as structures, systems, or organized groups. The field does not seem to be moving in that direction; as a matter of fact, the predominant trend is an ever-growing tendency to study communicative processes through cybernetic models which has swept the imagination of most practitioners. Family therapists are divided into the following groups: the structuralists (e.g., Minuchin), the strategic therapists (e.g., Haley), the homeostatic systemic therapists (e.g., the group formed at the Mental Research Institute in Palo Alto, California—henceforth referred to as MRI), and the evolutionary systemic therapists (e.g., the Milan group).[1] In chapter 3 we had an illustration of the structural approach, in which there were two ideal types of well-functioning and dysfunctional families. We saw that this formulation was somewhat cursory, and that, in the end, the therapist followed the guidelines of his own practical reason in his effort to restructure families. The main therapeutic strategies, as we discussed, were seen as straightforward interventions over power asymmetries, with the therapist making the greatest use possible of his power superiority (conferred upon him by his expertise), and a rich repertoire of rhetorical maneuvers destined to persuade the patients to follow the therapist's guidance. We now turn to the other three approaches in family therapy.

The strategic approach of Jay Haley is similar to Minuchin's structuralism (they were associates at the Philadelphia Child Guidance Center for a number of years). On one hand, Haley's followers give more emphasis to the power hierarchies within the family and in the therapeutic system (therapist plus family), but on the other hand they dilute the structural view by blending it with systemic insights.[2] Haley was one of the original members of the Bateson research group in California (1952–1962), which constituted one of the seeds from which family therapy grew. (I will say more about Bateson and his group later on.) Another member of the team was Don Jackson who founded the MRI in 1959, however, Bateson's research project of communicative matrices and MRI's studies with families grew apart, although eventually there were periods of mutual collaboration. The MRI therapists today are not so interested in families per se as they are in communicative matrices, but families happen to be an outstanding social group supporting communicative flows, and as such interest them. However, the communicative matrix is not complete without the therapist, and hence they study these therapeutic conglomerates in which everything the therapist does or says has a certain impact over that matrix. As a consequence, his best communicative skills are called upon in order to enable him to monitor the session. The MRI therapists envision these communicative matrices striking a homeostatic equilibrium, that is, as self-regulating. Finally, the Milan group also regard these communicative matrices as cybernetic mechanisms, but differently from the MRI therapists, claim that the systems are in a constant process of evolution. The very search for a therapist is an evolutionary step, indicating that the family is ready for change.

If Minuchin and Haley propose a therapy with little knowledge of the family, and with a heavy use of power and rhetoric, the systemic therapists regard themselves as merely entering and leaving cybernetic mechanisms, that is, power for them is part and parcel of those mechanisms. Examining their project from another perspective, however, we immediately see that they are rhetoricians. In order to fully understand this characteristic of their therapeutic project, we should examine their assumption a little more closely.

The chronological beginning of all this is to be found in Bateson's research project to study the double-bind. Influenced by his family heritage in the natural sciences, by Bertrand Russell's theory of logical types, and by the then-emerging cybernetics and systems theory, Bateson set out to study communications in humans, as well as in other animals, with the working hypothesis that there were different levels of organization of communicative messages. He observed that otters employed the same gestures in both fight and play, but while in the former they would bite each other to shreds, in the latter they only tickled each other. There was a good indication of the existence of a communicative level different from that of the messages, guiding the behavior towards fight or play. Among humans the phenomenon revealed itself more clearly. Each communicative action was attached to a higher level, so that in learning how to knit, a person also learned, subliminally, how to learn. If, in addition to knitting, the instructor also taught how to learn to learn how to knit, the person would subliminally learn how to learn how to learn how to knit, and so on.

Two types of communicative units revealed a conflict between levels: paradoxes and double-binds. In the command, "Don't read this message," the reader disobeys the instruction in the very act of obeying it. In this paradoxical command there is a conflict between the meaning of the message, its semantics, and the act of issuing it and obeying it, its pragmatics. A typical example of double-bind came from the observation of the interaction between a mother and her schizophrenic son. The young man was hospitalized, and upon a visit, he greeted his mother effusively, putting his arms around her shoulders. She immediately stiffened, and he pulled his arms back. Then she asked him if he did not love her anymore, and noticing his embarrassment, she said: "Dear you must not be so easily embarrassed and afraid of your feelings."[3] It was a situation in which the patient would be damned if he did express affection towards her, and damned if he did not. At one level, the mother wanted her son to love her and so to express himself, but at another level she was uneasy with the intimate situation. Double-bind messages were regarded then as missiles fired by the speaker, missiles against which the addressee had no defense whatsoever.

Other researchers, following Bateson's wake, rolled up their sleeves and got their hands into empirical studies of the double-bind. The surprise was great, and probably the disappointment, too, when they began to discover that double-binds were part of a much vaster array of communicative actions, which they called "transactional disqualifications," and could hardly be restricted to units of communicative exchanges, but needed to be sought for in broader stretches of verbal interactions.[4] The disqualifying maneuvers were similar to the rhetorical arsenal of the Sophists in ancient Greece (see chapter 7). They consisted in evading or changing the subject, in pretending to answer a question with a statement that cannot serve as answer, in denying or disqualifying the speaker's assertion by questioning his right to make it, or the appropriateness of its expression, as well as numerous other maneuvers. What the researchers failed to realize—as had the Sophists twenty-five centuries earlier—was that such rhetorical ruses were not amenable to collection and classification as "specimens in natura." They could be newly coined in every communicative situation, they were not entities, but part of a creative habitude inherent in communication.

The double-bind as well as its correlative sophistic maneuvers amounted to a struggle to control the other. In other words, these rhetorical moves were power strategies. But Bateson did not think that power could be the arena of rhetorical skirmishes. He envisioned a global system of meaning and grounded it on a biological and ecological base. Double-binds, disqualifying transactions, power claims, or attempts to control were meaningful, not in and of themselves, but insofar as they were mechanisms in the cybernetic life machine conceived by Bateson. He was careful, however, to keep separate his assertions of biological and mental determinisms.[5] The mind fluctuated through two cybernetic processes: calibration and feedback. It received signals from the environment and changed in adaptation to new conditions. This terminology was largely expanded and applied in family therapy. Like cybernetic mechanisms, the family's communicative matrix presents negative and positive feedback loops. In the first case, the matrix functions like a thermostat, introducing small degree changes to compensate for environmental modifications. The environment is the family itself. A child reaches adolescence, becoming more independent, the mother enrolls in a college course in order to compensate for the change. In the case of positive feedback loops, the changes are drastic, and not mere accentuations of degree. The family divorces, has a baby, or mother and father exchange controlling roles. The example of the thermostat is illustrative. In negative feedback loops, the exterior temperature rises, thereby stimulating the thermostat to trigger the air-conditioning and keep the house temperature stable. This is a process of morphostasis. But suppose that in the middle of the summer, instead of rising, the exterior temperature drops to freezing. The thermostat is not prepared to deal with that change, someone needs to change the switch from "cooling" to "heating." If the system of refrigeration/heating tries to handle the abrupt reversal, it has to undertake a large leap of change in response to this positive feedback loop, developing a morphogenesis, that is, generating a new structure capable of striking equilibrium under the radically new conditions.

Bateson continues to be regarded as a founding figure in the family therapy movement, but many writers in this field, in an eager attempt to deepen their theoretical basis, went further into the fields of cybernetics, systems theory, and biology. While Bateson preserved the independence of the mind, the scientists propose a universe entirely ruled by biology and reflected in "microorganisms" such as the family. They claim that our knowledge of families has been misguided by a series of "centrisms":

ego-centrism, family-centrism, ethno-centrism, social-centrism, ideolog-ical-centrism, and language-centrism. Our discourse strategies induce us into the illusion that we occupy some sort of central position in the universe, when we interview a family or write about therapeutic prin-ciples. Humberto Maturana, who has become the favorite biologist of systemic family therapists, argues, for example, that given the absolute impossibility of centrality, all objective knowledge is impossible.[6] The consequence of this is that knowledge cannot aspire to be global and complete. But is this not a knowledge claim steeped in globality and completeness? The family therapists understood that what was at stake was a radical critique of causality. They started to observe in family transactions that the traditional way of punctuating reality, in terms of who causes what, or what causes what, was misleading, because no system of causality ruled with consistency in family life. The husband who yesterday was the cause of all evil, today becomes a companion and affectionate father; the loss of a job in a city which yesteryear had caused the family life to collapse, one year later resurfaces as a blessing in disguise, leading the family to move to another city where they become much happier. On a microscopic level, these therapists realized that when they conducted an interview with a family, oriented by the traditional beliefs in causality, they were proceeding "linearly," that is, with the assumption that reality was well ordered in a linear sequence. The opposite was a "circular" conception of reality, according to which, a question not only elicits information, but also conveys information to the interlocutor, thus exercising a certain determination over his answer. In asking "What is the problem?" "What is wrong?" or "What can I do for you?" the therapist was conveying the message that there was a prob-lem, that something was wrong, or that he could be helpful. To avoid these connotations, commenting on the weather, or talking about inter-national politics was not a better alternative, because it implied a denial of the reason why the patients had originally looked for therapy. Thera-pists started to think about the impact their questions and statements had upon the entire group, and what is more, proceeded to listen to the interventions of each client as a coded move within a system which had been in existence before therapy and which the therapist was now about to join.

If the biological philosophy is unsparing of knowledge, it is even more so of power structures. In the same way that reality cannot be organized linearly into relations of cause and effect, it cannot also be organized into hierarchies. What we regard as power relations or endeavors to control are to be seen as "epistemological errors," as Bateson liked to say, because every act is a response in an interlocked relation inside a mechanism which is either repeating itself in morphostasis, or renewing itself in morphogenesis. An obvious implication of this bio-cybernetic view is that systems of relations evolve according to their internal rules, and the will of individuals is not determining of their course, but determined by it. The consequence of such an assumption for therapy is that it does not "cure" or "change" a communicative matrix, it is attracted to it by a wider force, the institutionalized existence of the therapeutic establishment. The therapist, like the patients, does not exercise will, but realizes his position within the system and reacts in patterns which are largely predetermined by his training and by the absorbing transactions the family will have with him. The bio-cybernetic point of view eliminates will and reduces behavior to a system which is "structure-determined," whose mechanism is postulated but cannot be understood. The therapist is supposed to behave as someone who is floundering in the rapids: he does not know what he will encounter ahead, all he can do is to cope with the obstacles presented along the way, a rock sticking out of the water, a rough curve, or a whirlpool. If he is successful at each and every obstacle, he will arrive safely at that part of the river where the waters are calmer. However, a failure here or there does not jeopardize his descent of the rapids, it only imprints a certain history upon the journey.

The cybernetic view of therapy portrays the family and therapeutic system as a multiple-layered mechanism in which the flows of symbols in the discourse of each person are more complementary parts of the whole than meaningful descriptions, even if only that which is said by one person alone is under consideration. Other possible layers in addition to the multiple discourses are a certain habitude of punctuation, certain habits of relations (forming coalitions, opposing conjunctural but regular adversaries, etc.), doing certain things within familiar contexts and drawing on experience to cope with new contexts, and finally, integrating narratives of the past with projections of the future. The therapist cannot interfere with all these levels of symbolization as a *deus ex machina*, but he adds another discourse to this bundle of complementarities. He will be all the more successful at influencing the system if he realizes his relative position, and instead of struggling to overcome the impossibility of swaying all those levels of complementary symbolizations, he goes along with them.

As was discussed in chapter 3, Minuchin is concerned with developing a theory of how families function, but his principles are so general and detached from his clinical practice that such a theory turns out to be more enunciated in his therapy than in his writing of principles. It constitutes an ad hoc set of guidances developed in the heat of the here-

and-now therapeutic session, and it follows common sense injunctions such as: it is better to lead the parents to fight than to let an anorectic adolescent starve to death; every intervention must be preceded by some probing, and if smoothly accepted, carried out; and so on. Like Minuchin's, the cybernetic and biological discourses about the foundations of family therapy generally hide more about their working assumptions than they reveal, although it is inevitable to recognize that different schools of family therapy have different approaches, and have much more in common than the eagerness of their leaders to assert identity and independence from one another allows one to realize. (I would like to stress these commonalities and overlook the discrepancies.) While Minuchin "theorizes" about families, the strategic and systemic family therapists "theorize" about their clinical practices. Both discourses meet on the familiar ground of common sense procedures, and are made even more alike by the intimations of their reconstructive endeavors.

The books of family therapy, unlike those of psychoanalysis, are replete with transcriptions of sessions, and minute descriptions of the meanings of the patients' and therapists' discourses. These sessions often reveal more of the underlying working assumptions than the introductory theoretical chapters these books contain. For one thing, most of these therapists are clinicians, not scholarly writers; for another, family therapy has not, in fact, developed a theory either of family life, or of treatment. Perhaps they do not need such a theory, given that their craft springs from the practical reason that we exercise in our everyday lives, and not from scientific reason. For most therapists, such a conclusion is an anathema: they seem to want to present their practice as scientific, and for that purpose attempt to harness it to concepts in biology and in cybernetics. Freud was caught in the same dilemma, clothing the psychoanalytic project in scientific garb, but now, one hundred years later, very few insist that psychoanalysis is science, particularly because this claim overshadows the psychoanalytic contribution of the loftiest value: that it created a new interpretive procedure, a new system of knowledge, relation of power, and rhetoric of persuasion, side-by-side with its co-cultural sisters, such as science and politics. Possibly, the family therapists will come to the same conclusion and abandon their current interest in biological determinism, especially because they have the psychoanalytic example to reflect upon.[7] But the comparison between psychoanalysis and family therapy is the subject of the next chapter.

The epistemological problem for the foundations of systemic family therapy is that their clinic, similarly to the structuralists' clinic, springs from practical reason, the common sense reasoning that we exercise in our everyday life, underscored by the moral beliefs which constitute our worldview. It is extremely unrewarding to write theories of practical reason, because the unwieldy results are likely to be denied as soon as they are put into practice. Perhaps it is for that reason that the theoreticians in this field turned to biology and cybernetics which, with their nonteleological and noncausal thinking, looked like a reasonable formulation for a conception of open-ended practice. But practical reason is indeed refractory to theory. I would like to convey the sense of practical reason from which family therapists derive their clinical inspiration independently of the loaded jargon they have borrowed from the natural sciences. I will do this by outlining their therapeutic program and presenting some of the stunning conclusions they have come to, after observing families' dynamics for a number of years.[8]

Therapy begins even before the client makes his first call. The customers, as family therapists call their clients, may be seeking treatment spontaneously, or may be coming to therapy through the coercive referral of a government agency, which is trying to make a truant return to school, or quarantining parents under the suspicion of child abuse. The referral often sets the mood with which the prospective clients will call the therapist: hope, anger, reluctance, fear, and so on. During the first telephone call to schedule an appointment, the therapist must be careful not to fall into the traps set by the referring source, or by the client's expectations. He will not want to admit, for example, that, yes, he is the best specialist in town for that kind of problem, or that, yes, he will be able to help the family, because he does not know yet the weight that each of his statements will have for his interlocutors. Fisch, Weakland, and Segal discuss several instances in which prospective clients try to frame the therapist in the first telephone call, and suggest "rules of thumb" as they themselves call them, for the therapist to avoid such pitfalls.[9]

The first interview is of the utmost importance. In some cases the family only has one interview with the therapist. As we saw in Minuchin's special technique for treating anorectics, the first session is very long and works as a sort of map for the entire treatment. These famous family therapists often serve as consultants in different cities around the world, joining together with the family and their present therapist, which restricts their contributions in many treatments to a one-session intervention. The transcription which will follow, with members of the Milan group, illustrates the impact of these single sessions. The goal of the initial interview is evidently to retrieve information. However, the therapist is not eliciting information alone, the patients are also evaluating and portraying him. His questions have to take both aspects into consideration, and furthermore address the needs of the immediate situation. The patients may, for example, need some prompt reassurances which the therapist will wish to give without jeopardizing the possibility of future interventions. It is impossible to design questions capable of meeting the challenges of every situation; Fisch, Weakland, and Segal, as well as Haley, review a series of possibilities of patients' attitudes during a first session, and make recommendations fitting particular circumstances. Haley divides his first sessions into four stages: "(1) a social stage in which the family is greeted and made comfortable; (2) a problem stage in which the inquiry is about the presenting problem; (3) an interaction stage in which the family members are asked to talk with each other; and (4) a goal-setting stage where the family is asked to specify just what changes they seek."[10] He proceeds by describing scenarios that may possibly occur at each stage, and provides practical suggestions to the therapists, such as, that conclusions should be kept tentative, that the therapist's observations should not be gratuitously shared with the family and so on. The spirit of this text is candid and earnest. Haley writes, for example: "When asking about the problem and encouraging people to talk, the therapist should observe how everyone acts as well as what they say. He *should not* share his observations with the family."[11] Different from psychoanalytically oriented therapies in which the analyst listens to the patient trying to decode the underlying meanings of what the patients say, the family therapist turns his attention to "the exact wording of [the] patients' remarks."[12]

Each of these schools of family therapy describes its strategies in great detail through the transcription of sessions in books and videotapes for training purposes. Minuchin, for example, begins by responding with intervening remarks from the earliest verbal exchanges in the first session. Haley proposes a more rigid division between eliciting information and applying directive interventions. The MRI therapists design their program similarly to Haley, but argue that the therapist's attitude is of great importance already in the early stages of gathering information, so much so that the successful description of symptoms by the patient depends on the successful positioning of the therapist. The Milan group conducts a hairsplitting questioning of the patient's declarations, and through these questions the therapists direct the family on to a track on which they will develop their intervention, thus paving the ground for it. Despite all these strictures, what we see in practice is that these therapists have such modest goals, and such enhanced rhetoric that, since the very beginnings of the treatment, they are already carrying out interventions toward the resolution of the problem. The planning of these interventions may be more or less formal, at times with a break in the session for the therapist to consult with his colleagues who are observing behind the one-way mirror, at other times with the choice of one session, usually the last one, to cast the interventions. However, as the transcription of Minuchin's session so well illustrates and the forth-coming transcription of the Milan consultation will emphasize, these therapists arrive at a diagnostic of the situation very early, and the break for the planning of interventions usually serves only to sharpen a plan which has already taken shape in the therapist's mind.

The client presents a problem, her child is difficult, her husband drinks, his daughter is anorectic, his wife too controlling. The presented problem usually has a long history of attempts to resolve it, so much so that, as the MRI therapists like to say, the solution has become the problem. The therapist's planning thus involves blocking that solution, or reframing the problem, or a variety of other alternatives which are not outlined in any theory, but stem by and large from the therapist's trial and error experiences with his clients, and also takes into consideration matters such as gravity and urgency of the problem, economy of means and family's acceptance of the interventions, among the infinite series of considerations capable of arising in practical reason. As Fisch, Weak-land, and Segal put it, "While the resolution of a problem requires the abandonment of the patient's attempted solution, a patient cannot simply stop doing something without doing something else instead."[13] In psychoanalytic parlance, one can say that family therapy operates symptom substitution. However, there is more to this program than meets the eye. The therapist evaluates and even tries different rhetorical maneuvers aiming at discovering what will be acceptable to the family, and reaching out, as deeply as possible, not to the heart of the individual's ego or memories, as in psychoanalysis, but to the semantic roots of their problem definition. Fisch, Weakland, and Segal write about "framing the suggestion" and "'selling' the task,"[14] while Haley writes about "telling people what to do when the therapist wants them to do it, and telling them what to do when the therapist does not want them to do it,"[15] but only expects them to rebel against the task.

One of the most interesting contributions from family therapy has been the observation of sequences of interpersonal behavior presenting astonishing regularity across a variety of families. In one sequence, the father is an absent figure, timid, incompetent, uninvolved, or disen-gaged. The child develops wayward attitudes and starts to create trouble at home and in school. The mother, who is closer to the child, tries to control her son, but fails. Then the father steps in to aid his wife and subdues the child. There follows a period of good behavior by the child, until the father has a relapse into his usual depressed state. In another sequence, the grandmother takes care of her grandchild and complains that her daughter does not know how to look after her child. The mother becomes withdrawn towards the child. The child starts to do bizarre things, or presents serious symptoms. The grandmother becomes over-whelmed by her grandchild's behavior and increases her complaints and accusations to the mother's incompetence. The mother abandons her withdrawal mood and joins in as a fighter, competing with her mother for the control of her child. She finally wins and goes on taking care of the child. The grandmother resumes the complaints that her daughter does not know how to properly look after the child, and eventually takes the child over again under her own care. The cycle starts over again.[16]

Insofar as the therapist's power position is concerned, Minuchin overtly makes maximum use of the power superiority he conveys as a therapist, as a famous family therapist, and as an expert in the treatment of certain problems such as anorexia nervosa. Haley also uses the therapist's power to effect changes of behavior in the patients, main-taining the therapist in a position removed from the family system, as an outside bearer of the right to make decisions. Families, of course, go to therapy looking for help and generally welcome these authoritative standings. The MRI therapists and the members of the Milan group have a different view. They claim that power is just another metaphor in systems of relations, as meaningful as the metaphor of anorexia, way-wardness, or any other symptoms because, after all, these statements are not worth what they mean but the use that they are put to. Conse-quently to say that someone is subordinate or superordinate to some-body else, is tantamount to doing something, and the therapist has to find out what the speaker is doing with that statement rather than meaning. This idea is drawn from the biological and cybernetic concep-tions that reality is a flux in a constant process of change and any attempt to impart structure or hierarchy to it does violence to its systemic ecology. The therapist uses metaphors of power according to his own discretion, at times claiming superiority, at other times equality or even inferiority.[17] Therefore, power is not an autonomous sphere of action or of meaning, but a metaphor to be given rhetorical use by the therapist in the name of treatment, as it is used by the family members in their attempts to change their situation by goading the other family members. Therapists from different schools like to see each other developing different strategies for the employment of power positions in thera-peutic tactics, and it is generally agreed that while followers of Minuchin and Haley use the "oneupmanship" (as they like to call it) to underscore their therapeutical advice, the followers of MRI and of the Milan group disclaim power superiority in relation to the patients, and do therapy from a "onedown" position, which leads the families to rely less on the therapist and understand that if anything is to change, it has to be through their own effort. This use of the concept of power is misguiding because it fails to recognize a wide spectrum of nuances through which power insinuates itself. To begin with, it fails to recognize that there is a power accruing from the social position of the therapist which is different from the power stemming from the actual attitude of an individual therapist. The latter cannot cancel out the former. The therapist naturally realizes when the patient's overestimation of his power is counterproductive, or when he has to make a statement backed by authoritative forcefulness, among several other circumstances in which one carries out these evaluations and acts according to his interests in that particular interaction. These interactive strategies, however, are part of practical reason available to all those who have the fundamental competence to engage in social interactions, and it is awkward to have this common sense ability presented in the frame of theory as a therapeutic stratagem. Again, therapists do use this fundamental intuition about power positions for therapeutic purposes, and evidently will continue to do so, but there is no need to raise this ability to the status of theory.

Fisch, Weakland, and Segal declare that the goal of their therapy "is to influence the client in such a way that his original complaint is resolved to his satisfaction."[18] In some cases this will entail a change in behavior, in other cases just "[the] altering [of] the client's view of the problem."[19] The assumption underlying this line of reasoning is that reality is always a reflex of symbols used in speech and consequently is constructed by language. This evidently is a viewpoint very similar to that espoused by the psychoanalytic project in the direction it took after Freud abandoned the seduction theory, and decided to interpret symbols without anchoring them to concrete events. In the case of Freud, nevertheless, the organization of these symbols had to be shuffled with the psychoanalytic narrative about the onset and growth of the psyche. Family therapists do not have a narrative with which to combine the patients' narratives. They really take in earnest the family members' discourse describing their discomfort: a husband's complaint that his wife has become too much of a feminist and in addition suffers from premenstrual tension; an adolescent's complaint shared by the family that he became mentally disturbed when he was hit on the head by a surfboard, and that since then he periodically sheds hair and his skin color changes;

or the children's complaints that the problem in their family is that the parents speak too loudly. These statements are regarded as truthful not insofar as their semantic meaning is concerned, but only in their pragmatic meaning, that is, the meaning of the actions consisting in saying those things.

The technique in dealing with symbols regarded in this way consists in folding the patient's narrative onto itself, following the patient's own agenda for cure. A family therapist will never insinuate, like a psychoanalyst would, that the patient's description of problems is a symptom standing for something else that has been repressed and therefore could not find its way into consciousness. Family therapists do, however, have their own agenda steeped in common sense, and since it is so, it is identical to the patient's own guiding principles: a suicidal client should not be allowed to kill himself, while a boy whose presented problem is masturbation will be allowed to persist in his symptom for a while; a couple, in which the man is thirty-five years older than the woman, and bases their relationship on a trading pact between the wife's youth and the husband's money should be allowed to further adjust to this model and live as happily as they can within it. Practical reason stretches the limits of tolerance of reality. I believe that upon first impression, the opposite would seem truer, that is, that theoretical reason can explain more and, therefore, restrain the realm of absurdity, but as we can see, it is just the other way around in theory and practice in family therapy.

Anyhow, family therapists are not resigned to using practical reason as the springboard of their clinical practice, and if on one hand they do not aim at theorizing about family life and conduct a therapy based on common sense, on the other hand their efforts in coining rhetorical maneuvers is intense and ever growing. As a matter of fact, what distinguishes the different schools of family therapy indeed is the repertoire of therapeutic interventions each employs. It is impossible to carry out a complete inventory of these maneuvers, because they can be invented afresh upon every new communicative situation, and by raising them to the position of theoretical dictamina, family therapists come close to the Sophist philosophers in ancient Greece, who believed that they could stave off discrepancy of opinion by developing the ultimate mastership over rhetoric. They failed in the first place because excellence in rhetoric was no guarantee of triumph over knowledge, or of power superiority, and in the second place because however much enhanced rhetorical skills conferred advantage in debate upon the trained discussant, untrained speakers could always conjure up the most astonishing rhetorical maneuvers, and defeat the trained ones. The lesson to be learned from the Sophist experience, which we will discuss in chapter 7, is that rhetoric is no match for power superiority, or for systems of knowledge, and that even systematic training in the art of argument is no assurance that the skilled discussant will never be defeated by an impassioned neophyte.

As I said in the foregoing discussion, the different schools of family therapy assert their identity by embracing certain sets of rules of thumb and refusing others. I have presented a sketchy portrayal of each school, and will proceed no further in this endeavor, because I believe they share much more common ground than their divergences allow one to realize. In addition, a school of thought or even of clinical practice cannot be defined in terms of a certain repertoire of rhetorical maneuvers. To assume that they can is tantamount to claiming that the use of a certain subset of words in the English vocabulary defines a theoretical standing, because speech tropes are as much part of our common language patrimony as words.

The history of family therapy itself provides us with a wonderful example of how rhetoric is insufficient to define anything. In the 1950s the Bateson project was researching the use of double-bind in its pathogenic implications. The research team was studying the onset of schizophrenic symptoms in people brought up by parents who communicated with their children by means of these distorted and paradoxical messages. Twenty years later, the double-bind ceased to be a symptom of pathology, and entered the realm of treatment techniques. Family therapists developed a large variety of distorted and paradoxical messages destined to confront and break down the patient's dead-ended diagnostics. One of these techniques is referred to as "prescribing the symptom." The patient comes in complaining that his problem is that he cannot have sexual intercourse with women. The therapist advises him initially that he should abstain from sexual intercourse. A family comes to therapy complaining that they cannot get along with one another, and that instead of separating, they wish to overcome that difficulty. The therapist tells them that in the weeks following the session they will have as little contact with each other as possible, each member of the family keeping to his own and staying confined to his bedroom while at home. An agoraphobic patient in desperate need of help comes to the office of a therapist who was referred to him as an expert in that disease. After a few sessions the therapist tells him that his case is one of the most obdurate, and that he will probably have to learn how to live with his symptoms, as he has done so far, avoiding public places. The rate of success obtained through these maneuvers is not negligible, but the interventions do not tell us anything, either about the diagnostic or about the prescribed treatment. This knowledge family therapists have is still deeply concealed in the therapist's experience oriented by practical reason. The main therapeutic intervention in this modality of treatment consists in a rhetorical maneuver, which once was considered a sign of abnormality, that is, the distortion of discourse.

The fact that the therapist is always trying to persuade the patient of something, even of the fact that he is not trying to persuade his interlocutor of anything, is rather natural; it is an unexceptional occurrence. It is the glue between therapists and clients, and was established by the widespread acceptance of the therapeutic in the Euro-American cultural heritage. Evidently, therapists take advantage of the "glue" factor, but the ways in which they do this vary from attacking the attachment to therapy as transferential resistance, to welcoming it, and making maximum use of it in order to encourage the patient to resolve his problems with greater hope. The therapeutic attachment is triggered by the institutionalized establishment, but its use in therapy does not necessarily conform to the establishment rules; the help patients obtain from their therapists is often derived from our ability to conduct ourselves in everyday life which is steeped in habit and shapes therapeutic methodology.

We should now turn to another remarkable session of family therapy, this time conducted by two members of the Milan team, Luigi Boscolo and Gianfranco Cecchin. The session takes place in North America and is conducted in English. The family had already been in therapy for treatment of the problem of a daughter who suffered from epilepsy, hallucinations, and fits of temper. The girl had recently tried to live by herself, but after a while went back to her parents' home. She was beginning to increasingly miss therapy sessions when Luigi Boscolo carried out this session of consultation with the family and their therapist. Gianfranco Cecchin teamed up with Boscolo as a consulting partner behind the one-way mirror.[20]

Excerpt 1

BOSCOLO: I would like to start by asking you, "How do you think the therapy is going?"

FATHER: Are you asking me, Doctor? Okay. We have been going to parental therapy in a group meeting, and I think it's helped us a whole lot.

BOSCOLO: And who do you think got the most out of therapy, you or your wife?

[...]

FATHER: It's hard to tell.

BOSCOLO: Let me ask your wife.
FATHER: Sure.
BOSCOLO: How do you think therapy is going?
MOTHER: Well, I wouldn't call the group we go to a therapy group insomuch as it's a support group. Um—as far as Mary's therapy—it hasn't moved along as well as I think it should. There again, I don't know . . . where the trouble lies. I'm beginning to question whether as much has been done as should be done, from the medical viewpoint. Why the medication does not hold at certain times, I. . . .

Keeney and Ross comment that Boscolo starts searching for hierarchies within the family, but the mother interrupts that line of inquiry by asserting that Mary's problem is medical. This theme will remain concealed throughout the entire session, only surfacing at the end in Boscolo's intervention.

Excerpt 2

MOTHER: . . . Two interviews, I think.
BOSCOLO: Two interviews. Do you get the impression that those two interviews you had would help you?
MOTHER: Yes, in the sense that we've learned to evaluate the therapist's capabilities with handling Mary as a professional person and felt that she had an understanding of the problem. As I say, my questioning has been aroused as to what should be done with medical evaluation.
      [. . .]
BOSCOLO: So, from the age of ten to the age of eighteen—eight years . . .
MOTHER: Right.
BOSCOLO: . . . This epilepsy didn't give you much trouble.
MOTHER: No, no.
BOSCOLO: Because it was controlled with medication.
MOTHER: Right, right.
BOSCOLO: Once in a while she would have what? Can you describe what?
MOTHER: Um . . .
BOSCOLO: Did she sometimes have some . . .
MOTHER: I would say that as a child she was unusually emotional.

BOSCOLO: No. I'm talking about when she had the petit mal. How many times, from the age of ten to the age of eighteen?

MOTHER: I never saw it.

BOSCOLO: Ahh—never saw it.

MOTHER: Never.

BOSCOLO: So she started on medication from the age of ten to eighteen without having a seizure.

MOTHER: And there was no more indication of her having it during that time.

BOSCOLO: Well, still she kept taking medication. So you figured out that it was the medication that was keeping away the petit mal.

MOTHER: Right . . . that was controlling. . . .

In this segment Boscolo leads the mother to spell out the history of the disease and finds out that the epileptic seizures had been under control with medication for the past eight years. Despite the mother's earlier statement that the disease was physical, in excerpt 2 she introduces the notion that Mary as a child "was unusually emotional."

Excerpt 3

MOTHER: . . . Sensitive, crying spells . . . and often she would try to look for blame for herself.

BOSCOLO: Looking for blame for herself.
[. . .]

MOTHER: Putting herself down, regardless of how we would offer support, encouragement, and creating an atmosphere of love and concern.

BOSCOLO: Whom was she most attached to until the age of eighteen?

Now Boscolo can resume his initial search of allegiances and oppositions in that family.

Excerpt 4

MOTHER: Uh . . . uh . . .

BOSCOLO: *(looks to father for his response)*

FATHER: Well, I think probably her mother, because her mother has an office at home. She spent most of the time there when she was home from school in the afternoons. Due to my business, I traveled for some time and was away for weeks at a time, but then I quit. So during most of the period in the last six or seven years I was at home in the evenings, but Mary would be doing her studies.

BOSCOLO: You were on business. Often you were away. So when Mary was between the age of ten and eighteen, you were not very often at home, so she . . .

FATHER: Oh, I was at home, yes, during a lot of that period. However, not during the day when she would need certain things. Her mother would take her in the car and . . .

BOSCOLO: You said that your wife was saying she was a very sensitive child. I'm talking about before the age of eighteen. She was sensitive, she was attached to her mother, you said.

Keeney and Ross call the readers' attention to the fact that Boscolo reframes the mother's description of Mary as "emotional" by "sensitive," and discovers that the alliance here is between mother and daughter. Notice that Minuchin would be sniffing enmeshment between mother and daughter through the information obtained in these early segments of the session.

Excerpt 5

FATHER: I was aware of this, yes.

BOSCOLO: You were aware. But do you feel it was a problem? That it was too much attachment? Did you have some impression that this was too much?
[. . .]

FATHER: Well, no. In fact, she was seeing her pediatrician at the time, so this apparently was part of the medical problem, see.

BOSCOLO: I see.

FATHER: They were dosing her apparently about as much as . . .

BOSCOLO: Has your wife ever told you, for instance, "I'm a little bit worried about Mary. She is too attached to me"? Has she ever talked to you that way?
[. . .]

FATHER: Oh, no. I don't think that ever came up.

BOSCOLO: Never came up.

FATHER: No. Of course, she always showed a lot of affection for me. I guess, being the only male of the family.

BOSCOLO: Who had more?

FATHER: Mary had . . .

The Rhetoric of Insight

BOSCOLO:	Mary . . .
FATHER:	Yes.
BOSCOLO:	Yes?
FATHER:	Well, certainly. I mean, she loved us both. She showed a lot of affection. Of course, when I came home, I had my share of it, too.
BOSCOLO:	Your share.
FATHER:	Oh, yeah.
BOSCOLO:	So she would be with you when you came home.
FATHER:	Oh, yeah, as much as possible.
BOSCOLO:	As much as possible. Was your wife pleased?
FATHER:	Oh, I'm sure she was. Yes. We never had any . . .
BOSCOLO:	Also in that period, until the age of eighteen, was Mary attached to relatives?

Note how Boscolo punctuates the client's discourse as if he were editing a text. As the father tries to bring the medical problem back into the interview, Boscolo cuts his timid and hyperbolic remarks, "They were dosing her apparently about as much as. . . ." The father vacillates in his statements, "Mary had . . .," while Boscolo wedges in the components of an intervention that is gradually building.

Excerpt 6

MOTHER:	No, we don't have any family that lives close. We have always been away from the family. My husband's mother, when she was alive would come to visit us frequently when she was in Florida, and she was in Carolina. She would stay with us and those were nice times, but we've never lived close to either side of the family.
FATHER:	We're about six hundred miles from the nearest one, huh?
MOTHER:	So there hasn't been close contact there.

Keeney and Ross point out the importance of the paternal grandmother in this family constellation. They inform us that in an earlier part of the interview not included in the transcription, the mother had characterized herself as "introverted." The diagnostic hypothesis under formulation has the mother as lonely, and in need of Mary's company.

Excerpt 7

BOSCOLO:	Your mother says she's kind of introverted while your father is extroverted. No? He's always had friends. Do

you remember, over the years, having an impression that father wished that mother would be more extroverted? And father would wish that mother would go more out with him. No? Do you have the impression that he kind of felt left out a little bit over the years?

Boscolo establishes a contrast between the "extroverted" father and the "introverted" mother and Mary indicates that she would rather be like her father.

Excerpt 8

BOSCOLO: I see.

DAUGHTER: *(crying)* But I'm really sorry about my death phobia and everything. If I had everything to go back and live over again—I'm saying this with great pain—I don't ever think I'd do the same again because the way I did it, it was just so foolish. My life is just so foolish.

BOSCOLO: Listen. Let me ask this, Mary. You said, "I wish I'd been extroverted like my father—to be more like . . ."
(gatekeeping of information)

DAUGHTER: *(crying)* I wish I would have had all the friends in the world. I wish I wouldn't have had a death phobia.

BOSCOLO: Yeah—but listen to my question now. Hm? When you say "I wish I would be like my father . . ."
(more gatekeeping)

DAUGHTER: *(crying)* The way you talked about me—I just feel ruined.

BOSCOLO: What did you say?

DAUGHTER: *(sobbing)* I said, the way you talk about me, it reminds me about all the bad things in my life. It just makes me feel ruined.

BOSCOLO: Well, let me ask this question again. Listen to me. When you said, "I wish I would have been like my father, more extroverted," did you sometimes have inside yourself the feeling that if I am extroverted like my father and like to have friends, maybe even like to go out with my father—Do you feel—that mother would have been left out because mother is introverted? She might feel kind of out if you became like your father? Or if you would have liked to have gone with your father? Do you feel this sometimes? That if I become too sociable, too extroverted, I might get into such a

good relationship with my father that my mother
would be left out?

Boscolo proceeds in forwarding his hypothesis that the mother feels
lonely, then turns Mary into her companion. Mary wants to free herself
from that bondage, but feels torn and develops symptoms. As we see,
this portrayal fits perfectly with Minuchin's descriptive categories: an
enmeshed pair, mother and daughter, vis-à-vis a disengaged father. The
therapy consists in pulling mother and daughter apart by bringing the
father into the picture. Mary irritably resists Boscolo's line of reasoning.
Boscolo tries another avenue, turning to her personal life, as the following excerpt will show.

Excerpt 9

DAUGHTER: Well, no I don't feel that my mother would feel left out
at all. I feel that she wants to do what she wants to do.
And I just feel that I want to do what I want to do, that's
all. It's just very plain and simple.

BOSCOLO: Then, suppose—suppose, Mary, that you become
extroverted like your father, all right? You would have
friends and maybe you would like to be a sportsman
like your father. He likes sports, maybe you would
have gotten involved with sports, and then your
mother would have felt kind of left out, wouldn't she?

DAUGHTER: Well, no, I don't think she'd feel left out because it's her
personality—she's an introvert. I don't think she'd feel
left out.

BOSCOLO: I see.

DAUGHTER: Not at all.

BOSCOLO: Do you have the impression, over the years for
instance, that somehow there was some sadness inside
mother?

DAUGHTER: There is what?

BOSCOLO: There was some sadness in your mother—you know
she was introverted. Didn't you sometimes think
that. . . .

DAUGHTER: No, not at all.

BOSCOLO: Hm?

DAUGHTER: Not at all.

BOSCOLO: Do you think?

DAUGHTER: (agitated) Not at all.

BOSCOLO: Do you sometimes think, for instance, that if you would

have gone out with your friends, somehow your
mother would have felt kind of alone?
DAUGHTER: No.

First he explores the consequences that Mary's development of her
social life would have upon her mother, and he then proceeds to scan
Mary's life outside her home, discovering/establishing that it is virtually
nonexistent.

Excerpt 10

BOSCOLO: Have you ever had a close relationship with a boy? A
sexual relationship?
DAUGHTER: Sometimes . . .
BOSCOLO: Have you ever had sexual relationships?
DAUGHTER: Like what? You mean kissing and stuff like that?
BOSCOLO: Even more than that.
DAUGHTER: No, I never went past the kissing stage.
　　　　　　[. . .]
BOSCOLO: Do you talk to your mother, for instance, when you
doubt whether to pass the kissing stage? Do you talk
with her?
DAUGHTER: Yeah, I asked her like at what age I should really kiss a
boy, and at what age I should go out on dates.
BOSCOLO: What advice did your mother . . .
DAUGHTER: What age I should accept a marriage proposal.
BOSCOLO: So you asked your mother what to do.
DAUGHTER: What?
BOSCOLO: You would ask advice of your mother? You confide in
your mother about your boyfriends?
DAUGHTER: Oh, yeah. Sure. I did all the time.
BOSCOLO: Was she good at advising you?
DAUGHTER: She was normally pretty good.
BOSCOLO: Yeah—What advice did she give about boys? What
would she tell you? You should go slow or fast?
DAUGHTER: She advised me to take things very slowly in the
relationships I had. Not to push the boy into anything
he didn't want, and not to let him push anything in—
me into anything I didn't want to do.

From the therapist's point of view he is advancing his hypothesis, or
according to Keeney and Ross, he is scanning the territory of relations
and reinforcing the hypothesis that Mary is completely devoted to

seeing that her mother does not feel "lonely," and her father does not feel "left out." Simultaneously with making these discoveries, Boscolo's questioning reveals the hypothesis he is construing, both to us, readers of the transcription, and to Mary, too, but she probably only perceives him as eliciting information whose ultimate implications she is not aware of. Nevertheless, Boscolo somehow paves the way for the family to accept his description of their situation by molding powerful caricatures: "the lonesome and sad mother," "the excluded father," and "the ambiguous Mary, split between helping her parents/curtailing her freedom, or letting them down/pursuing a life of her own."

Excerpt 11

BOSCOLO: *(to mother)* You said that in the beginning of the marriage was a period in which you were outgoing. You were with your husband. It was a period that . . .

MOTHER: More of a social period of our lives, which I think is perhaps normal in most marriages.

BOSCOLO: Did you enjoy that period?

MOTHER: Yes. It was a very pleasant time in establishing a social group, or becoming established in one, perhaps as a married couple instead of a dating couple. [. . .]

DAUGHTER: Well, I feel that both my parents are now kind of closing in on their retirement age and I don't want them to work as hard as they used to. . . . I don't want to see them unhappy in old age—wondering what they're going to do for the rest of their life.

BOSCOLO: You are worried about them?

DAUGHTER: Well, yeah, I'm concerned about what their retirement age is going to be like.

BOSCOLO: But when you said that you would like them to take trips without you, did you say that because you feel otherwise they will be unhappy? Do you feel they are unhappy?

DAUGHTER: Well, not necessarily unhappy, but it just gives them something to do together.

BOSCOLO: Because they do not do much together?

DAUGHTER: My parents haven't been together in a social life for really a long, long time, and *(crying)* before they die I want them to see and be a part of the world they live in. And, you see, that's very important to me.

BOSCOLO: Who do you think needs this more, your father or your mother?

DAUGHTER: I think they both equally need it.

BOSCOLO: But, for instance, what do you think if you were not alive, for instance, if you were not here if your parents did not have any child. . . .

DAUGHTER: Yeah. . . .

BOSCOLO: . . . Do you think it would be easier for their future, or more difficult? How do you see their future without you?
          [. . .]

DAUGHTER: I don't know.

BOSCOLO: If they did not have any children, how would you see their relationship in the future, hm?

DAUGHTER: I don't know. I really couldn't answer that question.

BOSCOLO: Let me ask your mother. How do you think your life with your husband would have been without children? Without your daughter?

MOTHER: My life and my relationship with my husband, I think would have been the same.

BOSCOLO: You said you worked. As a mother it was not satisfying?

MOTHER: Yes, yes.

BOSCOLO: It was not satisfying for you?

MOTHER: Yes, it was.

BOSCOLO: It was.

MOTHER: I have always said that my daughter was a delightful part of my life. . . .

BOSCOLO: I would like to ask you, "How would you have spent your life with your wife without your daughter?" How do you think it would have gone—your life with your wife?

FATHER: With just my wife?

BOSCOLO: Yes. You and your wife, without a daughter.

FATHER: Oh, I imagine that knowing my wife, we probably would have settled down about the same way. Maybe we wouldn't have been in the same location, I don't know, but I think that life itself would have been approximately the same.

Now the idea of the two parents living without Mary has been brought out and fully examined. Notice that the theme of the medical problem has been entirely passed over. According to Keeney and Ross, by proposing scenarios of life in the future without Mary in the home, Boscolo places the idea of change on solid grounds, making it tangible for the family.

Excerpt 12

BOSCOLO: I would like to ask you, Mrs. Brown, "Do you have brothers and sisters?"

MOTHER: I have a sister.

BOSCOLO: You have a sister. Older or younger?

MOTHER: Older sister.

BOSCOLO: She is married?

MOTHER: I have no idea. I haven't had any contact with her since I was eighteen years old.

BOSCOLO: Where is she?

MOTHER: I have no idea.

BOSCOLO: You don't have any idea? You had a fight? Or you broke up?

MOTHER: No. At the time we were both living at home, and then she moved away from home and cut off contact with the family through her own choice due to a disagreement she had with my father . . . We weren't raised together. My parents were divorced when I was very young. . . . She lived with my father, I lived with my mother.

BOSCOLO: Ah—you lived with your mother, she with your father. I see.

MOTHER: Until I was thirteen.

BOSCOLO: Thirteen. How was your life with your mother?

MOTHER: Very good.

BOSCOLO: Didn't your mother miss your sister?
[. . .]

MOTHER: Yes, she did. I know that she would have liked the two of us together.

DAUGHTER: . . . I'm not really that interested in my mother's side of the family because she let me know that her sister wasn't interested in her. . . .

BOSCOLO: She doesn't talk much about her first life?

DAUGHTER: . . . You know.

BOSCOLO: You're more interested in your father's, you say?

DAUGHTER: Yeah.

BOSCOLO: You are interested in your father's side of the family. I see. Also, your mother is more interested in your father's family than hers?

MOTHER: Um-hum.

BOSCOLO: I'm asking you, "Is your mother more interested in your father's family than her own?

DAUGHTER: I'd say, yes.

BOSCOLO: Yes. Whom is your mother more attached to in your father's family?

DAUGHTER: She was very attached to my Grandma Elsie, before my grandmother died.

BOSCOLO: She was very attached to your paternal grandmother.

DAUGHTER: That was the only one I know that she was attached to. [. . .]

BOSCOLO: I see. When did your grandmother die?

DAUGHTER: About ten or eleven years ago.

BOSCOLO: Was she very attached to your mother?

DAUGHTER: Yeah.

BOSCOLO: You were attached too?

DAUGHTER: Oh, yeah, I was attached to Grandma Elsie, too.

BOSCOLO: Yeah? When you think about her, do you think—"old"?

DAUGHTER: I think about an old lady standing somewhere in a hat. *(family laughs)* That's what I think about. Grandma Elsie always wore a hat.

MOTHER: She was famous for her hats.

BOSCOLO: Was she close to you? I mean, did you have a good relationship?

DAUGHTER: Oh, yeah, very close.

BOSCOLO: Very close. I see.

DAUGHTER: She always used to come visit me.

BOSCOLO: I see. So you lost a sister, I mean, you don't know anything.

MOTHER: No. There is no contact.

BOSCOLO: Your mother died seven years ago. Do you have much contact with your father? Or not much? [. . .]

MOTHER: Oh, I had lived with my father from the time I was thirteen. . . .

BOSCOLO: Yes. . . .

MOTHER: . . . then until I was nineteen.

BOSCOLO: During those years you lived with your father? Your sister was also there?

MOTHER: Yes, for part of that time.
BOSCOLO: How did you get along with your sister for part of the time? How did you get along?
MOTHER: All right.
BOSCOLO: There was no closeness . . .
MOTHER: No, there was conflict between she and my stepmother, but not between my sister and I.

Boscolo explores the family backgrounds of each parent. First he focuses on the mother's side, and little by little a picture emerges in which she is partially disinherited from affection in her family of origin by being separated from her father and sister. Later on in life she finds solace in her mother-in-law Elsie, but she dies. Her daughter Mary represents her last outpost against loneliness. Now Boscolo turns to the father's side.

Excerpt 13

BOSCOLO: *(to father)* Your sister is closer to you or to your brother?
FATHER: I guess to me.
BOSCOLO: Do you call her sometimes? Do you see her?
FATHER: Oh, yes, yes. We talk and we write letters.
BOSCOLO: Letters. And then sometimes do you go to see her? When you are on trips or . . .
FATHER: Well, when we go anywhere near the Carolinas, we'll stop there.
BOSCOLO: Oh, so when you go for your trips, you stop there.
FATHER: Yes. Sure.
BOSCOLO: Is that often that you go?
FATHER: Well, every two or three years. Maybe four years. Yes, we'll go.
BOSCOLO: That pleases them, they look forward to that then.
FATHER: Oh, yes.
BOSCOLO: How about your parents?
FATHER: My parents are both deceased.
BOSCOLO: When did your father die?
FATHER: My father died in nineteen-forty-six.
BOSCOLO: And your mother?
FATHER: My mother? Um . . .
DAUGHTER: About ten or eleven years ago.
FATHER: No, honey. It was, yeah, I guess it was about twelve years ago.
MOTHER: Mary was eight and she's twenty-three now, so how

	many years ago was that?
FATHER:	Thirteen years. Now wait a minute. . . .
DAUGHTER:	I'm twenty-two now.
MOTHER:	Twenty-two.
BOSCOLO:	Excuse me, Mrs. Thomas, your mother-in-law, whom was she most attached to of the children?
MOTHER:	Her children?
BOSCOLO:	Of her children.
MOTHER:	Oh, definitely her son.
FATHER:	I was the baby.
MOTHER:	. . . We enjoyed each other. I would look forward to her coming for a visit.
BOSCOLO:	So it was a deep blow for you when she died. [. . .]
MOTHER:	Un-hm.
BOSCOLO:	I see, very big. *(to mother)* And did you also enjoy your sister-in-law?
MOTHER:	Well, I'm not really that well acquainted with them over the period of years. You see, I see them when they come to visit us or when we go there, but over the period of years I was most attached to my mother-in-law, and I suppose that had a lot to do with Mary because Mary is the only girl grandchild. . . .
BOSCOLO:	I see.
MOTHER:	And so we would write long letters and she would call and she always wanted to come down and visit and we sent pictures every week, you know, the weekly development. . . .
BOSCOLO:	How old was Mary when Mother died? She was eleven, hm?
MOTHER:	No, no she was about seven because we were in Downington. You were seven or eight years old.
BOSCOLO:	When did she die? What year?
MOTHER:	*(sighs)* What year were we in Downington? I can't remember.
DAUGHTER:	About nineteen-sixty-five, I think.
BOSCOLO:	Sixty-five? Fifteen years ago.
FATHER:	Sixty-five, sixty-six.
MOTHER:	About that.
BOSCOLO:	I see.
MOTHER:	It's hard to remember.
BOSCOLO:	It was a loss. Did you feel you had almost a better

	relationship with your mother-in-law than with your own mother?
MOTHER:	No. There were so many years in between that I couldn't compare the two. You see, the two were not part of my life at the same time.

The loss of the grandmother/mother-in-law is stressed as a great setback for the family. When Elsie died Mary was eight years old; two years later she started to present the symptomatic behavior.

Excerpt 14

BOSCOLO:	Is there any other woman ever since that's taken her place in your life? I mean, any other relationship?
MOTHER:	No-no-no, I think I probably felt that way about her because of her interest in Mary as a grandchild. . . .
BOSCOLO:	I see.
MOTHER:	. . . and knowing that I'd married her favorite son. You know, that's . . .
BOSCOLO:	So you married her favorite son.
MOTHER:	Right.
BOSCOLO:	And she was a girl, which was important for her because she had all male grandchildren. . . .
MOTHER:	All male grandchildren. She was delighted when we had a girl.

Notice that the mother persistently presents herself as associated with her daughter in the relationship with Elsie. The importance of mother and daughter to the grandmother stemmed from Mary, the only grand-daughter of Elsie's favorite child. The mother is not important to the mother-in-law for her own sake, but because she is Mary's mother. She needs Mary as her trump card in order to be relevant to Elsie. Boscolo now turns to the benefits of therapy, possibly with the goal of pushing further the theme of change, by bringing out the idea that the parental group that they are attending may be helping the parents change their attitude towards their daughter.

Excerpt 15

BOSCOLO:	It is your impression, Mary, that since they have been going to this group, this group of parents, that they are helping you?
DAUGHTER:	They are what?

BOSCOLO: Since they have been attending this parents' group.
DAUGHTER: I'd say that they've been pretty happy over me.
MOTHER: Helping.
DAUGHTER: Oh, helping?
BOSCOLO: Do you think they are helping you at all?
DAUGHTER: Oh, helping me. Yeah.
BOSCOLO: How about you? You have been in therapy, no? Do you think you are helping your parents, too?
DAUGHTER: Helping my parents?
BOSCOLO: Um.
DAUGHTER: Yeah.
BOSCOLO: As in what—what problem do you see in your parents?
DAUGHTER: I don't know, I don't know. It's all very fuzzy to me. I don't really know what you're referring to.
BOSCOLO: You don't?
DAUGHTER: No. I don't know how I could possibly help my parents. I know that they're the ones that help me.
[. . .]
BOSCOLO: But do you see a problem in your parents?
DAUGHTER: No, I don't see any problem with my parents.
BOSCOLO: You don't see any problem.
DAUGHTER: No. It's not that I'm trying to be ignorant or anything.
BOSCOLO: Is the problem the future that worries you with your parents? How will their life be in the future?
[. . .]
DAUGHTER: What problem? I don't—I don't know what you're talking about.
BOSCOLO: I'll stop here. I'll now have a discussion with my colleague, and I'll come back with our conclusion.

Keeney and Ross register that Mary issues contradictory messages, giving information that she is helping her parents and that she is not helping them. Mary went along with the topics of conversation introduced by Boscolo, but in the last segment of the transcription we had a glimpse of her reaction: while she agreed to talk about her family situation, which is not the problem from her point of view, she asserts that she does not know how she could help her parents, since they are supposed to help her. Boscolo calls for a break in the session to consult with Cecchin who was observing behind the one-way mirror. After the intermission the session is resumed with Boscolo summarizing the team's conclusions to the family. The family listens "in a trance like posture,"[21] as Keeney and Ross observe.

Excerpt 16

BOSCOLO: My colleague and I have reached the conclusion that I
now give to you. What impressed us a lot is the life of
the parents. We are very much impressed with the life
of Mother. It was a life, before getting married, that was
somehow solitude. She had a sister, but somehow she
couldn't have a meaningful relationship with the sister.
She had a mother, but she was separated by the father
and sister. Then she separated when she was thirteen
years old from the mother and went to Father with the
older sister. And then the sister left. So we are very
impressed with your life, Mrs. Thomas, before you got
married. We feel a lot of solitude in your life.
[. . .]

MOTHER: Maybe I didn't realize it.

BOSCOLO: From what you told us, really, we felt you could not
have a, how do you say, a "warm relationship." Your
family was all broken up somehow and we think that
when you got married, there was a period when you
were very happy.

MOTHER: Umm.

BOSCOLO: . . . Where you felt satisfied on all levels. And then we
are also very impressed about Father and his solitude,
after he lost his mother. His mother died when Mary
was about nine years old. And in those first nine years
of Mary's life, somehow, the parents—Mother and
Father—had a life, maybe for the first time. *(mother
nods in agreement)* Especially for Mother, a life—a
relationship—not the solitude that you had before
getting married. And in those nine years your mother-
in-law was very important. You could make contact. It
was a very meaningful relationship also for your
husband. He was in a very intense relationship with his
mother, and the family was maybe in the best period of
your life.
[. . .]

MOTHER: Um-hm.

BOSCOLO: Mary was coming out, it was going well—was going
well. But then Mary, at a certain point when her
grandmother died, deeply felt that her parents were left
with an emptiness. Mother had lost a very important

person: mother-in-law. Daddy had lost a very important person: his own mother. So Mary somehow started to think and deeply started to constrain her tendency towards independence. Other boys and girls start slowly to become more independent: they get more and more involved in an outside life. Mary, however, started to say, "I've got to do something for my parents," and somehow she took the position of the grandmother. She developed all kinds of behaviors—ways of looking, rotating the eyes, fidgetiness, and withdrawing. She avoided relationships, particularly intense relationships with boys typical of her age. At the maximum, she would give a kiss, but she wouldn't get very involved because she deeply felt that "I have to fill the life of both my mother and my father, who have become empty after the death of grandmother." *(daughter turns and stares at mother)* So, somehow she took this role, as she has been doing for you all these years, by developing all these kinds of behavior. By developing all these kinds of behavior, she has both Mother and Father thinking about her all the time. By doing this she gives them the opportunity to parent her around-the-clock every day. And by doing this, their life is filled and is not void.

We are very impressed, Mary, by what you have been doing for your parents. And your parents have the opportunity, thanks to what you are doing for them, to have a life less lonely than they would have if you would not have taken on this task after your grandmother died. Did you feel, "My grandmother, when she died left a tremendous emptiness," so you decided to fill it? You are doing a great work for them by giving them the opportunity to continue being parents for you.

Now, lately, you have somehow introduced the idea of separating a little bit by deciding to go out and live in your own apartment. This is also a good thing in that it tests how your parents could do without you. You're also very sensitive in calling them and coming back when you feel it is too premature to leave them. Now, we think you are doing well and for the moment we think you should continue like this. Furthermore, we think the therapy that you have been doing is going well in the sense that the therapy keeps things as they are for Mary. We would be alarmed if Mary suddenly started to change and become more independent— because she would leave unfinished work. Then her parents might go back to their loneliness where there might come out some emptiness. So I think, for the meanwhile, therapy with Mary is going well in the sense that change at this point would be kind of risky.

You *(to therapist)* told us that Mary doesn't come to the appointments regularly when she comes. This is good because if she comes regularly to the appointments she might get too involved with you *(to therapist)*. If she got too involved, she may think she has to leave the parents. So meanwhile, it is too premature. We think that the therapy should go on like it is going on now.

We also think it is very positive that the parents are going to continue to go to this group that they are attending with other parents. This may help the parents develop some kind of relationship for the future. Mary may even feel that now there is somebody else who can fill the void of the parents. Mary will decide herself in the future. We think this is very good. If your parents go to these groups you may see them find their life: maybe the group will substitute for your grandmother.

You have been taking the place of your grandmother since the age of nine to help keep the life of your parents, as I said before, not lonely and not empty, and allowing them to be continuously good parents for you. And now with these groups they are attending, they might find some meaning that enables them to take away the constraints on your own independence. So in the future you might try, like all the other girls your age in adolescence, to find your own life. For the moment we think you should continue because your parents are not ready yet. You understand, Mary, what I am saying?
[. . .]
DAUGHTER: I think I do.
BOSCOLO: Anyway, if you don't understand very well, maybe

your mother or your father will explain what I told you
when you go home. . . . *(to therapist)* So, meanwhile, we
think things are in equilibrium and that you should be
very sensible that change doesn't occur for the moment
because Mary has taken that task upon herself for her
parents. We want to add that we saw Mary crying
before when she said she was worried for her parents'
future: "What will happen to my parents, and their
retirement plans? I would like very much that they
would enjoy. . . ." These are things the grandmother
would have thought about.

    (to Mary) So we think that you, Mary, should
continue like this until you feel in the future that maybe
your parents have started to feel less lonely, less empty
with you starting to make your life. Do you
understand? Your life becoming more independent like
the girls of your age. Meanwhile, we think that the
behaviors, the attacks are very important because it
keeps your parents helping you, trying to do things for
you—this fills up their life.

    (to parents) I'd like to say something about the
point made in the beginning of the session when you
said, "How about the medical problem?" Hm? You
asked me, "What do you think about the medical
problem, the medicine, the diagnosis?" We would like
to give an answer. We have a lot of experience with
these situations; many situations similar to this. We
think the problem of epilepsy is an organic problem.
We think that in your situation, most likely it's not
organic, but it's not possible in our experience to clearly
say that it is not organic. We are more inclined to say
that it is not a brain—

    [. . .]

DAUGHTER: Tumor?

BOSCOLO: Not a tumor or brain lesion. But we are not certain
because you can never be certain. We are more inclined
to think that there is not a brain lesion. Anyhow, we
think even if we are more on the side that there are not
brain problems, all the behavior that Mary has is
behavior for her parents—in the sense that we were
saying before. This behavior helps the parents in not
having a void, by giving some meaning to their life by

being parents. In this sense we think you should continue to take the medicine and tests the doctors prescribe. By doing these tests, she keeps going along with the task she has taken upon herself since she was nine years old in helping the parents have a life that is not alone, not empty. So maybe in the future—as I said—Mary may feel that the parents can live without her, maybe with the help of the group therapy they're following maybe in time to see herself as not needing medical tests or medicine. For the moment, however, we think things shouldn't change.

[. . .]

MOTHER: I agree that the anticonvulsant medicine is controlling the epilepsy, but what I'm concerned about is the depth of the hallucinations that she still has, the violent behavior that she exhibited in the past year that was never part of her life before.

BOSCOLO: You see, this violent behavior—even if there is an epilepsy—though we doubt it very much—we don't say there isn't, you understand what I mean? But we doubt very much that there is an epilepsy. Even if there were an epilepsy, which means a lesion of the brain— which we doubt very much—even with respect to what you describe in the last years as being more violent we understand why she exhibits this behavior.

[. . .]

MOTHER: I don't. I don't and Mary doesn't.

BOSCOLO: We understand. See, she has been exhibiting this behavior over the past years because somehow as she grows the push toward *independency*, particularly *independency* in leaving the home is more powerful. Understand what I mean, leaving the home? I mean a regular relationship outside like the girls of her age. So she must constrain herself more in order to continue to be worried for her parents. "How can I have them continue to be parents?" "How can I have them not feeling alone?" She has to make more efforts. That's why it comes out with more of this kind of odd behavior.

MOTHER: You mean that explains the behavior of her beating her head against the wall, and her wanting to kill herself, and attempting suicide?

BOSCOLO: Well, even this one—beating her head against the wall —is more difficult for her. We understand it is more difficult for her in the period when she is twenty-one or twenty-two years old because she is growing. It's more difficult to constrain the physiological, natural impulse that everybody has at her age toward making a relationship outside, or starting to think of making her own life. I understand it's very hard for you to understand because on the one hand she has this full-time work she has been doing for the parents since the grandmother died. Now, simultaneously, as she is twenty-one or twenty-two years old, there is also a strong physiological force that strives to make her have the life that all the other girls of her age. . . .

[. . .]

DAUGHTER: I don't agree with that.

BOSCOLO: . . . And so it takes more the effort in this period. The idea of death or the idea of beating her head against the wall is also because it is really tough for her in this period. But when she feels in the future that she deeply starts to perceive that both her parents will be able to have a life between themselves, then she will diminish this work she's been doing. Then she'll have the possibility of finding her own life.

DAUGHTER: I don't agree with that.

BOSCOLO: As a matter of fact she cried before. By crying, Mary said, "I'm so worried about my parents. About their retirement plans. I would like them to travel around to enjoy. . . ." *(daughter turns around and stares at mother)* Somehow, this is the worry for you. When she perceives in the future that there are no more reasons to worry, she will see the parents as able to have a satisfied life without solitude. The constraint will go away and she will follow the physiological forces that an adolescent girl has toward making relationships. *(knock on door, consultant leaves)*

[. . .]

BOSCOLO: *(enters room)* My colleague says he thinks that maybe the parents have lately started to not have the feeling of loneliness—the idea of being alone without their daughter—and they might be in a position for feeling well. Also, Mary is very prudent—she goes slow. All

this year she has done this work for you and so she has
not developed during the year, that is, developed
outside relationships with girlfriends or boyfriends.
She doesn't yet get much training from the outside. At
the same time, her parents may be more ready at this
point to think that if our daughter goes out, maybe
even gets married and makes her own life, we will be
able to have our life: not an empty life, but a
meaningful life. Mary, you see, at this moment it is very
important to say, "go slow"—Anyway, that's our
conclusion and now we will turn you over to your
therapist and add that we think the therapy should be
continued like it has been continuing. Okay?
[. . .]

MOTHER: Thank you.
DAUGHTER: Thank you.
FATHER: Thank you.
BOSCOLO: Eventually, if Mary has some doubts—if there's
something that you don't understand very well about
what I said, eventually Daddy or Mother will explain it
to her.
FATHER: Hopefully we'll be able to.
MOTHER: Okay.

Boscolo and Cecchin's intervention begins by remarking that the
mother has indeed led a solitary life. The father is associated with the
mother and described as solitary, too. Elsie's death was a great loss for
both parents, and Mary, sorry for them, decided to replace her grandmother in giving meaningfulness to her parent's lives. She accomplished
this by developing her symptoms and sacrificing her freedom as a
teenager. Boscolo does not present this narrative as an accusation, or a
diagnostic, but as laudable activities performed by Mary under those
circumstances. He underscores his statement with a prescription-of-the-
symptom move, by recommending that Mary should not change, otherwise her parents might feel let down. Mary's withdrawal from therapy is
equally praised, because therapy means change, and it may be premature for Mary to move out of her parents' home. The intervention will
be successful if it is accepted as truthful, if it unearths what a psychoanalyst would regard as repressed material, freeing the patient so that
they may come to grips with what the real issue is. The intervention,
however, although cast as encouraging continuation of the patterns,
carries a rhetoric destined to fuel change, and Boscolo registers the

possibility of change by associating it with the parents' work outside therapy, with the parental guidance group, because therapy is an activity in which the three family members enact their entanglement.

Boscolo disqualifies Mary as the one responsible for the family, by commenting that even after she has admitted to having understood what he said, that if she did not, her parents will explain it to her later. As to the question of epilepsy, which probably throbbed throughout the entire session under the discussion of the family issues, Boscolo addresses it by means of a double paradox: First, it is a fake and it is true: "We think that in your situation, most likely it's not organic, but it's not possible in our experience to clearly say that it is not organic," he says. Second, he states that they are experienced in these matters, but concludes that in their experience they cannot say it definitely. The goal of this paradox is to introduce the idea that in Mary's case, epilepsy is a behavior symptomatic of family difficulties, without completely denying the family's diagnostic that it is an organic problem. The mother steps in, expanding the picture of symptoms, by bringing in the "hallucinations" Mary has, clearly opposing Boscolo's reframing of the medical complaint; however, he does not heed her intervention, but gives her an answer in the most evasive way, repeating the paradox he has already placed in the family's hands. The mother does not give up and insists, "You mean that explains the behavior of her beating her head against the wall, and her wanting to kill herself, and attempting suicide?" His response continues in the same way. Mary also rises against Boscolo's description of the situation, but comes up against the same wall of resistance, as he continues to talk to mother, insisting on the paradox and completely ignoring Mary's two voicings of her disagreement. At this point Cecchin interrupts the session, which can be regarded as a rescuing mission to save the besieged Boscolo. Upon his return, he basically repeats his message. In the final exchange Boscolo repeats that if Mary should have some doubts, her parents will explain it all to her, to which the father replies, perhaps sarcastically, "Hopefully we'll be able to."

It is natural for Mary to want to leave her parents' home (and hence "not help them," as Boscolo puts it) and still feel insecure about it, and come back after her first initiative ("to help her parents"); this could hardly be regarded as an ambiguous message. There are no doubts that change is about to take place in this family, with Mary's moving out; it has been a difficult process, aggravated by the epilepsy (whether medical, or just a communicative symbol within the family, or both); and therapeutic help to steer these unfoldings in the family is certainly welcomed at this point. Instead of describing the situation in these simple terms, we could have used Minuchin's terminology and talked about a mother and daughter enmeshed and a disengaged father, in a psychosomatic family in which the daughter holds her life hostage against the threat of seeing her father marginalized and her mother saddened. However, despite the fact that she is mired in this plight, Mary still had energy to struggle for her own emancipation, and thus she fights back. Or we could use the cybernetic jargon and say that the grandmother's death destabilized the family matrix and Mary was called upon to fill in for Elsie. She was not cut out for the function as her adolescence pulled her away from it, and consequently introduced ambiguity into the system with symptoms that are now physical ("epilepsy"), now psychological ("emotional"), as well as ambiguous attitudes towards her parents, at times struggling to reestablish the family homeostasis, at other times struggling towards morphostasis, but without knowing exactly in which direction she should go. In this session Boscolo portrays the homeostatic picture of the family and introduces the theme of change, which was already present among the family members when Mary left home. He works as a sculptor, carving the rough piece of wood into the shape already suggested by its rawness, and then further transforms it. But all this process is merely spoken about and furthermore in a convoluted and distorted way. Evidently the point of therapy is that the truths of life are often missed, resisted against, repressed, disguised, or deliberately ignored for fear that they may entail unpleasant realizations, and therefore it is not enough to merely mention them to the person. The failure to heed these truths is not a matter of comprehension, but of acceptance. However, therapeutic discourse accomplishes a great deal more as it often defines what these truths are.

If in the session with Minuchin we are left with the sense that something was accomplished with that family by virtue of the fact that Minuchin coached them into accepting the view of matters he presented—and we must hasten to say that the family cooperation in that regard could not have been more forthcoming—in the session with Boscolo it appears that the view of matters is only formulated, and the family leaves unassuaged. The ways that the therapists perceive the problems are very similar, and so are the steps they undertake towards treatment. Minuchin's style seems to be warmer and the results he obtains with the family more successful, although it is difficult to say whether the success is more a consequence of his charming personality, or of the family's cooperating mood. The other relevant feature is that Minuchin's session was the beginning of a treatment to be conducted by him while in the case of Boscolo, it was a consulting visit. It seems quite clear that the definition of the problem as well as its treatment in both cases was the product of common sense judgment, although the style of implementing therapy was different on account of personalities and conceptions of therapy. Evidently, it was not raw common sense that anyone could exercise, but a special knowledge developed throughout a long experience, deeply plunged into practical reason.

If the therapeutic discourse in family therapy feeds itself on practical reason, in what way does it differ from other forms of nonspecializing discourse that we employ in our everyday lives? What, after all, is it that cures patients? Since therapists define by and large what are acceptable ways in which we should lead our lives, are they not foraying into moral philosophy and establishing that which constitutes a good life? If this is the case, should they not make explicit what a good life consists of? And once they do so, would their rhetorical "sleights-of-hand" become ethically acceptable? With these questions I wish to introduce some of the themes discussed in the following chapter. Those issues are not exclusive to family therapy—they are equally central for psycho-analysis—and since the two modalities of therapy rest on opposite poles of clinical practice, they will serve us well in characterizing therapeutic discourse and its crucial dilemmas.

5 PSYCHOANALYSIS AND

FAMILY THERAPY

We're constantly correcting, and correcting ourselves, most
rigorously, because we recognize at every moment that we
did it all wrong (wrote it, thought it, made it all wrong),
acted all wrong, how we acted all wrong, that everything to
this point in time is a falsification, so we correct this
falsification, and then we again correct the correction of
this falsification and we correct the result of the correction
of a correction and so forth.
Thomas Bernhardt

The decisive question to be asked about therapeutic discourse is, indeed, "What is it that cures?" We saw in the preceding four chapters that both the practice and theory of therapy have wandered among a variety of possible answers. Freud claimed that cure is obtained by means of the correct application of the principles of his metapsychology; cure is consequently a matter of knowledge of what is wrong, and what constitutes the adequate means to resolve it; and furthermore this knowledge is initially a reconstruction of the problems and later on a set of procedures to deal with the problems. This knowledge is therefore the product of observation and reflection. The analysts in the object relations school agree with that assumption, but argue that the momentary impact of the insight is not enough, that the patient has to be exercised over the substance of the insight for a certain period of time. Consequently, the knowledge has to be couched in a certain practice facilitating its reception. Merton Gill claims that the pursuit of interpretations in depth (interpretation of genetic neurosis) is wasteful, while the analysis of transference, which brings under the analytic lens the most visible manifestation of distorted discourse, is far more rewarding, in addition to being a steadfast way to get to the core of the neurotic symptom. The family therapists deny the importance of the underlying meaning of symbols, claiming that symbols are worth only that which they are used for, and propose that cure is the replacement of symbols, which they can obtain by employing powerful rhetorical maneuvers.

They also notice that the power asymmetries between therapist and clients can be used by the former as leverage to accomplish the symbol substitution constituting the goal of their treatment.

There are at least four models of therapy and therapists which are largely employed by all schools of clinical practice. These models derive more from the interactive situation than from the therapeutic strategy, although it is in the latter that therapists make use of them. They are the following: therapy/therapist (1) as a mirror of the patients' problems; (2) as a system of knowledge which the therapist teaches, replacing the inadequate knowledge the patient previously had; (3) as play, in which the therapist makes himself available as a toy, or transitional object, with which the patient plays until he overcomes his symptoms; and (4) as an interpersonal relation. These four relational attitudes are a consequence of the therapeutic interaction which casts the patient, expecting to be helped, against a therapist, trained to help professionally by means of verbal actions. In similar counseling situations in life, bringing together relatives, friends, or lovers, the help is preceded by empathy and emotional attachment, and although it may also appeal to reason, that is not its hallmark. The main line of communication in the therapeutic setting is one of affection, the appeal is designed as rational, in spite of the fact that it aims to effect changes over emotions. This state of affairs calls for hypertrophied means of persuasion, and these four models of therapy/therapist are natural extensions of the effort to convince, cutting across all forms of therapy based on the use of speech.

The mirror model is that which serves the rhetoric of insight; the therapist shows the patient what is wrong with him. Family therapists also employ this model in several maneuvers such as emphatic repetition of what the patient says, or what is probably the most universal therapeutic technique: describing to the patient what he has just said in order to provoke the impact of hearing what he said in somebody else's voice which, although a repetition, often surpasses the awareness-awakening effects of thinking in the seclusion of self-reflection. The mirror model is not exclusive, because the therapist always applies touches to the patient's portrayal. The psychoanalysts do so by deconstructing the patient's narrative and rebuilding it interwoven with the psychoanalytic narrative, while the family therapists do so by reframing the patients' discourse. As a consequence, the mirroring must be almost always combined with the teaching model, since under the guise of repetition, new information is smuggled into the therapist's discourse and conveyed to the patient. In psychoanalysis the new information introduced in the repeated message comes from the psychoanalytic system of knowledge of the psyche, but in family therapy, it derives from guidances lurking in practical reason. The transitional object or toy model casts the therapist as a coach, training the patient in the new ways of his life. The training model is also very frequent in all types of therapies, because when an interpretation or intervention fails, the alternatives are either to backtrack and (a) try a new one or insist on the same, (b) train the patient in the acceptance of the therapist's point of view, or (c) try to persuade the patient with a more powerful rhetorical argument. There are therapists, such as the psychoanalyst in chapter 2, or the family therapist in chapter 4, who insist upon hammering on cold iron, stubbornly repeating their message; nevertheless, even this most unimaginative procedure can ultimately produce the desired results and change the patient's mind, as we saw with the psychoanalyst's client.

This apparently easy success of therapeutic interventions is due to the eagerness surrounding the patients' will in therapy. Although therapists often talk about "resistance" and "defense" as common attitudes among patients and obstacles to treatment, a therapeutic clientele culturally trained in the ways of that institution facilitates the task of the clinician, revealing an informed zeal about going through the procedure. This eagerness can also have detrimental effects for clinical practice, since it leads many patients to erect therapy as a permanently supporting system in their lives, thereby rendering the analysis interminable. One of the strands of family therapy is precisely the challenging of the entrenched belief in therapy as a panacea. Still, in a culture dominated by the triumph of the therapeutic, even before the therapist tries out his persuasive moves, he can count on the willingness of the patient who, by virtue of seeking therapy, has already been converted into a follower of the movement, however meager his belief in the system and hesitant his surrender to the therapist may be.

In the three texts of therapy transcribed in the preceding chapters, we do not find any outstanding examples of the therapist leading the session as a personal relationship. This happens for two reasons: first, despite Merton Gill's proposal for an analysis of transference, which inevitably renders the interaction more personal, therapy remains by and large a technical matter; second, most transcriptions of therapeutic sessions aim at illustrating clinical aspects and are, therefore, chosen through very slanted criteria. However, in therapy there are always moments in which, from a therapeutic point of view, the clinician does not know what to do, or in which the conversation wavers towards themes unrelated to the patient's problems, among several possible nontechnical situations. In these moments the interaction becomes casual, just like a personal relationship, if the therapist does not feel obliged to thwart it, or makes efforts to establish links between the nonchalant conversation and his diagnostic. (Freud's clinical reports and letters provide us with wonderful examples of his casualness, at times, during sessions of psychoanalysis.) Finally, certain themes brought in by the patient may stir up the therapist's emotions, and he may choose to hide those feelings, channel them into a therapeutic intervention, or just express them without censorship or technical clothing. Evidently one cannot advocate that therapy become a personal relationship, because that would deny its definition as a professional service which is paid for. However, in a relationship of this nature, focusing on the most intimate and personal facts of a person's life, it is extremely difficult for one of the parties to remain entirely impersonal, because the distance brought about by neutrality increases the emotional weight of the patient's verbal testimony, by imparting to it an aura of exceptionality which it does not necessarily need to have.

As these four models of therapy/therapist intermingle in practically every clinical approach and in every treatment, it is obvious that the relationship between therapist and client has not become completely technical. In addition, the claims for independence and originality by different schools becomes untenable since these therapies are based on verbal action and consequently cannot avoid the dialogical procedures of mirroring, teaching, training, and conversing intrinsic to dialogue. The curing element, however, is not the persuasion strategy independent from the power which bolsters it and the system of knowledge which stokes it. We shall examine each of these spheres in therapeutic discourse, narrowing the gap between psychoanalysis and family therapy, as well as broadening the base of therapeutic discourse.

Philip Rieff is shrill in separating therapies of detachment from therapies of commitment.[1] From the point of view of therapeutic strategy, a disapproval of the world can either lead to the desire to transform it (commitment), or to a disenchanted attitude of critical skepticism (detachment). Jungian psychology is an example of the former. Freud's psychoanalysis is obviously an example of the latter. Family therapy is also a therapy of detachment, because it does not develop any efforts to change the world, and perhaps it is even more so than psychoanalysis, because of its refusal of the notion of pathology. Family therapists assume that the communicative procedures they identify among their patients are normal facts of life identical to the procedures that they themselves will employ to help the family pursue their goals. Whatever these are, family therapists regard them as in a permanent process of change typical of any communicative matrices. What these therapists lack, when compared to psychoanalysts, is the critical and disenchanted attitude; nevertheless, both groups share the refusal to become committed crusaders, as would be more likely among political or religious proselytes. The notions of commitment (engagement) and detachment (disengagement), more than good criteria to classify therapies, constitute an analytic dichotomy very typical of the Western heritage, both in its intellectual and common sense traditions.[2] The criticism of Oedipal behavior, for example, entails a condemnation of commitment, while the criticism of narcissism entails a rejection of detachment.

The rhetoric of psychoanalysis is subdued because, as we saw in chapter 2, the patient must not be persuaded by the strength of the argument, but by the correctness of the insight. This posture held by psychoanalysts indicates that what cures for them is the knowledge they have of the psyche. Family therapists, on the contrary, assign all meaningfulness of behavior to speech and sternly deny that meaning may remain concealed underneath that which is talked about. If the two approaches to therapy are at variance in what concerns the qualification of the patients' discourse, we can find no discrepancies in the ways both employ therapeutic discourse. In fact, psychoanalysts and family therapists accomplish their therapeutic goals by showing the patients what was ignored, by persuading them that things are different from that which they thought, by exercising pressure over them to change their outlook, by being silent or reticent, by mirroring exactly what they say, or by revealing skepticism, among several other possible rhetorical strategies. The key word describing cure in both therapies is "change." But there are several kinds of change possible, from a different phrasing, to a different way of feeling and behaving, including the misconception that things have changed when they have remained the same. Therapeutic discourse cannot gauge emotions directly, and its knowledge must always be filtered through words. Consequently, cure is to a large extent the result of an agreement between therapist and patient about the change taking place, if it actually has, and if it was the desired one. Since there are no fixed conventions determining what counts as change—at every moment in the thread of life there are experiences which can be either regarded as novel or as repetitious—the realization of change depends on the uses of argument. Psychoanalysts have some criteria in their theory of the psyche which they use to determine when change has taken place: the patient overcomes her hatred towards men improving her relationship with male friends. Family therapists resort to practical reason, and decide that change occurred when the anorectic girl increased her weight, or the truant boy went back to school; or they take a radical attitude establishing that change is the product of agreement with the patients under the impact of a rhetorical intervention. They may persuade the family that the anorectic girl changed by leaving home, or even persuade themselves that the truant's family, who abandoned therapy outraged at the inefficiency of the therapist, changed for better, by relinquishing their dependence on the therapeutic establishment and trying to deal with their truant child on their own.

It is clear, however, that the "changes" based on agreement need a certain amount of support from common sense, the girl's leaving home and the family's leaving therapy are understood in plausible terms, in ways very different from those explanations of them being "cured" or "changing" behavior. Those explanations flounder in the absence of the buttressing of practical reasoning, and if they linger in the patient's acceptance for a while, they only do so as long as the patient remains spellbound by the therapist's authority, questioning the rightness of his own common sense. The rhetoric that opposes practical reason can further thrive if it is backed by a prominent power asymmetry. The patient may be too humble, the therapist too arrogant, the therapeutic establishment too awesome, the population of patients too ordinary. Otherwise, a rhetoric dispossessed by practical reason can live on, out of a system of specialized knowledge hovering above common sense, and thereby avoiding its challenges. The categories of expert knowledge are too abstract, too complex, inaccessible to the reach of common sense.

Therapeutic discourse unfolded in opposition to religious and political discourses, developing persuasive maneuvers cleansed from coaxing appeals, and deeply steeped in a relationship characterized by an accentuated power asymmetry, and in a complex and specialized system of knowledge. It developed a subdued and underhanded rhetoric. However, it met with such a widespread success in the cultural heritage of the West that it misled many into thinking that the triumph of the therapeutic was due to rhetoric. We saw that this is misleading because the rhetoric of therapeutic discourse owes its strength to the knowledge which stokes it, and to the hierarchy which guarantees its deployment. If, on one hand, these facts do not make the therapeutic rhetoric more acceptable to common sense, on the other hand, they do not justify the attempt to found this mode of discourse on rhetoric alone.

The therapeutic relation is characterized by a distinct bond. The patient is drawn to the therapist as an expert who can resolve, or at least help him to resolve his existential difficulties. For the therapist, the patient is a client and, however compelling his problems may be, the clinician is not expected to have sympathy for them from a humanistic point of view alone. To put it in different terms, the therapist's perception of the problems can be totally humanistic, but it ought to be competently so, that is, it ought to be professional. This was the novelty introduced into our lives by the triumph of the therapeutic: the existential discomfort which, in the past, used to be transcendental, meta-physical, and which could only be dealt with by moral systems could now be handled by a professional, in what was more of a technical skill than of an art or a calling. Since the beginning, psychoanalysis developed as power therapy, in the sense that the individuals' problems were caused by ambiguity, by a lack of assertiveness, or by the exercise of an assertiveness leading to the control and domination of others. This was rather evident in Adler's project for psychoanalysis, which considered the inferiority complex as the abode of neurotic behavior. However, it seems to be a main characteristic of power that it thrives better when concealed, and perhaps, for that reason, while Adler's proposal foundered, Freud's succeeded. In Freudian psychoanalysis, power is extricated from interest and progressively expunged from its forms of cultural, social, and interpersonal expression. The process of purification of power passes through resistance, defense, transference and counter-transference, and repressed and expressed wishes, mechanisms which are disruptive of the harmony among forces within the ego and in social life. What emerges from the ashes of such an unrelenting conjuration of symbols is a much stronger will, capable of a wider exercise of power which steers away from surrender and domination.

This Freudian conception of power bears many resemblances to Nietzsche's and Foucault's, by condemning the traditional (Christian influenced) critique of power which had it as a negative element under all circumstances.[3] The Christian attitude towards power, as the Socratic attitude which we will discuss in the next five chapters, was contradictory, because if, on one hand it carried out an intransigent denial of power, on the other hand its strategy to accomplish this objective laid an outstanding claim for power. Like Nietzsche before him and Foucault after him, Freud realized that the time was ripe to restore the faith in power, placing its embryo in the individual's inner life, before it received the meaning pasted onto it by culture, society, and family life. The analyst, who stirred up like a "teacher," a "coach," a "friend," a "lover," a "mirror," or an "instrument" this willful power in the patient, could not be anything less than a powerful figure himself, because in addition to all the above-mentioned functions, he also served as an exemplary model for the patient.[4] This was his response to positive transference, the "unobjectionable" one, a function very similar to the Christian and Socratic testimonial. In summary, the outline for the psychoanalytic project of therapeutic discourse according to Freud was the following: a restrained rhetoric (influenced by modern culture dominated by science), unfolding in the interstices of concealed power (a modern conception of power), which, however, did not develop into domination. The project maintained two elements of classical culture: the belief that unassuming rhetoric could be more persuasive, and the principle that the message must be backed by the speaker's testimony, which was restricted to the therapeutic session in psychoanalysis. Outside that context the analyst was no longer under obligation to his vows, for he was not a priest but a professional.

The question of power in the Nietzschean-Freudian-Foucaldian tradition is indeed rather complex, because it is conceptualized as an autonomous sphere preceding action and meaning, and consequently can only be assessed through approximations, as if its pursuers were archeologists condemned never to find the artifacts they look for. The power of therapeutic discourse is present in the institutional establishment and in the formidable social reverence it arouses, as the power of healing does in most cultures, to the extent of being exempted from other spheres of power such as politics. The individual therapist enjoys a great deal of this power and furthers it according to his skills. Is psychotherapeutic power—that which is awakened in the patient, and that which is commanded by the therapist—a characteristic of self, an effect created by the metapsychology, or a combination of both? In the same way that we concluded that rhetoric could not stand up on its own, power only comes into existence through actions—and since we are talking about discursive actions, we can say through rhetoric—as well as through a system of knowledge which simultaneously defines it and leans on it to be reinforced, preached, or challenged.

A system of knowledge is a constellation of symbols organized in a particular way. Some of us regard such systems as atavistic, that is, deeply steeped in the selves of their carriers. Others regard them as flexible instruments entirely manipulable by those who hold them. The atavistic notion of symbols owes a great deal of its recent inspiration to Freud's theory of symbols, which casts them inside recondite recesses of the self (ego). Anthropologists, although equally contributing to the atavistic explanation, have also consistently argued that symbols were good to think with, to be raised into the role of a bulwark under certain circumstances, or discarded outright under others. As a matter of fact, our contemporary regard for symbols as ephemeral entities is largely a consequence of the anthropological travelogue, which, by inventing symbol descriptions for others, led anthropologists to realize that cultural symbols were constructable and deconstructable.[5] Symbols can be atavistic or instrumental according to the choice of their users. Psychoanalysts pursue atavistic symbols in their patients' minds, and if the symbols reveal themselves too fleeting, the therapist will find in this an indication that they are red herrings, that is, symptoms, and that he must look for underlying meanings standing for symbols which are atavistic to be sure. Family therapists broke with this view and adopted the belief that symbols are instrumental, expressions of actions whose meanings are not to be found in the symbols themselves, but in the cycles of exchanges in which they are used. Symbols therefore do not mean qua texts, but only qua actions of inscribing into texts.[6]

Therapists are not so concerned with the status of the symbols they employ in their clinical discourse, or in their theoretical writing; these symbols are taken for granted as textual. When there is a polemic between two schools of therapy, the contenders do not consider their opposing positions as a pair of meaningful complementary actions, but as discrepancies involving statements of right and wrong. The symbols which are contextual and flexible, insofar as they call for responses on the part of the therapist, are those employed by the patients. Once these symbols are reconstructed in the therapeutic writing as procedural explanations, they regain a textual status and are chucked into the upholstering of theory. A patient's reference to an object that can be associated with a phallic symbol is a flexible and contextual communicative action which can or cannot be interpreted as representative of a repressed sexual motive. However, once this becomes written down into the statement that there is a category of objects qualifying as phallic symbols it becomes textual and gains in rigidity.

The quandaries about the system of knowledge in therapy are not restricted to the textual and contextual nature of symbols, or to the atavism and flexibility with which symbols become invested. The moral implications of the meaning of symbols is equally puzzling. The situation would be unproblematic if therapeutic symbols referred to trivial facts; but they do not. The symbols reframed and interpreted by the therapist are not only reflexes of psychological mechanisms, or fillings in communicative channels; they also constitute guidances about how people should lead their lives and, as such, function as a vicarious moral philosophy. In psychoanalysis this philosophy is historical, in the sense that it regards present symbols as condensations of the past, and projections onto the future. Symbols do not become morally validated in psychoanalysis insofar as their semantic meaning is concerned, but provided that they run on the correct path in the interior of the psyche, integrating the history of the individual in a satisfactory manner to the inner mechanisms such as consciousness, memory, ego ideal, ego preservation, securing of pleasure, and redemption of reality. Notice that unlike the detective, the psychoanalyst has no interest in discovering whether the events for which the symbols stand actually took place. The moral philosophy of family therapy is antihistorical and, in point of fact, antimoral. It does not have any regard for temporal sequences, from past to present and into future, but looks instead for interlocked patterns of actions forming cycles and repeating or changing, but constantly undergoing these evolutionary leaps ignited by internal functions. As it can be realized, it is a model similar to the psychoanalytic one, differing only in that instead of thrusting the mechanism into the psyche, family therapists place it inside communicative matrices. Both clinical practices are under the sway of scientific influences which, though stemming from different sources (nineteenth-century natural sciences, "Naturphilosophie," and medicine in one case, and twentieth-century cybernetics and biology in the other), converge in the common quest to replace religious morality by scientific reason. A therapist well informed about the origins of his métier, once questioned about the moral orientation of his practice, would answer that there is none, because he deals with the intrapsychic or with the communicative mechanisms preceding the formation of moral judgments in time for psychoanalysis and in relevance for the here-and-now for family therapy. However, despite all those caveats surrounding the considerations about the function of symbols and wrenching away their meanings, it is undeniable that therapists do issue moral directions to their patients. They shy away from making explicit the ethical imperatives underpinning therapeutic discourse, but the moral judgments are there, in the cases of both psychoanalysis and family therapy, springing from the exercise of practical reason. This is fortunate for those who believe that common sense is the best forum for judgment, and unfortunate for those others regarding practical reason with suspicion, and opposing to it the special reasons: scientific, religious, or political.

When therapists are called upon to discuss the ethical imperatives of their practice they do not talk about divorce or permanence of the family, about legitimacy and illegitimacy, about piety and impiety, about punishment and reward, about the adequacy of behavior to the prevalent social mores, or about justice and injustice. They talk about whether they should disclose to the patient all they know about him or not, and how far they could go in the deployment of rhetorical maneuvers. The morally acceptable standing for a psychoanalyst is the well-poised functioning of the psyche as defined by the metapsychology, and for the family therapist, the free-flowing communicative matrix that does not inconvenience any members in that circle, to the point that he or she thinks something must be done to alter the system. However, above and beyond all this Cartesian imagination, therapists do influence people's lives in moral terms, deriving their moral judgments from common sense and ideology.

The Rhetoric of Insight

Moral concepts are fleeting and change with the times. The prevailing standards of Viennese society at the turning of the century are hardly acceptable today in European and American societies. As a matter of fact, all constellations of symbols are subject to change and to manipulations which look arbitrary. Systems of knowledge have no greater independence than power hierarchies and rhetorical repertoires. These issues will be rendered significantly clearer in chapters 11 and 12, when we will compare therapeutic discourse to Socratic dialogue and discuss the cultural seat of the Western paradigmatic struggle to integrate the trinity constituted of knowledge, power, and rhetoric, or to break it and proceed with one or two of the spheres. But before we reach this conclusion, we must turn now to a very similar expression of this dilemma in Greek philosophy, pitting Socrates and the Sophist rhetors against one another, twenty-five centuries ago.

PART TWO

PLATO'S LEGACY:

REASON OR RUSE?

6   MIMESIS VERSUS METHEXIS

To read what was never written. *Such reading is the most
ancient: reading before all languages, from the entrails, the
stars, or dances. Later the mediating link of a new kind of
reading, or runes and hieroglyphs, came into use. It seems
fair to suppose that these were the stages by which the
mimetic gift, which was once the foundation of occult
practices, gained admittance to writing and language. In
this way language may be seen as the highest level of
mimetic behavior and the most complete archive of non-
sensuous similarity: a medium into which the earlier
powers of mimetic production and comprehension have
passed without residue, to the point where they have liqui-
dated those of magic.*
Walter Benjamin

In fifth-century Athens, education commanded social
prestige and the ability to read was one of its foremost components.
Unlike the Egyptian and Chinese traditions, literacy was available to all
educated people and not exclusive to those bureaucrats in service to the
rulers. In ancient Greece the ability to read and write was a collective
property and as such mattered. Literacy, however, had not yet settled in
the Attic culture to the exclusion of all dispute. The grip of oral culture
was still strong and harbored a constant potential of challenge to the
expansion of writing. One of the most important cultural artifacts of the
time was the *Odyssey*, a written epic poem celebrating the Greek traditions of a period of oral culture, thus bridging the gap between the
spoken and the written. Plato's dialogues established an additional link
between literacy and orality, by examining the philosophical implications of an oral quest for truth in written texts.

In an oral tradition, evidently the cultural memory is not stored in
written texts. It is transmitted in narratives and recitatives, myths and
poems. Knowledge is memory and the authority of the speaker stems
from his capacity to remember and to command respect for his statements. If he is a physician he has learned his art from someone else, but
his declaration will be enough because statements are based on sincerity, not truthfulness. It then follows that what takes place in face-to-

135

face interactions is decisive because there is no media other than oral discourse to retrieve knowledge. What is known must be present in memory and surface in discourse.

A cultural framework resting on literacy is very different.[1] The written text substitutes for memory, the concern with truth replaces the rule of sincerity, and the authoritativeness of the said or written is enfeebled. Truthfulness comes to the fore but does not establish a peaceful rule. The written truth is kept long enough and spread widely enough to undergo challenges sooner or later. Also, the author of the text is not present before the reader to defend his statements. As a consequence, the power of assertion is reduced both in its substance and in the form of the representation conveying it. Literacy also represents language, and by casting it beyond man, raises his awareness of it, drawing him ever deeper. There is a point at which he believes there is nothing outside language. It is time to question the power of language, an ever-growing concern among us.

In our post-Saussurean, post-Jakobsonian, and post-Chomskian world, the concept of language has gained a very specific and technical meaning within the science of linguistics, to the extent that we now move from language structure to cognitive structure, without any pause at the content of the thought and saying. We have pushed this distinction between form and content to the extreme and landed ourselves on the paradox of talking about cognitive and linguistic structures as empty entities lying outside language. We have learned to think that what matters are the operations we apply to concepts, not their meanings. Plato's philosophy points in a different direction. Before the *mythos* and before the *logos* ("language") there is something of value to be recognized, something prelinguistic which for that reason can hardly be talked about. This is the *agathon* ("good"), which is neither the referential relation between things and words nor the indexical relation between speakers and speech. It is not a collection of cultural motives, although in trying to unravel it we run the risk of "linguistifying" it, or of culturalizing it, which immediately makes us lose its grasp. The philosopher cannot begin his search anywhere else other than in the territory of language and culture. The dialectic method is precisely a procedure destined to establish discriminations in the linguistic and cultural universe. When the conceptual entities become reasonably ordered, the philosopher comes in touch with the *agathon* revealed through the crevices between the categories of knowledge, through the *différences* as Derrida puts it,[2] or through the disassembling of the language games in Wittgensteinian parlance. The essential content of our knowledge, therefore, is not something that we can link up by means of reference, or establish pragmatically in the discovery of who is saying what to whom, or encompass in any genre of expression; it is something we come into touch with in the spaces and intervals we create by tidying up our house of knowledge. However, it does not come from without, but from within, because it exists within the human soul.

Plato's model of dialectic dialogue claims that the fusion of form and content establishes the right of discourse. Indeed the Socratic dialogue presupposes a total engagement of the speakers in the dialogical situation in the sense that the rhetoric of persuasion and the effluence of internal motives become one. Reflection is produced by dialogical circuitry, not by the individual's stepping back from the debate. The reason that counts is not individual, but emerges from the group engaged in the debate. The immediacy of the speech situation is preserved. The participants speak with the full brunt of their knowledge and convictions, they do not withhold anything nor contrive ad hoc arguments without foundations in the group's memories and beliefs. As a consequence of immediacy, each dialogue is a whole in and of itself, rather than a stage towards something else. Each dialogue takes up a complete subject and gives it a complete examination insofar as the abilities of the participants go.

Speech can be *mimēsis*, that is, "imitation" of something else, or *methexis*, the "participation" of some things in others. These two categories of action—copy or imitation on one hand and classification or participation on the other—were cultural pillars in ancient Athens. The Greeks aimed at a high form of culture, *paideia*, characterized by the fulfillment of the loftiest qualities of body and mind, such as strength, dexterity, proportion, beauty, modesty, piety, justice, intelligence, wisdom, and temperance. Despite the appearance of these many qualities, they are all encompassed in one quality, *aretē* ("virtue"). The collective *aretē* was the *paideia*. To imitate or copy was a waste because mimesis stood in the way of the true cultivation of these values. To imitate a behavior, to imitate a way of speaking, to imitate the reasoning contained in an argument created by somebody else, or to imitate the gait of an acquaintance, or the looks of a friend was always less desirable than to develop these qualities from within, from the fountainhead of one's own potential. These forms of imitation, however, were not the worst of evils. The truly insidious mimesis lurked in forms of expression which at first glance would look unsuspicious, such as poetry and writing.

If it were possible for us to organize our knowledge of the world in terms of clear-cut categories which did not mingle or coalesce and remained autonomous around unequivocal self-definitions, then we would not be entitled to talk about methexis. But our cosmos is characterized by several possibilities of interrelations among its descriptive categories. This interwoven plurality requires from our knowledge a practice naturally in conflict with mimetic activities, which consist of copying the categorical setup of the world through a medium of representation. The mimetic copying surmises that all categories are either discrete or their interrelatedness is not problematic. In either case it is assumed that we can copy these categories before we sort them out.

It is very tempting to assume that the cosmos is divided into discrete and mixed categories, and that we apply mimesis to the former and methexis to the latter, but that cannot be the case. If it were, we could not know beforehand which categories were mixed with which, and so we would always have to begin with methexis. The other tempting and equally inadequate solution to integrate mimesis with methexis would have the latter preceding the former in time; however, this is yet another unsustainable hypothesis because if that were the case, once methexis had completed its work, it would be ruled out and replaced by mimesis, so that the two would still be incompatible. The mutual exclusion of these two concepts urges us towards radical decisions about whether the categories of knowledge are related or unrelated to one another, and if so whether the connections are discrete or ambiguous.

Plato argues that the categories of knowledge are related in an equivocal manner and that the function of knowledge is to reorganize them, not to copy them. But how can we organize these objects without representing them in some medium? Or do they have an essential autonomy accessible to us and independent of any medium of representation? That is the central question of Plato's inquiry, which inaugurates the Western tradition of philosophizing. Plato begs the question of the absolute essentiality of categories of knowledge, but is unable to find a satisfactory answer to it. Instead, he continues to discard systematic organizations of knowledge, and ends by leaving us holding our breath, and realizing that his very research bears testimony to the confused interrelation of all things. Therefore the only possible intervention is methexis. But where does the intelligibility come from, if the universe of knowledge is muddled? Why should we conclude that at the other end of the tunnel entities turn out discretely in their absolute essentiality, thereby justifying our methetic search? Why should we not conclude that the confusing tangle of relations is the state of affairs of all things, and that there is no alternative for us other than to try to copy the muddle as best we can?

Plato tries to find an ontological foundation for ideas by extricating them from the mind and differentiating them from the qualities of the objects. Several objections can be raised against this, but we will focus on one, introducing it with a series of questions. If ideas are independent of objects and concepts, is the network of their relation also independent from relations in other realms? If they are, we must apply our methetic organization of the cosmos to this domain as well, in which case it can no longer be the guiding light of methexis. If the relations among ideas are not independent from other domains, how can ideas themselves constitute a domain apart? What would be the force underwriting man's effort to grasp ideas before they congeal into complete reification? Plato provides an answer to this question in the *Republic* by referring to the link between ideas and knowledge as "intelligence,"[3] but this does not tally with Socrates' untiring preaching of the self-cultivation of virtues, because these latter qualities are at rest in the human soul and do not constitute a realm of their own. An alternative would be to have virtues independent of ideas and concepts, but in that case a dilemma would still persist as to which should have the ultimate sway over knowledge, ideas or virtues? It is not our goal to meddle in a philosophical discussion of Plato's ideas, but we cannot overlook the issues of ethics and speech which are crucial for our discussion of therapeutic discourse. In the first chapters of this essay we discussed whether therapeutic discourse could feed itself exclusively on the art of communication, or whether it was in need of an ethical grounding. The relation between ideas or virtues and concepts is critical for this subject matter.

In the following chapters, we will examine this issue in some detail, reviewing Plato's attempts to found knowledge on independent grounds, to thrust it into the mind and finally into the soul. But for now let us pursue a bit further this line of reasoning. If methexis is our only possible action of knowing, and if it consists in a complete rejection of mimesis, then we may fall into a reductio ad absurdum, foreclosing the possibilities of our own research. In order to avoid this, we must produce the ontological self-sufficiency according to which the categories of knowledge need to free themselves from those objects founded on perception, from languages founded on representation or copy, and from the entelechy founded on cultural traditions, concept formation, or other systems of ideas incapable of claiming for themselves absolute essentiality. In summary, the question we will be pursuing in our discussion of the dialogues is whether they found ideas on independent grounds, or alternatively how they accommodate mimesis with methexis. In conclusion we will see that Socrates finds a *tertium quid*, something that comes across quite eloquently in the dialectic dialogues, particularly in the *Parmenides*, to be discussed in chapter 10.

The problem which struck Socrates in the fifth century B.C., and which continued to tantalize Plato in the fourth century, was that the Greek paideia seemed to have reached a stage of self-complacency. As a consequence, the Athenian thinkers took for granted that things were well ordered and could be elegantly represented or eloquently imparted to those who wished to learn. Socrates rose against this state of affairs attacking writing, poetry, and Sophist philosophy. At the same time he showed an alternative through his dialectic of cross-examining ideas and revealing their ill-foundedness. He did not write down any of his arguments, but Plato, who became one of his disciples, wrote the dialogues to honor his master and forward his philosophy.

The dialogues contain many puzzles which have haunted philosophy for twenty-five centuries, among them the tense and precarious balance between mimesis and methexis, almost always recast in new terms in each dialogue. At this point, a methodological observation is in order. Plato's dialogues can be studied from three perspectives: according to the content of the ideas, the logic of the argument, or the weaving of the dialogue with the threads of the cultural context. Most philosophical studies focus on a combination of the two first approaches. Many regarded the dialogical form, chosen by Plato to present his philosophy, as mere idiosyncrasy, but it is unlikely that Plato considered the dialogues simply as a form of presentation, because, in these texts, the conversational situation is interwoven with the content and logic of the argument in delicate philosophical filigrees. Our reading of Plato takes the three lines into consideration and derives its hermeneutics from the new way of studying the dialogues introduced in the beginning of the nineteenth century by Friedrich Schleiermacher, pursued through one and a half centuries of Platonic studies in Germany, and today especially championed by Hans-Georg Gadamer.[4] This tradition of scholarship unravelled the inner work of the dialogues in which the conversational situation is of the utmost importance. Thus Socrates attacks Sophist philosophy when in presence of representatives of that school, or slays poetry when he meets a candid rhapsode such as Ion. The argument on many occasions follows the rhetorical needs created by the situation, or unfolds as a direct response to the shrewdness or weakness of the participants. Many parts of the arguments refer to specific historical situations, such as the political atmosphere in post-Pericles Athens, the trial and condemnation of Socrates, the bad reputation in which public opinion held the Sophists, or the current concepts of medicine.

Once we take into consideration the conversational, historical, and cultural aspect of the dialogues, it becomes possible to tell Socrates from Plato. The resemblances and differences in their philosophies are mapped throughout Plato's maturing. At first, all his efforts go to immortalize his master. Later, he begins to take exception to Socrates' ideas, but still pursues a line of reasoning compatible to the two. In later dialogues he excludes Socrates; however, their philosophies constantly encompass a common ethical imperative. For the purpose of our essay, Socrates' dialectic, his critical inquiry into virtue, and his onslaught against mimesis will be of greater interest than Plato's doctrine of ideas or of forms and insights into logic, and for this reason we will restrict our inquiry to Socrates' philosophy.

The dialogues convey an astonishing contemporaneity to our times and some are so delightfully plotted that as philosophy they are as exciting to read as drama. Unlike the Sophists, the participants in the conversations do not lecture each other, but pursue their inquiry together, led by Socrates' implacable questioning. The result, more often than not, is that the discussants realize that they do not know as much as they thought. In this way, the dialogues lead to negative situations rather than to positive assertions of facts. Many are inconclusive and it is particularly these that arouse the deepest interest in Plato's scholarship, because their inconclusiveness is intended and does not stem from philosophical clumsiness.

The art of methexis, without the pretension of carrying its teleology through to completion, is fully illustrated in these dialogues, which are probably the first effort of critical philosophy in the Western tradition. No other activity or speech genre could be more destructive for mimesis than argumentative dialogues. Nevertheless, they stand on a basic assumption that a certain representation of states of affairs is both necessary and possible. The discussants rebuff all proposed copies of states of affairs and explore the unrewarding domain lying beyond representation, but remain aware that in order to do these philosophical gymnastics, they need some representation in order to strike at that which they claim to be misrepresentation. This, however, is a tricky undertaking which Socrates embraces by replacing positive assertions about states of affairs with his critical questioning. If this inquiry is to have a positive side it can only be grasped a posteriori, by reconstructing Socrates' procedures. At this point, the readers of the dialogues come close to Socrates' interlocutors who had only benefited from the debates in the long run, first by realizing that what they thought they knew was precarious, and second by sharpening their critical skills.

The confrontation between mimesis and methexis is present in all dialogues either explicitly as in the *Ion* or in the *Republic,* or implicitly as in the *Philebus,* the *Sophist,* the *Statesman,* and the *Parmenides.* But the implication of the discussion can always be traced back to the basic question between methexis and mimesis. Sometimes it flares up in a reflection on passing in the course of the debate, as in the *Theaetetus*, when Socrates interrupts the discussion about knowledge and muses upon what he and Theaetetus are doing. He reminds his interlocutor that upon numerous occasions they have said, "We know," "We do not know," assuming that they made sense to each other, but the topic of their conversation is knowledge and they "still know nothing about knowledge," as Socrates concludes.[5] The implication of this remark is that in looking for the meaning of knowledge, one is led to make certain assumptions about knowledge in order for the conversation to proceed.

Unlike the Sophist teachers, who stripped discourse of its moral content, Plato proposes a methexis which unfolds from mimesis. An initial worldview is necessary from the start even when the speaker's project is to build a new one. Methexis is this process of disassembling the initial worldview as the new one is elaborated. As we descend the string of dialogues, we learn that all worldviews are fallible, and that the process of piecing them together is all that matters and that which truly redeems the human soul. However, Plato constantly warns his readers and Socrates his listeners that the keen eye that promptly understands that fact, hastens to abandon the task of building up mimetic worldview, and, while seizing upon the hermeneutics of methexis, ends up empty-handed. The true dialectician must display, from the beginning, the commitment to the whole picture building activity, however shattered the motivation for that commitment may become as it runs the gauntlet of methetic experiences.

We have to be careful in our use of these words "methexis" and "mimesis," because in the dialogues they do not have the central function assigned to them in this essay. Instead of methexis, Socrates talks about dialectics, and the attack of mimesis, although sometimes explicit, often appears as a critique of belief. There are, however, two subjects that bear the brunt of his critique of mimesis: poetry and literacy. The main attacks on poetry appear in the *Ion*, and in Books 3 and 10 of the *Republic*. *Ion* is a lighthearted dialogue in which Plato plays jokingly with Ion, a young rhapsode who gives recitals of Homer's poetry, and is enthralled by the Homeric artistry. Socrates points out the artificiality of poetry recitals, saying that Ion enacts feelings that he does not have, and induces his audience to have emotions about things that did not happen. The greatest falsity, however, must not be blamed upon the rhapsode, but on the poet himself. The reciter is one possessed by the gods, a critique that pleases Ion, and yields his proud agreement, but he who is possessed is also deprived of reason, something that Ion finds equally edifying, because for him, as for the poets, according to Socrates, the ravishment of aesthetic ecstasy, and not reason, is the supreme form of knowledge.

In the *Republic* the critique of poetry is fully spelled out. Poetry is a form of representation, "three removes from nature."[6] God creates the class of couches. The carpenter, in a second remove, imitates God's creation by making couches. Finally, there comes the poet imitating the carpenter. The imitator, however, only copies the appearance of objects.[7] He copies or imitates a phantom, not the truth.[8] It is for that reason that it is so easy for mimetic art to reproduce just about anything, because it does not undertake the true art of creating real objects. The distortions imparted to reality by mimetic art fall "nothing short of witchcraft."[9] What Plato fears the most is the perfect imitator who can copy all things, introducing a confusion between reality and his make-believe reality. The wizards of imitation should be praised, Plato recommends, but chased out of the utopian polity he constructs in the *Republic*.[10]

Poetry presents the gods as humans, weak, overtaken by base sentiments. Another evil of poetry is the instigation of the fear of death in man, because it corrupts the desire for freedom leading many to prefer life under serfdom. Plato rises against any form of representation of speech, and suggests that in a poem all quotations should take an indirect and reportive form.[11] Poetry numbs man's sense of justice by extolling contemplative virtues to the detriment of action founded on reason.

The main target of the criticism is not art in itself, but the uses to which it can be given, particularly in troubled times. Plato wished to emphasize those arts which could contribute to the uplifting of the polity and ban those which diverted man's consciousness from his political tragedies. Homer had become a sort of Attic consciousness, a repository of the social, political, and religious identity of a city which oscillated between the recent memory of the Persian invasion and the fear of a defeat before Sparta, its arch-rival. Homer's poetry fulfilled the role of inflaming the polity's pride by glorifying the Greek past of heroic wars and deeds. His poems were read in every home like a covenant of cultural values. For Plato, however, while they elated the Attic spirit, they fell short of inducing the citizens to political action. Thus, he makes Socrates inveigh against poetry, proposing that it be replaced by philosophy which could more easily awaken the souls and save the city-state.[12]

Plato is known to have written tragedies in his youth before, influenced by Socrates, he decided to become a philosopher. In addition to being a philosopher, he is an accomplished artist, and the highly dramatic plotting of some of the dialogues unrelentingly engage the reader for their aesthetic qualities. How could this refined artist forward such a bold condemnation of art? Moreover, how could this outstanding thinker fall into the elementary contradiction of attacking the mimetic copy of reality, while he himself writes imitating his master Socrates?

It is in the *Phaedrus* that Plato unleashes his full-fledged attack upon writing. He compares it to painting, both silent copies of the world which sever the medium from the source of expression. A painting creates the illusion of a sight, but it conveys the experience of the moment portrayed on the canvas after it has been deprived of life. Writing likewise imitates speech after it has deprived the discourse of voice. The topic of discussion in the dialogue is love. Socrates and Phaedrus go for a walk in the country, while Phaedrus reads a speech about love written by the Sophist Lysias. The conversation between the two strollers is permeated by irony and good humor. The weather is good and the countryside beautiful. Phaedrus is dazzled by Lysias' piece, and Socrates invites him to read the speech rather than forward his own ideas on the subject since, he says, "I am not altogether inclined to let you practice your oratory on me when Lysias himself is here present."[13] Here begins the irony in the assertion that a written text represents its author. Coming from Lysias, Socrates already knows what to expect, and since his friend Phaedrus is so enthralled with the sophist's speech, he spares him the embarrassment of advancing uncritical ideas about love, and instead has him read Lysias' text. After the reading, Socrates discards the speech as repetitive, a mere "piece of rhetoric,"[14] and refuses to give his own speech on love. Phaedrus begs him insistently to speak, "I swear that unless you deliver your speech here in its very presence [a plane tree], I will assuredly never again declaim nor report any other speech by any author whatsoever."[15] There is great irony in this, because Socrates would obviously prefer that Phaedrus talk about his own ideas rather than report those of others. Socrates agrees to speak, but says he is going to deliver his speech with his head covered, so that he can "rush through . . . without looking at you and breaking down for shame."[16] Lovers feel shy when they make love declarations, either for fear that they may be rejected, or because of the uneasiness of disclosing intimate feelings to another who, although the object of that feeling, has not yet come to share such intimacy. Socrates' speech is a hoax. It is elegant in form, but effects a syntax and a rhetoric typical of written text as opposed to that of speech. It presents love as a peril worth the caution of its carriers. These are not ideas held by Socrates. He covers his head because of the lies he is uttering and the shame of delivering a speech in written form, a shameful speech which hides its author, defending him from being called to task for his lies.

The deceit created by writing is comparable to that of poetry. While writing conceals the liar, poetry reveals the "possessed."[17] Both hurt truth and reason, each in its way. After his hoax speech, he tells Phaedrus he was joking, "sinning,"[18] and that now he is going to speak forthright, with a bare head in order to restore to love its due.[19] Phaedrus could not report the ideas conveyed in Lysias' speech because one does not "learn" what is written, but only memorizes words without grasping their meaning. In this sense, writing can be placed on a par with myth and with poetry, opposed to *logos* ("language," "speech"), deprived of knowledge. The myth teller repeats a story he has heard before. The writer also repeats what he or somebody else thought/said. The reader remains at the level of the words, repeating the symbols used by the writer without participating in their choice and piecing together. A written text cannot speak for itself, and therefore cannot be held responsible. This is the case with every medium of communication, we might add. Writing, however, makes a claim for self-sufficiency, by dispensing with memory. It is as if writing pleaded with us to not worry about recollecting knowledge or struggling to bring things together, because it does that for us, although Socrates claims it really does not and urges us to choose a medium capable of expressing our thoughts both immediately and completely.

Plato, like Freud, is constantly emphasizing the need to distinguish the human faculties from their products, such as intelligence from ideas, or memory from that which is remembered. He wants to tap the container, but, like Freud, has to proceed by shuffling contents which he treats as indices to the container. Differently from Freud, Plato does not build a theory of symbols, never describes the nature of the container, nor proposes a theory from within which the puzzles of meaning should be solved. His aim is to underline the immediacy between that which is in the human soul and the discourse that expresses it. He distinguishes the knowledge existing as memory, the *mnēmē*, from the knowledge retrieved as remembrance, the *hypomnēsis*. He proclaims a speech with *mnēmē* and without *hypomnēsis*, that is, a speech which is more immediate than mediated, more insertion than extraction, more giving than taking, and more anticipatory than recollecting.

Phaedrus asks Socrates how to become a "master of persuasion," and in his reply, Socrates rephrases the expression with a "finished performer,"[20] that is, the speaker who knows how to make his speech fit his audience. This adjustment becomes impossible in the face of a written text. The need to match speech and audience resides in the nature of the object "on which our discourse is brought to bear": the human soul.[21] To different types of discourse there correspond different types of soul, and the rhetor must know the "ways in which souls are affected . . . what kind of speech can be relied on to create belief in one soul and disbelief in another."[22]

Socrates tells Phaedrus a fable about the god Theuth, who, having created writing, went to the Egyptian king Thamous, and urged him to adopt the new invention, so that all Egyptians could become more educated and more able to remember. The king refused Theuth's offer, refuting his claim that writing would enhance memory, because the result of literacy would be quite the contrary, it would "implant forget-fulness" in his kingdom, by creating the illusion in those who read that they knew.[23] Derrida analyzes this dialogue, focusing on the myth of the Egyptian king and on a central word in the *Phaedrus*, *pharmakon*, which has multiple meanings: medicine, poison, drug, and filter.[24] He claims that Plato is keen on employing words like this, in which the conceal-ment of the underlying meaning common to all others makes the word ambiguous and constitutes a philosophical problem. The two main meanings of *pharmakon* are poison and medicine; poison in the sense of a foreign and artificial substance entering the body or the soul and thus intoxicating it. Medicines, of course, can be poisonous and produce the same effects. Socrates compares the texts brought in by Phaedrus to a *pharmakon*, a medicine/poison destined to kill something inside man and replace it with something else. Men may not be able to express love, but since they are all capable of loving, they contain love in their souls. If a speech with wrong ideas about love persuades its listeners, it may kill or numb that natural feeling, replacing it by a distorted concept, estab-lishing, for example, that love is a good sentiment to receive, but a dangerous one to give, and that every man should, therefore, make others love him, but refrain from loving them. A text or a speech can be poison or medicine to the soul as much as a medicine can cure or poison a patient. Since we cannot avoid texts, speeches, or medicines, we ought to restrict our consumption to those substances closer to nature, because they will be less likely to poison our organisms and souls. A written text is undoubtedly far removed from the naturalness of oral speech.

Health and virtue come from within, not from without, Socrates teaches in the *Gorgias*.[25] Consequently, healing and knowledge cannot be exterior to man; they ought to be developments taking place from within. It follows that medicines and texts must always be applied in harmony with the *agathon* ("good") of health and knowledge lying inside man. The medicine/poison substances have the potential to endanger the health, or irritate illness. The philosopher's task is therefore to clarify the meaning of the ambiguous words by using explicit words, those which do not belie that which lies in man's soul.

In the beginning of the *Phaedrus*, Socrates does not rush to debunk literacy. He keeps a neutral position, he attacks the content of Lysias' speech, not the medium in which it is cast. The assault on literacy is carried out through the irony lying between the lines, by the myth of Theuth, and by the myth of the cicadas, in such an indirect way that Socrates only advances his criticism from a one-step-removed position as a report he conveys. He also points out to Phaedrus the redeeming features he finds in writing, such as the immortalization of the speeches of the great men. He goes as far as saying that "there is nothing shameful in the mere writing of speeches."[26] The choice of style or medium does not matter so much if it is compatible with the situation of the speaker and the listener, and does not jeopardize the argument.[27] He draws the anatomy of rhetorical speech showing how it can be elegant and dazzling, independent of its content.[28] Oral discourse cannot be raised to an absolute alternative to written discourse, because if the latter has a natural inclination for wrong, the former can also forward the purposes of evil. In the same way that it is not sufficient for a doctor to know the right treatment, since he must be able to choose who needs the treatment,[29] the rhetor must also be able to choose the right form of speech for his given audience.[30] Plato, then, is justified in having reported his master's debates in the written form, and Socrates' criticism of writing does not absolutely oppose it to oral discourse.

Socrates' attack on mimesis and exemplary demonstration of methexis in his dialectic method is a cultural and historical tribute of the passage from an oral to a literate context. The new medium of writing overcomes the old of speaking, but does not sweep it away. The fervor with which people adhere to a cultural novelty such as a new medium of expression is unbridled, and leads to a temporary neglect of the over-ridden but indispensible qualities of the previous medium. As writing comes to the center of the culture, speech becomes literacized, that is, the organization of speaking is submitted to the prerequisites of writing. Socrates raised his voice in defense of the qualities of oral discourse which it seemed was being jettisoned in the Athens of the fifth century B.C. Today, as our culture of literacy shows signs of obsolescence, and is replaced and incorporated into a cultural setting progressively dominated by the electronic media and the age of computers, it is opportune to examine the values intrinsic to the media of speech and writing swept away by the irresistible appeal of the new and unexpected.

It seems that in the oral context of the Greek culture, reflection was collective and not individual and self-centered as we know it today, within our literacized and Christianized traditions. Socrates argues that the critique and clarification of subject matter is the product of dialogue rather than the withdrawal of the individual mind to think the issues over. The reflective function of reason is then performed in group and woven in the turn-taking of conversation. The concluding thoughts reveal a consensual basis in the means of discussion and a clash of opinions integrated by the persuasiveness of certain arguments. This kind of reflection can more easily be accomplished in oral than in written discourse.

The main value of oral discourse in Socrates' contentions is that it is cast on the validity claim of sincerity as opposed to truth introduced by literacy. The authority of knowledge resides in the sincerity of the speaker. Socrates pays tribute to the earlier Homeric stage of the Greek oral culture, in which authority and sincerity were grounded on hierarchy in the myth of Theuth, because the ultimate decision about the worth of literacy does not depend on evidential proof, but on the authority of that one who rebuffed the new art, King Thamous. The king of Egypt is superior to the god Theuth because he is the god of gods. Socrates, however, also puts in the king's mouth a strong argument, that literacy produces precisely the opposite results to those forwarded by Theuth; that is, writing enfeebles memory by dispensing with its practice. His quest is not to go back to the supremacy of sincerity, but to create a new culture in which sincerity and truth become fundamentally integrated with the claims of discourse.

The variety of issues discussed by Socrates are congealed in the polarization of mimesis and methexis. Writing accentuates the inclination to produce mimetic copies of reality, and thus tends to dispense with methexis. It is prerequisite of the written text that it present a definite state of affairs, that it function as one conversational turn in a broader dialogical situation. The written text is potentially endowed with more completeness because it is not strung together with other texts, as clauses in an oral dialogue are. The inconsistency between two statements made by the same speaker in the course of a conversation is easier to point out because the statements are closer to one another in time, and their author is present to react against any objections. The written text and its author are protected from all those checks. The prerequisite of oral discourse, as conceived in the Socratic dialogues, is that speech questions and disassembles states of affairs. This, however, is not the responsibility of a speaker alone, but the result of the dynamics of dialogues which harness all participants to the best argument.

Once Plato has marked the boundary between methexis and mimesis and vowed to capture the essences of both, he is free to write beyond his critique of literacy and to compose his dialogues with the inspiration of a poet or tragedian, and even to tell myths in these texts. Likewise Socrates crusades against the Sophists and feels free to employ Sophistic maneuvers in the persuasion of his sterner adversaries.

The targets of Plato's dialogues are the mimetic copy performed by poetry, the mimetic repetition present in writing, and the empty-shelled discourse of the Sophist, who by making speech into an end in itself, creates a gap between word and deed, between the said and the meant. In order to circumvent the claims of truth and sincerity, the Sophist philosophers argued that the belief in all possibilities was realistic and not hypocritical. The issue of sincerity and truth could no longer be raised for all that mattered was the cunning of speech. The Sophists, however, were not cynics and espoused ideals as lofty as those of Socrates. Maybe it is for this reason that they became his main adversaries. In the following chapter we turn to the polemic between Socrates and the Sophists.

7   THE SOPHISTS' EXCESSES

The movement of the Sophists in ancient Greece is extremely important for us because one of the major critiques that can be levelled against therapeutic discourse in general, and that of the family therapists in particular, is that it employs sophistic techniques and is therefore unethical. The Sophists' philosophy is also important because it led to a radical application of the concept of methexis as a verbal art, characterized by spontaneity and immediacy, an absolute praxis completely divorced from theory. Socrates himself cannot be fully understood if removed from the context of sophistic philosophy which he made profession of faith to combat and on which he so extensively drew in order to supply his arsenal of rhetorical weapons. Jaeger and Gadamer recognized the affinity between the Sophists and Socrates, and although heeding Socrates' opposition to his rivals, they interpreted his philosophy in the light of the Greek cultural milieu of the time, which was by and large influenced by the Sophist teachers.[1]

The Sophists were travelling teachers of wisdom in the Greek speaking world during the fifth and fourth centuries B.C. Etymologically, the word *sōphistēs* means a professional or expert in wisdom. As a matter of fact the Sophists claimed that they could realize the highest ideal of *paideia*, that is, to teach *aretē* ("virtue"). The word "sophism" retained in the European languages the negative meaning it connoted in ancient Greece: in the definition of the *Concise Oxford Dictionary*, "false argument intended to deceive." The Sophist rhetors were reputed to strive at any costs to win all arguments, irrespective of whether they were right or wrong, including using deceitful speech maneuvers. The Sophists travelled from one city to the next, teaching rhetorical skills to the children of the rich and charging payment for their services. They generally were followed by a retinue of apprentices hoping to join the profession one day. Depending on their background knowledge, they could also teach mathematics, geometry, astronomy, or any other subject the teacher was competent in and the student wished to learn and could afford. The main subject of their instruction, however, was rhetoric, and that is the field in which their contribution has found a long-lasting presence. They came mainly from cities smaller than Athens, but this great cultural center was the marketplace for their craft. Describing the Sophist gathering in Callias' house in the *Protagoras*,

Plato writes that they were for the "most part foreigners—Protagoras draws them from every city that he passes through charming them with his voice like Orpheus, and they follow spellbound."²

The Sophist education was primarily aimed at those hoping to become politicians in the Athenian democracy. Two of them, Alcibiades and Critias, eventually became rulers in the tyranny of the thirty, set up in Athens by the Spartans (404 B.C.). The idea of teaching rhetorical skills was pervaded by the democratic ideal that the aspiring newcomers, without family wealth or reputable name, could be given a chance to reach the world of high politics. On a more mundane level, the Athenian youth was fond of a good argument, and eloquence was among the main predicates for a young man who wished to have social appeal.

The Sophists sparked a cultural movement probably similar to that spearheaded by positivism and science in the beginning of the present century, rising against the old values of religion in the contemporary case and of traditional culture in the ancient example. They demoted sacred cows, invaded areas of thought preserved by long-standing prejudices and attacked the Greek religion, the epic poems, and the moral code of paideia. In their ravaging onslaught against tradition, they outlined a new cultural practice, that of education. Jaeger makes the interesting point that the idea of "vocation" is of Christian origin, entailing a different range of meanings than the Greek *technē*.³ Arts or technique such as carpentry, masonry, or chariot driving could be taught to anyone, while a vocation identified a limited group of people with a particular art. The idea of *technē* in the education of the arts implied that the transmission of that knowledge was opened to all, thus embodying the high democratic ideals of ancient Greece.

A few metaphors captured the imagination of the Greeks in their founding conceptualization of education. The Sophists liked to compare it to agriculture or to gymnastics. In the first comparison, the soil stood for human nature, the farmer for the teacher, and the seed for the spoken word. But knowledge did not germinate in man in quite the same way. Actually, the Sophists' very experience of teaching bore witness to the inappropriateness of the metaphor, for they knew it was not enough to mention the objects of knowledge, it was necessary to persuade the student, as well as to take several other rhetorical precautions in order for the imparted piece of knowledge to remain in the learner's consciousness, undisturbed by rival opinions. A second favorite metaphor, that of gymnastics, did not fare much better. The idea of training was given relief, but the Sophists' experience had also led them to realize that the acquisition of knowledge was not a matter of repetition conditioning the mind to perform a particular task. A more interesting metaphor, that of medicine, was also used by the Sophists and Socrates. The normal state of an organism was equated with a latent state of knowledge in the soul. The disruption of this state in medical terms was disease, while in philosophical terms ignorance. The physician and the philosopher restored health and knowledge respectively. The challenge to this metaphor naturally resides in the question whether the untaught mind would be knowledgeable; likewise, would the body never tainted by disease be healthy? We will come back to the medical metaphor of education later on in this chapter.

The final metaphor is not one carved by the Greeks, but by contemporary students of the Greek paideia who see in Sophist-Socratic education a practice bearing close resemblance to psychotherapy. The dialogues have numerous references to healing souls in their state of thinking that they know what they in fact ignore. Gorgias, one of the leading Sophists, wrote that "the power of speech over the disposition of the soul is comparable to the effect of drugs on the disposition of the body. As drugs can expel certain humors from the body and thereby put an end to sickness, and even to life, so can words equally produce grief, pleasure, or fear in the soul."[4]

The great concern about education revolved around the dilemma of whether to preserve a paideia ("education," "culture") under stern criticism or create a new one. According to Jaeger, "[the] oldest meaning [of aretē] is a combination of proud and courtly morality with warlike valour."[5] In the aristocratic times described by Homer, the Greeks started to shape a notion of individual, founded on the person's ability to sustain his honor. This aretē, however, was the privilege of nobles and warriors who faced the social pressure to maintain their leadership and exemplary attitude. The breach of honor would put one to shame. But honor was not only military prowess. It was also the correct observance of the cultural norms, respect for the code of values. In this sense, aretē bridged material and spiritual values and remained in the polity after the death of its bearer as an example to be mirrored. Naturally, the main channel of transmission of aretē from one generation to the next was the epic poetry praising the accomplishments of the erstwhile heroes such as Agamemnon, Achilles, Odysseus, and Ajax.

In the democracy of the city-state the nobility had been replaced by a bourgeoisie much larger in numbers than its preceding ruling class. Honor was no longer the distinctive emblem of the hero, but something to be pursued for personal advantage. The failure to achieve it did not put the individual to shame, but invited a new try. In this context the paideia that could link body and soul was wanting in its goal of aretē. There were forms of education for the body such as gymnastics, as well as ennobling disciplines for the soul such as music, but nothing capable of bridging the two. The individual identity inherited from the Homeric times pitched the individual on the ground of the polity and consequently *aretē* needed to be a collective value. However, if the Homeric poems had a widespread penetration and hegemony over education, under the democracy of the fifth century no form of education could claim the same universality. Moreover, the Attic intelligentsia had come to the conclusion that in order to maintain democracy, they should better educate the leaders in the traditions of paideia, as well as in its critique. The *polloi* ("the crowds") seemed beyond reach and did not count in that democracy. A public leader needed to be eloquent in public speeches because his main task was to persuade his constituency as well as his adversaries to support some measures as opposed to others. Thus the *aretē* of education in democratic Athens was the ability to speak persuasively. The politician was called a rhetor, that is, an orator.[6] The values of cunning and intelligence, the gift to woo people and deceive adversaries through wily maneuvers had a long standing in the Greek culture. The epic poems are replete with praise for such qualities and so are the myths and fables. The qualities of the fox and of the squid are extolled because these animals represent the highest skills in hunting and in deceit respectively.[7] It constitutes no surprise that these features became mixed with the ideal of persuasion through eloquent speech. Nevertheless, *aretē* also means "appropriation of the beautiful," and although eloquence is a beautiful quality, it is not substantial, but more a means to an end. The content of paideia to be imparted to the leaders was virtue, and not the new rhetoric in which it was supposed to be transmitted. Socrates insisted that virtue was a whole, while the Sophists split it into constitutive parts such as justice, courage, holiness, piety, temperance, and the other qualities current in the Greek paideia. But the Sophist philosophers were regarded as advocates of the teaching of eloquence for eloquence's sake.

In spite of this fame, what the Sophists really did was to carry out their educational program whose goal was to teach virtue through sophisticated rhetorical means. For these rhetors, the mind contained an internal structure which handled the objects of knowledge, defining and classifying them in Attic order. Education was confronted with the choice of either filling the mind with objects, as in encyclopedic teaching, or developing the classificatory structures through formal training.[8] While Socrates set out to piece together the puzzle, combining encyclopedic with formal education, the Sophists became tangled in the multiple vines of the project, and went on teaching rhetoric at the expense of the transmission of values. The integration of encyclopedic and formal education is proposed in the *Republic* through the fusion in the ruler of the philosopher and the king. For Socrates the field of knowledge for the integration of encyclopedic and formal education was philosophy; for the Sophists it was politics, although there was no consensus about political values. Pericles' democracy had been a golden period, but in the wake of that regime, the Athenians realized that the excellent leadership had taken them to the brink of tyranny. There were no models in the past, or in neighboring city-states to serve as examples of the polity that the philosophers and rhetors wished to build through education. Consequently, their propositions unfolded toward the imagination of a utopian polity, or toward a concentration of reflection upon the discourse developing those utopias. Both directions are illustrated in the *Republic*. The consequence of this educational effort cum critique was that paideia ceased to be a state of affairs to be extolled and passed on, becoming a goal, a situation never before experienced, something to be sought after and built through education. This dissatisfaction with the existing culture coupled with the struggle to create an ideal culture, became a basic tenor of the Western, Euro-American conception of culture, particularly in Anglo-Saxon countries.[9]

The Greek culture of the fifth and fourth centuries was thus characterized by a profound discontent with the society, politics, and culture of the city-state, followed by the assumption that it was possible to live within a cultural setting entirely produced by the applied rationality of man, a cultural setting which was not the result of historical injunctions. The Greek paideia was not regarded as a self-reproducing tradition, but as one that, like the phoenix, burnt itself and rose from its ashes with renewed vitality. Like the swan, it sang melodiously when it foresaw its end, in Homer's poems, in the tragedians' plays, and in Plato's philosophy. The meaning of paideia comprised both the content of culture and the process of acquiring it, but in the first denotation it moved away from mimesis and propounded not a copy, but the creation of a new reality. The second denotation was clearly a methetic one, subordinate to the utopian paideia that could arise from any of the reformative projects, either Sophist or Socratic and Platonic.

The Sophists were caught in the middle of this Greek cultural puzzle. On one hand they wished to educate their contemporaries, which implied that their teaching should have for content a certain cultural object. This object was *aretē*. On the other hand they were not satisfied with the *aretē* culturally defined in paideia and, therefore, their project also adumbrated the redefinition of *aretē* and the recreation of culture. The attempt to teach a culture that at the same time had to be re-created resulted in the loss of content in Sophist teaching at the expense of the swelling of the pedagogic techniques. Note that eloquence was also a virtue in the Olympus of the ideal Greek paideia, hence the means of education could also be taken for at least one of its ends. Socrates seems to have been more successful than the Sophists because although caught in the same dilemma, rather than sliding all the way toward a rhetoric of persuasion which could be put at the service of any ideas, he developed a rhetoric of critique through whose mesh only those very fine ideas could pass. In the studies of Plato's philosophy the formulation of a doctrine of ideas is generally attributed to Plato, while the critique, the dialectic method of cross-examining opinions is credited to Socrates. This view, however, belies the spirit of the dialogues, which are a great deal more concerned with the dialogical handling of ideas than with their postulation. The *Republic*, considered Plato's political treaty, devotes only one third of its length to the description of the utopian city-state. The other two thirds are occupied with criticism and pedagogy. Unless we are willing to say that the dialogues are more Socratic than Platonic, it is necessary to recognize that Plato's concern with the rhetoric of critique is more important than his forays into the rhetoric of persuasion or his formulation of a doctrinaire worldview.

The Sophists allowed rhetoric to become uncoupled from truth and ethics.[10] In the *Gorgias*, Callicles attacks Socrates because he still does philosophy, an art that is a mere complement to education and consequently should only be practiced by the young who still have many things to learn. The thrust of his intervention in the dialogue is that education is a means for a political end, but his end is casuistic.[11] This separation between rhetoric and ethics opened a crack in the Sophist system through which Socrates was able to split it and eventually bring about its downfall. The Sophists' principles, such as Progagoras' "man is the measure of all things," turned out to be empty shells as we learned that the man in question was only a loquacious speaker and little else. However, the Sophists were not entirely off track; they were not the benighted traveller whistling songs to ward off his fears of ignorance. Their diagnostic of the times, culled out of political malaise, was indeed insightful. They realized that in their Greece it had become very difficult to decide the best argument because of the contentious atmosphere lacking in principles. As a matter of fact, it was difficult to make a good argument prevail over a bad one. Skeptical about the persuasive force of knowledge and deprived of power, the Sophists concentrated their efforts in the perfecting of the art of debating.[12] No matter how skilled their argument was, once confronted with a superior power, it was worthless, as Socrates eloquently demonstrated at his trial. Also the cunning of the argument was not enough to overcome the authority of knowledge, as their strifes with Socrates showed. Their strategy was to excel in the use of argument in order to overcome power and knowledge.

The art most intimately identified with the Sophist movement was eristics, the art of disputation aiming at victory and not at the establishment of truth. The word for a lawsuit or trial in Greek is *agon*. From it we derive the English cognate "agony," meaning mental anguish, bodily suffering, struggle; a state typical of someone who is in the throes of death. The etymological evolution of the meaning of this word finds an interesting parallel in the historical and cultural context of trial in ancient Greece. The practice of torture to extract confessions and of depositions sustained by oath were replaced by the proof of innocence or guilt based on logical argument. Evidently the argumentation was tortuous and the grappling between defense and accusation agonizing. The legal and political arenas were dominated by juggling eristics, which nevertheless were not sufficient to measure up to the power asymmetries in the declining polity.

In the Sophist rhetorical arsenal we find a copious stock of tautologies and half-tautologies. Typical is Gorgias' saying that "being is unrecognizable unless it manages to seem, and seeming is feeble unless it manages to be."[13] Another technique was to ask questions to which it was impossible to find an adequate answer, thereby confusing the interlocutor. Socrates himself contributed a few juggling maneuvers among which is the trademark of his repertoire, the elenchus. It consists in taking the adversaries' statement, let us say "A," asking him whether it does not necessarily imply "B," and whether "B" does not necessarily imply "C," and "C" "D," and so forth, and finally showing that "D" contradicts "A." But elenchus was not eristics because the line of reasoning was clearly expounded and could therefore be challenged at any point. It was more akin to a Sophist to refute an argument with a strongly differing opinion without providing the grounds for holding it. The effect of such a move was to create a standstill in conversation, the original statement becoming mired, but neither confuted nor proved. The Sophists would also pretend to agree with an argument, recapitulating it sarcastically, a maneuver only possible in the presence of a conniving audience. Another technique consisted in inquiring about the more elementary aspects of an argument, pretending not to understand its broader implications in order to prevent the speaker from proceeding with his reasoning.

The main goal of a discussion was to defeat the interlocutor and the use of every move to confuse him was acceptable. Another relished procedure consisted in forwarding absurd syllogisms which although logically correct denied reality. For example, a Sophist could argue that men are biped. Women are not men, therefore they are not biped. Writing about the Sophists' strategies, Gorgias enjoins his readers "in contending against adversaries, to destroy their seriousness with laughter and their laughter with seriousness."[14] The Sophists would confuse a sound argument by inverting its logical order or by branching it out onto numerous centrifugal arguments weakening the stem of the main argument; or still by adducing unrelated subjects which at first sight seemed related, so that the interlocutor would be distracted from his line of reasoning, trying to interrelate the awkward topics thrown into the discussion. Evidently these tactics were only possible in face of the interlocutor's earnestness and his willingness to repeatedly grant the Sophist the benefit of doubt. The other side of this benefit is, of course, the acceptance of the Sophists' power as knowledgeable teachers.

Of two final techniques in the host of examples, which were so widely employed by Socrates in his elenchus, one involved placing an argument into a much broader context than that originally intended by the speaker, so that the logic of the argument with which he had started could no longer be maintained. The other maneuver consisted in subdividing the argument into categories and proceeding with the discussion of each category until the whole became irremediably fragmented. These two rhetorical rules were: expand the argument if it is too focused, or reduce it if it is too broad, in order to break the logic of exposition.

A Sophist rhetor lavishly enjoyed polemics and looked for established values to topple. The Trojan War was among the dearest and most heartrending stories of the Greek mythology. Helen deserted her husband, King Menelaus, and eloped with Prince Paris of Troy, thus triggering the ten-year war so costly in lives for both sides. Helen was an antiheroine of Greek culture, beautiful but wicked. Gorgias took to defend and restore her reputation in his *Encomium of Helen*. The argument claims that she ran away with Paris owing to (1) a combination of chance, necessity, and the will of the gods, or (2) because she was abducted by force, or (3) because she was seduced by persuasion. In the first case she is not to be blamed, because the human will cannot thwart a god's will. In the second case she also deserves to be acquitted and the charges must be brought entirely against her assailant. Finally, if she was persuaded, she must not be considered at fault because "speech is a powerful force which can achieve the most divine results with a very minimum of bodily effort. . . . Persuasion by speech is on a par with abduction by force."[15] The *Encomium*'s argument obviously conceals the possibility that Helen either enticed Paris, or at least agreed upon eloping with him. It creates the impression that all instances were covered and the proof of Helen's innocence exhaustively demonstrated.

As we said before, the metaphor of medicine for philosophy was very compelling in Socrates' days. Medicine had earned great prominence through the pursuings of a school of practitioners who gathered around the research and teaching of Hippocrates (460-390 B.C.), a contemporary of Socrates.

The medical knowledge of the time was steeped in the thinking of pre-Socratic wise men such as Pythagoras, Heraclitus, and Empedocles. This knowledge was a combination of religious belief, magical practices, and experiential discoveries. It was held, for example, that the causes of sickness lay in an imbalance among the four basic elements: earth, fire, water, and air. Empedocles presented a theory according to which love (or mutual attraction) and strife (or mutual rejection) operated over the four elements, separating them or bringing them together. There were life cycles dominated by each of these forces, but the best times were those when both exercised equal influence, striking an ideal balance among the four elements. Sickness was also explained as an excess of fire in the body, an imbalance between cold and heat, while dropsy, colds, and congestions of the respiratory tract were attributed to an excess of water in the organism.

Hippocrates reproached these doctrines, because they were based on assumptions difficult to prove on empirical grounds. He found instead that it was possible to explain the body ailments through observable components of the organism, such as blood, bile, and phlegm. These juices *(chymos)* or humors were in a constant state of flux, and health and sickness could be understood in terms of quantities of each of these elements, but also and chiefly in terms of the speed at which they circulated in the body.[16] Illness was therefore a process with a beginning, a middle, and an end. The outcome could be prevalence of the ailment, which in some cases would bring about the patient's death, or its cessation with the completion of the cycle. The body itself was armed with healing forces, the *pepsis*, which acted by "cooking," or "grinding," or "decanting," or still "digesting" the surplus of humor. The physician's role was, therefore, to accelerate the process, when he believed the sickness was bound to complete a cycle and cease, or to slow it down, and even stop it, when its completion could be fatal for the patient. In every illness there was the right moment to act, the *kairos*, and there was a *krisis*, a turning point at which the ailment prevailed over the natural forces of healing. Sickness was as natural as health, and its treatment should be natural, too. It consisted of diets, relaxation of the mind, and physical exercises, but also of surgery and other forms of intervention over the body.

Since in the ancient Greek cosmology illness was natural, it should also have social and cultural correlates, because the tipping of the balance of humors in the organism could be triggered either by internal causes, or by external causes such as over- or undereating. The physician was expected to learn as much as possible about his patient's life in order to understand the illness. He proceeded by formulating hypotheses and testing them in his inquiry and physical examination. Furthermore, the treatment could only be successful if the physician were able to persuade his patient of the right course to follow. Medicine was consequently involved not only with *physis*, but also with the *logoi*, that is, language, for in addition to arriving at a precise knowledge of the pathology, the physician had to convince his patient that he was right, and persuade him to follow the prescribed treatment which could be painful and therefore undesirable.

It is hard to exaggerate the influence of medicine on the Greek culture of the fifth and fourth centuries. Jaeger writes that the conception of a world derived from "divine descent was now replaced by the general conception of *human nature*."[17] One of the staggering novelties in the domain of knowledge was the strategy of formulating hypotheses before the affirmation of a thesis. In the realm of medicine, this practice led to experimentation, while in philosophy it led to Socrates' dialectic, a method for questioning knowledge which should be given precedence over stating knowledge. In the *Phaedrus*, Socrates claims that the rhetor, likewise the doctor, must be able not only to administer the right treatment, but also to choose who needs the treatment.[18] Socrates says, "rhetoric is in the same case as medicine,"[19] about the adequacy of rhetorical styles/treatments to interlocutors/patients.

The Greek cultural scenario of that period must have borne some resemblance to Europe of the beginning of our century, when the brave new world of modernity broke through the grip that religion had over the moral order, and the belief grew that science could resolve all the problems of nature, while politics could take care of societal problems. In Greece, medicine arose as a rational and empirical practice, capable of subduing nature in the human body on a par with rhetoric, the art of taming the polity for good purposes. It is inevitable that a cross-fertilization took place between medicine and rhetoric, as it did in our own century between science and politics. This mutual influence unfolded both in methods—e.g. the formulation of hypotheses and the pursuit of a diagnostic through trial and error for the physician, and the systematic questioning for the dialectician—and in theories—e.g., the naturalness of health and illness and the call for the physician to intervene vis-à-vis the naturalness of virtue and ignorance, with the similar call for the philosopher to intervene and reawaken knowledge where ignorance had spread too far. Medicine became not just a metaphorical figure for rhetoric, but to a large extent its very model, as in our century science became a model for politics. The rhetoricians began to consider them-selves physicians of the soul, like modernist politicians who thought that the art of politics lay in management and economics. If on one hand rhetoric became imbued of the spirit of medicine, medicine on the other hand earned a philosophical status for asserting a kind of knowledge that was empirically demonstrable, existentially practical, and that could be proven correct against other arguments on the grounds of logic and reason. It was a knowledge breaking away from fearfulness of the divine powers, and from the power of the polity by carefully avoiding to challenge either. The Physician's Oath or Hippocratic Oath, still uttered by medical graduates at commencement exercises, begins by swearing upon Apollo, Asclepius, and all the gods and goddesses, and ends by pleading for good repute among men for all time. The métier of the physician began as a brotherhood, passed from father to son and kept as a secret among the initiates, much in the same way as Sophist phil-osophy. Like rhetoric, it was a new art, and upon entering the house of every new patient, the physician was expected to explain the nature of his skills. Medicine therefore depended on oratorical abilities.

In the first part of the *Gorgias*, a dialogue in which several compar-isons are drawn between medicine and rhetoric, Socrates entertains a debate with Gorgias himself, and with Polus, about the definition of rhetoric. In the second part, Callicles takes over the discussion, but he is not a real interlocutor and opposes Socrates' argument on the basis of his unrelenting animosity against the philosopher. Socrates, however, keeps him within the boundaries of the discussion, and tries by every means to make him overcome his monolithic and unreflective oppo-sition to philosophy. This dialogue, like several others, strikes an amal-gamation between the content of what is discussed and the act of discussing it. At the level of the said (explicit meaning), Socrates crit-icizes the Sophist notion of rhetoric and proposes his own which, by analogy with medicine, contains healing properties aimed at the soul. At the level of the act of saying this healing practice (edification of the soul) is illustrated by his efforts to break through Callicles' narrowminded-ness. He cures/enlightens his interlocutors, not by preaching in a mono-logical discourse (administering medicine), but by questioning their assumptions and thereby forcing them to develop stronger ones (monitoring natural processes). At one point he invites Polus "to submit nobly to the argument as you would to a doctor."[20] This intimation reflects the spirit of the whole dialogue which is an invitation for his comrades to undress their weak opinions and submit them to Socrates' examination. The work of their scrutinizing minds, under Socrates' lead, produces health, the recovery of their spiritual grace characterized by knowledge.

Socrates is not satisfied with the definition of rhetoric provided by Polus: "the noblest of the arts."[21] As the discussion unfolds, rhetoric is defined as the science of words that leads people to think about the subject matter of discourse. Socrates draws on this definition to show parallels between medicine and gymnastics, which also would use words, and therefore call for a differentiation from medicine. Gorgias tries one further distinction between the arts based on manual procedure and rhetoric which is exclusively concerned with words.[22] Socrates then brings up the case of arithmetic which involves no manual operations, asking whether that could be rhetoric, too.[23] No, answers Gorgias. But what, then, is the subject matter of the words employed by rhetoric? "The greatest and noblest of human affairs, Socrates," replies Gorgias.[24] But that is not a definition by any means more precise than that provided by Polus earlier, and Socrates insists that the answer must be refined. In his next attempt Gorgias claims that rhetoric "brings freedom"[25] to people in the courts, in the assembly, in the senate, "or in any gathering of a citizen body,"[26] by carrying out a persuasion "concerned with right and wrong."[27] This for Socrates is the crucial issue: how does one define right and wrong? Socrates goes right to the heart of the matter by asking if rhetorical persuasion creates a conviction based on belief or on knowledge. Gorgias answers that it is on belief alone, and Socrates concludes that, if that is the case, "then rhetoric apparently is the creator of a conviction that is persuasive but not instructive about right and wrong."[28] Gorgias remembers a biographical fact in support of his arguments, and tells how once he went with his brother Herodicus, a physician, to visit a patient who refused treatment. What finally persuaded the patient was none but rhetoric.[29] In addition, he argues, rhetoric may be used for wrongdoing, but this should be blamed neither on the art, nor on the teaching of the art, likewise a wrestler who beats his parents should not bring blame to wrestling or to his trainer. Socrates, in response, begins to unweave the argument that an art not founded on knowledge cannot produce right, and finally leads Gorgias to self-contradiction admitting that rhetoric can be used for evil purposes.[30]

Polus takes the discussion over, proclaiming himself the questioner, a position he believes easier to assume, maybe the secret of Socrates' success, and begins to question the philosopher. Socrates, in his answer, defines rhetoric as no art at all, but as a mere routine such as cookery destined to the immediate pursuit of pleasure, deprived of any considerations whatsoever with the good or evil the food will produce in the organism. He says that rhetoric is "the semblance of a part of politics."[31] Then he proceeds to argue this statement by showing that justice is to legislation as medicine to gymnastics. Rhetoric operates over legislation and therefore is only a semblance, not real politics. Justice, in addition, is only one of the virtues, and even if rhetoric could represent it, this would still be a very incomplete picture. In conclusion, Socrates says that people drink medicines for the sake of health and not because of the doctors' orders.[32] The motivation to pursue health and justice, therefore, does not depend on persuasion, but on an internal motivation. Rhetoric is entirely parasitical because it does not add anything to the arts. The remedy for poverty is moneymaking, for sickness medicine, and for intemperance and injustice justice, while rhetoric leaves these faults absolutely unaltered.[33] The happiest man is one who was never sick, happier than one who is equally healthy, but had to be healed. Consequently, medicine is not the covenant of health, it is merely a procedure for the treatment of the sick similar to the punishment of the unjust. Medicine is of no use for healthy people; likewise, rhetoric is of no use for those who do not intend to do wrong.[34] The physician only knows how to identify sickness as the opposite of health.[35] His knowledge of health, however, is not obtained through medical training, it is part of his *sensus communis*,[36] and so is the knowledge of justice and of virtue.

In conclusion to this discussion of the Sophists' tactics to win debates, I will examine a passage of the *Protagoras*, which brings into relief the question of power as opposed to the logic of the argument, as well as Socrates' use of a Sophist rhetoric with the greatest of all Sophists, Protagoras. Socrates does not contend only for the sake of winning but has a point to prove: man does wrong because of ignorance and to render explicit the steps of one's actions constitutes wisdom. In the *Protagoras*, as in other dialogues, there is an astonishing symmetry between the content of the discussion and the attitudes reflected in the postures adopted by the discussants. Protagoras and his disciples claim that they teach *sophia* ("wisdom"), the highest *aretē*. Socrates shows them that their conception of these qualities is wanting. He does this by means of a straightforward argument and of a tenacious wrangling with Protagoras, who is unwilling to abandon his powerful position as the most distinguished Sophist, and concede defeat to Socrates' arguments. Socrates wins on both fronts, he presents the best argument and forces

Protagoras out of his obduracy. In the end he persuades all his opponents of his points and earns their recognition.

The dialogue begins with Hippocrates' visiting to Socrates' house in
order to ask the philosopher to take him to visit Protagoras, who is in
town. Hippocrates wants to become a disciple of the great Sophist and
has the money to pay for instruction. But he is too young and has never
met the master, so he asks the experienced Socrates to go with him.
While they wait in Socrates' courtyard for the day to clear up and the
visiting time to be opportune, Socrates tries his young friend's mettle. If
Hippocrates were a disciple of his famous namesake, what would he
become? A doctor, naturally. Seeing Protagoras, in turn, what will he
become? A Sophist, of course. But as the Sophists are surrounded by so
much prejudice and controversy, would not Hippocrates be ashamed of
his new *epangelma* ("profession")? Socrates helps his friend out of the
cul-de-sac: Hippocrates is not learning in order to become a professional, but just to improve his general knowledge, a "liberal education."[37]
But does Hippocrates know to whom he is entrusting his soul? He
replies affirmatively "to a Sophist, he who has knowledge of wise
things."[38] But the same knowledge can be attributed to painters and
builders. What singles out the Sophists' wisdom? Hippocrates answers
that a Sophist is a "master of the art of making clever speakers."[39] In that
case, what is the subject matter of their teaching? The answer is that
subject about which the teacher imparts knowledge. Socrates follows up
in his relentless manner: What is that subject matter in the case of
Protagoras? Hippocrates does not know. How can he then entrust his
soul to someone who does not even know what it is he teaches? As
Jaeger puts it, commenting upon the same passage, Socrates "talks so
unassumingly and puts himself so simply on a level with Hippocrates
that the young fellow has no idea that the *real* master is walking beside
him all the time."[40]

Protagoras, in contrast, is pompous and aware of his superiority in
social prestige. He is staying in the house of Callias, the richest man in
Athens, and is surrounded by disciples and admirers. He agrees to talk
to Hippocrates and Socrates, and begins by explaining the nature of his
epangelma. Sophism is an ancient art, but since its practitioners did not
enjoy very high esteem, many found useful disguises under poetry or
music, but not him. He warns Hippocrates that as a consequence of his
teaching, the young fellow will become a better man next day and
thereafter better every day. But better in what, asks Socrates. Protagoras
then defines the subject of his teaching: "The proper care of his personal
affairs, so that he may best manage his own household, and the state's

affairs, so as to become a real power in the city, both as a speaker and man of action."[41] The subject of his teaching is therefore politics as Socrates concludes with his acquiescence. Socrates begins to besiege the master by stating that he does not believe that such a subject matter can be taught, since it is an *aretē,* and virtue cannot be taught. Protagoras answers, agreeing that it is true that every man has a sense of justice, but that there is also room for "instruction and taking thought."[42] Socrates goes on chipping at the master's pedestal, by leading him through an exegesis of *aretē* and its composing qualities.

The *Protagoras* has been considered as a synthesis and culmination of the earlier dialogues. In these, Plato discusses each of the virtues; justice, piety, prudence, wisdom, and courage. Now he takes them up all together and addresses the more encompassing issue of whether *aretē* can be taught. Socrates proceeds with Protagoras by exploring similarities between pairs of virtues. The great Sophist finds this line of reasoning rather puzzling since the custom is to differentiate the virtues as distinctively as possible. He leads Protagoras to a first contradiction, for after asserting that each quality has only one contrary, folly turns out as the contrary of both wisdom and temperance.[43] Furthermore, Protagoras is led to recognize in shame that his argument, as unfolded by Socrates with his agreement, posits that an injustice can be practiced with temperance. Socrates conducts himself carefully not to alienate his adversary by hurting his pride. He warns him that it "is the argument itself that I wish to probe, though it may turn out that both I who question and you who answer are equally under scrutiny."[44]

After the argument about whether that which is beneficial is good, the audience enthusiastically applauds Protagoras' eloquence. Socrates, noticing the disadvantage in which he finds himself by not having a cheering spectatorship, carries out a wily move that would not be unfamiliar to a family therapist. He says, "I am a forgetful sort of man, Protagoras, . . . cut down your answers and make them shorter if I am to follow you."[45] With this maneuver he obviously tries to curtail the space in which Protagoras usually shines. Protagoras replies in kind: "Am I to make them [his answers] shorter than the subject demands?"[46] Furthermore, who is supposed to decide how short they should be, he adds. Socrates insists that he make them shorter, flattering him in passing, by pleading that he does so not to be beaten by anyone in brevity. Protagoras, a seasoned discussant, is undaunted and says: "I have fought many a contest of words, and if I had done as you bid me, that is, adopted a method chosen by my opponent, I should have proved no better than anyone else, nor would the name Protagoras have been heard of in Greece."[47] Socrates then escalates the confrontation by taking an even more drastic step: "I have no wish myself to insist on continuing our conversation in such a way of which you don't approve. I will talk with you another time, when you are willing to converse so that I can follow."[48] In saying so, he rises to leave, but is stopped by Callias. Socrates insists that Protagoras should make his arguments briefer, and adds: "Personally I thought that companionable talk was one thing, and public speaking another."[49] Callias proposes that each one talk in the way better suited to him. Alcibiades breaks in denouncing Protagoras' Sophist maneuver of giving long answers in order for the audience to forget the original question. He also brings Socrates' sophistic tactic out in the clear, claiming that his bid to Protagoras to make his answers shorter is not to aid Socrates' memory, for he considers Socrates' presented reason "a little joke about being forgetful."[50] Critias also invites them to proceed with the debate and asks the audience to avoid taking sides. Prodicus downplays the contest character of the discussion and calls it a conversation among friends for the benefit of them all. Hippias also calls for the reconciliation of the two discussants, proposing that they both compromise, and that a referee be appointed as an arbitrator. Socrates, who has an endless sagacity to detect power maneuvers, rebuffs the suggestion on the grounds that the chosen referee would wither and be "a man of lesser attainments" or just one "like ourselves," and consequently, in either case, "the appointment would be superfluous."[51] He adds that there is no one there wiser than Protagoras, and suggests that the discussion should go on with Protagoras asking the questions and he answering, and bids that while doing that he will "try to show him (Protagoras) how, in my submission, the respondent should speak."[52] After that they will exchange roles.

Socrates uses the ruse of being forgetful in order to force Protagoras to shorten his answers and curb his appeals to the audience's sympathy, whose support of Protagoras puts Socrates in a difficult position. He knows that however good his arguments are they will be worth nothing if they are not able to persuade the audience. He thus threatens to end the discussion by leaving, although he obviously has no intention of doing so. He woos Protagoras to meet his request by vowing to put himself in a position which seems to present no threat to Protagoras, who will ask the questions while he will answer them. Socrates' maneuver is certainly deceitful and his answers to Protagoras' questions are often twice as long as Protagoras' own earlier answers. Is Socrates trying to shoulder Protagoras out of the Olympus of rhetoric in order to himself become the paragon of the art of persuasion? If he is to become the champion of rhetoric, he will not achieve that independently of the substance of his arguments. He closes the discussion by showing that

Protagoras, who claimed to teach *aretē*, does not even know what virtue is. It cannot be a whole composed of parts, it either is one or cannot be taught at least by the methods envisioned by the Sophists. But let us return to the debate.

Socrates begins the last leap of his siege of Protagoras by claiming that courage is linked to wisdom. Protagoras, of course, does not agree because, he argues, if it were so, "you might as well go on and conclude that physical strength is knowledge."[53] Socrates realizes that he has to backpeddle a bit and come on from further behind. He establishes the difference between "happy life" and "unhappy life." The former is agreeable and pleasant, the latter full of grief and pain. Protagoras cannot agree with this because for him one must distinguish between good and bad pleasures, pains that are evil and pains that are not, and even establish a "third class" of pains, "which are neither evil nor good."[54] For him, Socrates' proposition is too general and has little explicative value. His explanation is of the knowledge-building type, a classification of pains and pleasures in a refined degree of differentiation. He cannot grasp what Socrates is after because he assumes that Socrates is also building a classification, while Socrates is merely building a rampart scaffolding from which to disassemble Protagoras' edifice.

Socrates asks him what he thinks of reason and knowledge. He replies that they are "the most powerful elements in human life."[55] Socrates makes it obvious that he is espousing the opinions of the uneducated crowds, that it is the emotions—"now passion, now pleasure, now pain, sometimes love, and frequently fear"[56]—that govern people's actions, rather than knowledge. He protests to the contrary, that knowledge and reason are high and unattainable values, while Socrates claims that knowledge thus conceived is like a slave, "pushed around by all the other affections."[57] Socrates insists on the identification of Protagoras' opinions with those of the *polloi* ("the crowds"). Protagoras tries to move away from this examination "of the opinions of the common man, who says whatever comes into his head,"[58] but Socrates argues that this line of inquiry will help them establish the relations between courage and the other parts of virtue.

He proceeds by claiming that the acceptable actions are those which in the end produce pleasure, while the unacceptable pleasures are those ending in pain. He engages the audience, talking to them and avoiding further embarrassment to Protagoras, by forcing him to agree with statements that go against his beliefs, which, however, are progressively drawing him into a whirlpool of contradictions. Socrates proceeds showing that there is a difference between our perception of the appearances of good and evil and our understanding of it based on measurement. "The same magnitudes seem greater to the eye from near at hand than they do from a distance."⁵⁹ To set this matter straight one has to resort to the "art of measurement" which is then equated with knowledge and poised as the best guide for a good life. He says that if, at the beginning of the discussion, he had explained that what leads people to make the wrong choices of pleasures and pains is ignorance, they would have laughed at him, but now, if they laugh at all, it would be at themselves, because they have all agreed that the cause of mistake is lack of knowledge.⁶⁰ He reminds them that Protagoras, Prodicus, and Hippias "profess to cure" ignorance, and chides them for not promptly sending their children to be educated by the Sophists, which would be beneficial to them and the community.

The trick here is that Socrates spells out these statements by getting his audience's agreement, but carefully avoids imparting his own acquiescence to those conclusions. Protagoras begins the discussion by establishing similarities between the virtues, but separating courage against Socrates' wishes. Socrates reminds him now that he earlier stated that "men who are utterly impious, unjust, licentious, and ignorant, yet very brave," prove "that courage is quite different from the other parts of virtue."⁶¹ Socrates shows that the coward fears wrong, such as death, for example, while the courageous fear that which is dishonorable. Courage is therefore knowledge of the right, while cowardice is ignorance of what one should rightly fear. It follows that courage is wisdom, and as such, not different from any of the other virtues.

In the end Socrates comments, in bewilderment, upon the puzzle in which they now find themselves. The discussion began with Protagoras claiming that virtue could be taught while Socrates denied it. As the argument unfolded, Protagoras pushed virtue away and was progressively led to show that it could not be taught, while Socrates, by reasoning, taught virtue step by step. Courage was the issue at stake; the more Protagoras separated it from the other virtues, the less teachable it seemed, while in Socrates' identification of all virtues as a unity, it seemed more graspable and could be taught as wisdom. However, Socrates' argument led them to the doorsteps of another gigantic question: what is knowledge? This theme will occupy Plato in several other dialogues. It surfaces in the *Gorgias* and in the *Meno*. The *Republic*, the *Theaetetus*, and the *Timaeus* also deal with the question of knowledge.

The Sophists' excesses lay in their overvaluation of rhetoric. They did not discard knowledge, but believed that the frontiers of the known could be furthered through rhetoric. In the face of an adversary of Socrates' stature, however, rhetoric shifted from the pursuit of knowledge to the attempt at persuading because, confronted with more powerful reasons, they could not help but give in, while their persistence in asserting their points through the ruses of argument revealed their greater concern with winning debates than with arriving at knowledge. The rhetoric of persuasion goes hand in hand with the question of power, and their skills in this area cannot be underestimated. In the *Protagoras*, however, Socrates does not lose to them in either power or rhetoric. He also does not advance knowledge in any remarkable way. The conclusion of the dialogue is that virtue is whole, but ultimately depends on knowing what knowledge is, in order to be understood. We should therefore turn now to Socrates, the educator.

8 SOCRATES, THE EDUCATOR

Our knowledge of Socrates comes from Plato's dialogues, Xenophon's writings, Aristophanes' comedy *The Clouds*, and from several observations in Aristotle's works. Plato's own biographic will, the "Seventh Letter," as well as his philosophical doctrine, in contrast to his teacher's and main character's ideas, help us draw the profile of the most interesting Socrates. He probably was born in Athens in 469 B.C., and died in 399 B.C. by drinking hemlock, after being tried and condemned to death by the state, on the charge of corruption of the Attic youth with subversive ideas.

Three dialogues deal with Socrates' trial and execution. In the *Apology* he defends himself against the accusations brought upon him by the court. In the *Crito* his eponymic friend comes to visit him with a plan for him to escape from the prison. Socrates refuses because this would be against the law. In the *Phaedo* an account of Socrates' last day is provided to those friends who could not be there with him. He dies with stoicism and happiness, supporting his disheartened friends, drawing them out of their tears and reflecting with them about the immortality of the soul. The early dialogues, called by Aristotle "ethical dialogues," are concerned with the definition of each particular virtue. In the *Charmides*, Socrates discusses temperance, in the *Laches* courage, in the *Lysis* friendship, in the *Euthyphro* piety, and the *Protagoras* strings together the inquiry pursued in these earlier dialogues at the same time that it pushes the question to a broader level of analysis, in which the definition of virtue is the subject. This topic is pursued further in the *Meno*.

Another subset to be distinguished is that of the "dialectic dialogues," comprising the *Parmenides*, the *Sophist*, the *Statesman*, and the *Philebus*. The first is a controversial dialogue in which Socrates, unlike in most other debates, follows Parmenides, the founder of the eleatic school.[1] But they never seem to reach any conclusions about the topic of their discussion. In the *Sophist* Socrates is a mere spectator; the discussion between Theaetetus and a stranger aims at curbing the excessive Sophist claim that it was impossible to make a false statement, since that which was not, could never have been and, therefore, could not be stated. In the *Statesman* a young Socrates follows a stranger who outlines the qualities of the good statesman who rules with the minimum of laws necessary. The *Philebus* brings Socrates back to the fore in a discussion of which good is superior, pleasure or wisdom? Outside of these two major classificatory categories, earlier or ethical and dialectic dialogues, there are extremely important pieces resisting association with others. The first one naturally is the *Republic* where Plato sketches the contours of the ideal city-state, based on the philosophical (dialectic) education of its rulers. The *Symposium* and the *Republic* have been considered the two greatest dialogues, but even if they are not so, they are certainly the two most popular ones and the most frequently printed. The subject of the *Symposium* is love, as it is in the *Phaedrus* and in the *Lysis*. The *Theaetetus*, like the *Meno* and to a lesser extent the *Republic* and the *Timaeus*, pursue an answer to the question: "What is knowledge?" But while the latter somehow finds a solution to the problem through a picture of the genesis of the universe, in the *Theaetetus* the efforts of Socrates and his interlocutors bring them to the realization that they are far from understanding what knowledge is. The *Gorgias* addresses the question of knowledge as well, but also, and more centrally, the subjects of rhetoric and education, and it presents the only version of a Socrates who is out and out persuasive. Finally, in this briefest of summaries of Plato's dialogues, we must mention the *Laws*, the last one he wrote and also the only one from which Socrates is absent. It is a discussion of the best laws for an ideal state.

Werner Jaeger attributes the origin of the Socratic dialogue to the circle of Socrates' disciples, who wished to immortalize "the incomparable personality of the master who had transformed their lives."[2] Before the Socratic dialogue, there was the genre of the encomium, also destined to extol the qualities of an outstanding person. But Socrates called for something special, a genre that could at once revere his memory and picture his unique intellectual style, as well as teach its readers the Socratic weltanschauung and existential strategy. Thus the Socratic dialogue combined the spirit of the encomium, that is, the biographical memoir, with the idea of a dialogical communication, and with a new rhetoric of persuasion which appealed to the interlocutor's reason, not his heart.

Bakhtin, studying the origin of the novel in its marvelous manifestation in Dostoyevsky's writings, included the Socratic dialogues in his "serio-comical" genre.[3] This broad literary category included, in addition to the Socratic dialogues, the mimes of Sophron, the literature of the Symposiasts, the memoir, the bucolic poetry, and the "Menippian satire," among other genres. The serio-comic opposed epic poetry, tragedy, history, classical rhetoric, and medicine. These were monological genres with an impersonal and straightforward discourse, thoroughly serious in preaching some subject matter and exhorting the audiences to accept it. The serio-comic, according to Bakhtin, had three outstanding characteristics. These genres were imbued with a specific carnivalesque attitude to the world, with their "atmosphere of jolly relativity," weakening the "one sided rhetorical seriousness, rationality, singleness of meaning, and dogmatism" of the other genres.[4] The second characteristic was that they were not based on legend, but on concrete experiences. Actually, they elected the critique of legend as their main theme. Finally, these genres "reject[ed] the stylistic unity . . . of the epoppee, the tragedy, lofty rhetoric and the lyric,"[5] combining the mimetic with the methetic word, interweaving in their texts pictures of the world as well as dialects, languages, and approaches to picturing the world.

The Socratic dialogue was written by many contemporaries of Plato, but we only have fragments from the works of other writers. Bakhtin imparts five characteristics to this genre that was so popular on the cusp of the two eras of oral and literate culture in ancient Greece. First, the dialogues introduced the idea that the truth was not unilaterally and monologically asserted by a text or speech, but was generated in the dialogical exchanges between two or more truth seekers. Second, the dialogues were founded on the operations of syncrisis, that is, the juxtaposition of different themes, and of anacrisis, the elicitation of the interlocutor's words by means of which the speaker's reasoning proceeded. Third, ideologies took the place of men in the role of hero in these texts. Fourth, the context of production of the text or speech was made into part of the plot, what Bakhtin called "dialogue on the threshold."[6] Fifth, the dialogues were personalized, the anonymity of the author was dissolved because under the new genre, meaning was derived by the clarification of the equation "who says what to whom."

The dialogues generally took place in the gymnasium (a center for the practice of sports where the youth of Athens gathered), in the houses of wealthy and enlightened Athenians, and in symposia or parties in which the guests were supposed to show their verbal eloquence and wit in speeches about a proposed theme. To be skilled in proving an argument and defeating an opponent was among the most highly praised qualities a young man could have, on a par only perhaps with physical fitness. The two schools for the teaching of philosophy were named after two famous Athenian stadia for the practice of athletic exercises, the Academy and the Lyceum. The debates would ensue upon the casual encounter of friends, but a notable speaker like Socrates was sought out not only by those who wished to improve their own speech abilities, or just watch the spectacle of intellectual wizardry, but also by those others who tried to wield respect and admiration from their peers

Plato's Legacy

by defeating famous speakers in an argument. There was also a certain rivalry between different schools of thought such as the Pythagoreans, the followers of Eraclitus, and the Eleatics, but the most popular and controversial were the Sophists, whose rhetorical skills were shared by speakers from all schools. Athens breathed in an atmosphere of controversy, and virtually any topic, from politics to religion, including customs of everyday life, could kindle the fire of a heated discussion. Socrates, of course, was not interested in just any argument, and did not enter debates for the love of defeating his opponents.

Jaeger, in a brief inventory of the history of Platonic studies, casts into relief the opposition between those scholars, who drawing on whatever could be reckoned from the chronology of the dialogues, claim that their study should be based on the history of Plato's ideas, and those others, who prefer to examine the dialogues against their social, cultural, and political background, following the track opened by Schleiermacher. Within this latter tradition, Gadamer writes that each dialogue is a whole in and of itself, reflecting a concrete conversation with its "movements of discussion and thought."[7] He calls upon Plato's students to "avoid getting involved in that old and fruitless game played by scholars . . . of seeking correspondences with other dialogues."[8] We must be cautious not to take Gadamer's statement in too literal a fashion, otherwise we would have to regard the dialogues as recollections of scattered conversations, unrelated to one another. That is certainly not Gadamer's view. What he rises against, is the finicky search of inconsistencies and contradictions between statements from different dialogues and even statements within the same dialogue. The dialogues are not a collection of monological assertions about philosophical issues, but a dialogical discourse procedure from whose own weaving philosophy unfolds. In this sense, the philosophy of Socratic dialogues lies more in the nature of the genre than in the content of the discourse conveyed by it, but this is only a heuristic conclusion, for neither Socrates nor I wish to establish a radical separation between the content and form of discourse.

These remarks are necessary, because in the Western philosophical tradition there has been a true obsession with separating form and content, beginning precisely with the interpretation of Plato's philosophy.[9] As a matter of fact, many have regarded the dialogues as a cumbersome and awkward form for the presentation of argument, an unnecessary obstacle to the reader's understanding. Gadamer shows that this view entirely misses the point, and proposes that the distinction between form and content be replaced by the unity of words (*logos*) and deeds (*ergon*), which is the true quest of the dialogues. To ask "how" in most of the dialogues is more important than to ask "what," but naturally the pursuance of "how" by default of "what" would be as fruitless as its opposite, which according to Gadamer, had been a common trend in Platonic scholarship.

If the structure of the dialogues is so important, an importance all the more enhanced when we think about those texts as testimonies of an oral culture, it becomes interesting to find out how much in them is Socrates' teaching, how much Plato's writing. Socrates professes that the virtues lie inside human nature and the teaching of them is not a matter of transmission, but of awakening what is dormant in the soul. Human qualities such as "wisdom," "justice," "beauty," or "temperance" lack ontological status in Socrates' philosophy, because they do not stem from the objects of perception, nor seem to be entities with an autonomous existence; they are contained in the soul, which means that the discourse about them is composed not only of words, but also of the testimony of *ergon*. Plato hastened to find an ontological foundation for virtue by creating his doctrine of ideas, according to which concepts had an independent and objective existence. Thus Plato's world is composed of three classes of entities: men, objects, and concepts. Next he put his philosophy in Socrates' mouth, but it is extremely difficult to reconcile Socrates' dialectic with Plato's doctrine of ideas.

The doctrine of ideas is introduced in the *Republic*, and is also extensively discussed in the *Theaetetus*. In both dialogues opinion is differentiated from knowledge and the latter made into a process of critique of perceptions.[10] But if the ideas belonging to knowledge are right and eternal, they must have a meaningful form easily grasped by intellection. The quintessential Socrates, whenever approaching this threshold, falls short of producing a filling for knowledge. The *Theaetetus* is a wonderful illustration of this point, because it ends with the conclusion that even the search for knowledge may be illegitimate since it implies the assumption that the researcher has partial knowledge of something related to knowledge, at least to formulate the grand question, "What is knowledge?" or to make the humble assertion, "I do not know what knowledge is." In the first case it is assumed that knowledge is something, in the second that the speaker knows something, he knows what he does not know.

The *Republic* could not be acceptable without an explanation of how positive ideas come to be, because it contains a picture of the ideal city-state which otherwise would be facetious. Thus Plato proposed an epistemology in taxonomic form in which the overall category is knowledge. It subdivides into intellection (the being of things, the essence of what is known) and opinion (the becoming of things, what generates the unexpected). Intellection, in turn, subdivides into science and understanding, as does opinion into belief and conjecture. Knowledge formed as opinion is based on impressions, perceptions, and images, while intellectual knowledge is arrived at through interpretation, a process consisting in the critique of what is supposed to be known. Now, this critique is obviously applied to opinion, but it can also be folded onto itself, thus constituting intellection, and thereby producing the best approximation to knowledge that one can aspire to have.[11]

We may summarize the differences between Socrates' and Plato's philosophies in the following terms: (1) The heart of Socrates' philosophy lies in his dialectic which accomplishes the methetic function of showing false interrelations among things. (2) Socrates' philosophy also presents a conception of the world which in its crude incompleteness claims that the meaning of things is not present only in discourse, but stems from the unison between *logos* and *ergon*. (3) Finally, Plato does try to provide us with a picture of the world contained in discourse and, as a consequence, is forced into defining the ontological status of ideas, which puts his philosophy at odds with Socrates'.

Throughout the Socratic trajectory ideas are good only as long as they can be criticized. This does not mean that Socrates had a cynical view about the representation of the world, but that in his exemplary testimony, one cannot understand the substantiation of ideas without contemplating at the same time the dialectic in which they are assembled and disassembled within the mesh of the dialogues.

A comparison with the endeavor of translation will help us explain the nature of Socratic education. The translator assumes from the beginning that there will be a word to translate the phrase in the foreign language. If he cannot find that word, there will be a second best choice of a word which is close enough to the meaning in the original text. But even if this approximate word is not available, it is always possible to explain the idea through paraphrases at which point the translation becomes more methetic action than mimetic copy. No translator needs to throw up his hands and feel desperate because the language is always there to serve him. This state of affairs renders translation exciting and challenging only while the translator is searching for corresponding expressions in the other language. In the process the translator learns interesting facts; for example, he learns that there is no word for such-and-such in the other language, that a certain idea in the original language can only be conveyed by what appears to be a bizarre constellation of words in the second language, and furthermore, that it is only bizarre from the point of view of the first language. Once a decision is made toward one glossing or another, the flame of discovery is extinguished. If this coupling of words and phrases between two languages were automatic, translation would be a tedious exercise; likewise, a translator could not practice his art if he did not begin with the working assumption that all that is said in one language can be equally said in another language. This assumption must be grounded on the belief that there is semantic equivalence among languages. Similarly, the Socratic dialogues presuppose that it is possible to develop the conversation over a basis of agreement. This agreement, however, is not final; neither is it the goal of the undertaking nor its most exciting part. The genuine challenge of the dialogues resides in the search for possibilities of agreement, as in translation it lies in the search for matching words.

At this point it is opportune to invoke our discussion in chapter 6 about the role of education in ancient Greece that was not to pass a cultural system on to a new generation, but to arouse in the individual critical resources capable of generating culture. The Sophists stated that man was the measure of all things. In the *Theaetetus* Socrates concludes that if that were the case, one could no longer make distinctions between true and false.[12] The Sophist humanism contained in this principle distills an all-tolerant liberalism, while Socrates' humanism is critical and partisan. Socrates undoubtedly realized that his contemporaries were asleep with regard to the pressing issues of moral dissolution and political corruption, and carved for himself a model of reformer, as opposed to the predominant model of conformist. He was not the messianic leader who foresaw the path to salvation, but a *philo sophia* ("friend of wisdom") who undertook for himself the shaking up of minds with superior arguments, without ever giving them the numbing certitude of positive knowledge. In the same way that it is often possible to reconstruct the steps of translations and point out mistaken or inadequate paths, it is also possible to find a better word. Socrates, then, never claims to have the last say on any matter, but continues to reconstruct faulty trains of thought, and suggest better findings for the "translation" of reality, but always making sure that upon each finding, the exercise of reconstruction and critique must start over again.

The meaning we attribute to the verb "philosophize," to reflect or speculate or theorize, owes a great deal to the culture of literacy which acquainted us with thinking, writing, taking absence to think, reading the previously written, and writing again. This common conception of philosophy as abstract reflection is virtually synonymous with the notion of writing. For Socrates, who lived in the context of an oral culture, to philosophize meant something quite different. It meant to engage in conversation with other people about certain topics that mattered more than others, because they referred to fundamental issues of human nature and man's life. Philosophy, in a way, was potentially present in every man's soul, and Socrates philosophized by instigating this potential to manifest itself. In so doing he incited himself and sparked the flame of his own goodness. He asks questions of his interlocutors, and either proves their answers wrong or trivial, or in the absence of an answer, proceeds with his own speculation of what they would deem correct, only to prove them wrong again and lead the discussion to the brink of new and tantalizing questions. Upon a first impression, it may look to the reader of the dialogues as though Socrates has stored up his sleeves the answers to the questions he asks, but nothing could be further from reality. When he contends with a weak adversary such as Euthyphro, his answers suffer and ramble at the level of his interlocutor. Euthyphro repeatedly misses the point of Socrates' questions and often slips away from the subject matter of the conversation, the nature of holiness. In one such instance, after Euthyphro wavers in his response to a question, Socrates remarks that if only he had wished, he could have answered much more briefly. "But the fact is that you are not eager to instruct me," Socrates comments,[13] and continues, "had you given the answer, I would now have learned from you what holiness is."[14] His argument only advances as long as his interlocutor's does. Compare, for example, the *Protagoras*, when in face of a worthier adversary, Socrates excels in the filigrees of a most intricate argument, or the *Theaetetus*, where his partner, although not contentious, is a most stimulating discussant.

At one point in the discussion of the nature of knowledge, Theaetetus comments that despite the fact that he does not have an answer to the problem, he "cannot get the question out of [his] mind."[15] Socrates replies, "my dear Theaetetus, that is because your mind is not empty or barren. You are suffering the pains of travail."[16] In view of Theaetetus' astonishment at his comment, he says that he is the son of a midwife and practices the same art,[17] and goes on to explain the art of midwifery as a metaphor for his own maieutic art. Women only become midwives when they are too old to conceive their own children, but they must have accumulated a wide experience before they embrace the profession. "Nobody better than a midwife can tell a pregnant woman, bring on the pains of travail or allay them at their will, make a difficult labor easy, and at an early stage cause a miscarriage if they so decide."[18] Midwives are also the best matchmakers that there are, for skills in harvesting go together with skills in sowing. However, they do not pander; they matchmake with decisive competence. The midwives' toil, nevertheless, falls short of the philosopher's because women only bring forth real children and not phantoms, whereas the beginning philosopher can generate false ideas. The teacher of philosophy, then, had this additional task: to tell false from true about the goods delivered by those he facilitates. As Socrates explains: "Those who frequent my company at first appear, some of them, quite unintelligent, but, as we go further with our discussions, all who are favored by heaven may progress at a rate that seems surprising to others as well as to themselves, although it is clear that they have never learned anything from me. The many admirable truths they bring to birth have been discovered by themselves from within. But the delivery is heaven's work and mine."[19]

Socrates' teaching is therefore unique, with each pupil calling for a special procedure, because the participation of the interlocutor is indispensable for its completion. He teaches through his questions and answers, his maieutic method. Here Gadamer's ideas about the precedence of the question over the answer will serve us as a springboard for a brief reflection about the Socratic art of questioning. We begin to understand a text or discourse, Gadamer argues, when we suspend the prejudices informing our interpretation. Naturally, we cannot understand a text in the absence of any preconceptions whatsoever, but we can make ourselves aware of the nature of these prejudices. The first move to suspend them and bring them into light is a question. The more fundamental and elementary the question, the bigger the load of prejudices being lifted. But the question is inevitably posed within the historical horizons of the inquirer's times. It must strike a balance between the memory of the past and the fancying of the future in order to be relevant for the time of its formulation. The hermeneutical situation is the only source on which he can draw to formulate questions and address them to his object of study. If this object is placed within the observer's own historical horizon or cultural tradition, it becomes extremely difficult to completely illuminate it, for the observer cannot step out of his hermeneutical situation without trivializing his questions. Similarly, if the object lies in a different historical time or cultural tradition, it will be an answer to questions typical of that framework, and the observer can either try to reconstruct them, or apply the questions of his time and place, thereby transforming the object into something else, or try to do both things, rendering explicit both the familiar and alien questions. If this juxtaposition is not terribly relevant to the observer's understanding of the past or of the other, it is extremely revealing insofar as his consciousness of his time goes.[20]

The Socratic questioning stakes out the path of the conversation within the ideological framework of his interlocutors. Since the topics under discussion are strictly kept within the horizons of the understanding of all participants in the debate, chances that they might lose the thread of argument or build up concealed disagreement are minimal.

If opposition arises, Socrates tries to overcome it by recasting the conversation in terms acceptable to all. This, of course, is obtained by means of his unrelenting questions forcing every one to speak out, voice his opinions, and take a stand in relation to all statements. No opinions are allowed to lurk in the recess of a grudging mind and no argument is allowed to proceed in the absence of consensus and full understanding.

Plato's philosophy is a political project, while Socrates is the activist in the dialogues. It differs from politics, as we have come to understand it, in that it has an element of philosophy in the sense of a quest for the truth, an element of education that attempts to persuade its readers of the truth, and an element of therapy in its plight to unravel the truth within the soul of each interlocutor, thus redressing righteousness in him. Politics, in this context, is not just one sphere of life, side by side with others such as philosophy, therapy, education, or religion, but a whole activity encompassing all spheres of life. It is an existential posture grounded on the unity of word and deed, of *logos* and *ergon*. In the "Seventh Letter," Plato tells us that first he thought of pursuing a political career, but once he realized that the ills of his polity were much deeper and not exclusive of Athens, he decided to take a different path and write his philosophical dialogues in order to praise "the correct philosophy [because] it affords a vantage point from which we can discern in all cases what is just for communities and for individuals, and that accordingly the human race will not see better days until either the stock of those who rightly and genuinely follow philosophy acquire political authority, or else the class who have political control be led by some dispensation of providence to become real philosophers."[21] Instead of looking for a solution to the ills of the polity on the horizontal plane of alternative policies, he found the evil so deeply rooted that it was necessary to move upwards along a vertical axis, and found a mode of knowledge of a wider range than those available, but at the same time inextricably committed to practice.

In the "Seventh Letter," Plato acknowledges his debt and admiration for Socrates as a philosophical mentor and political example. Gadamer writes that Socrates is for Plato, "a man of inconceivable rectitude in the midst of a world which no longer had the slightest inkling of what such rectitude is."[22] Crito, for example, provides Socrates with all the justifications he needs to flee prison and escape his execution, but he refuses the idea, faithful to his principle that the law must be obeyed under any circumstances, even when its application is unjust and perverse. One thing was to educate leaders, and by dint of this practice try to change the state, while a quite different attitude was to subvert the state outright, ironically, the very charge under which Socrates had been condemned. Gadamer speculates that, "the question which Socrates' action poses for Plato is this: how is it possible for someone to be so detached from everything which surrounds him that his behavior could differ so radically from the norm?"[23]

Plato recognizes the failure of his political practice. He was involved in the succession of the Sicilian tyrant, hoping that his disciple Dion would improve matters in that polity, but the results were quite the opposite. He confesses in the "Seventh Letter" how Socrates' condemnation to death shattered his political hopes,[24] leading him to retire from politics. After this upset he looked for a more fundamental praxis and found it in philosophy, regarded as the art of educating the elite which supplies the state with rulers. Socrates had done that in his dialogues. Plato also created the Academy and thereby established his educational practice as an institutional endeavor.

The question of power in the dialogues is dealt with at two different levels of the polity and of the individual, which in the end are bound together by the ethical imperative. The anatomy of microscopic power in relations mediated by the individual is not a subject of the discourse of the characters, but is illustrated by the weaving of the dialogues themselves. The *Protagoras* illustrates both levels of power. At one point in the discussion Socrates asks his interlocutor whether the virtues the Sophist teaches do not fall within the realm of politics, and is answered in the affirmative. Here we have power at the level of the polity, and this cannot be the basis of the emancipatory quest. The interpersonal power is illustrated by maneuvers such as Socrates' threat to abandon the discussion if Protagoras does not agree to make his interventions shorter, which cannot found the quest for the emancipation of virtue in the human soul either. Socrates knows that someone surrounded by such social prestige as Protagoras earns students easily and finds an unencumbered path with which to forward his teachings. Socrates, on the contrary, lacks that power, but transforms his powerlessness into a trump card by exploiting the sorrow which the contemptuous and powerful display toward those who are in subordinate positions. While the prestigious rhetors, such as Protagoras and Gorgias, use their power as a stratagem in their effort to persuade, Socrates prefers to operate from an underdog position. The impact of his persuasive appeal is derived in large measure from the contrast he establishes between the boisterous superiority of his adversaries' untenable claims and the modesty of his inquisitiveness which proves them wrong. This triumph of the true and modest over the false and boastful is a typical trait of classical culture which has survived, carried unto the present by Christianity.

Plato's Legacy

Although there is no claim in the dialogues that power is a foundation good enough to produce knowledge, to persuade others, or to awaken virtue, it is quite obvious that power is necessary to educate the citizens of a polity, and in the *Republic,* the state is summoned in order to educate those who are likely to become rulers. Socrates also makes use of power in face-to-face interactions, alternating positions of subordination with positions of superordination. For Socrates, as well as for Plato, there is naturally a certain tension in the need to project their message and convince others of it. This cannot be achieved by default of power. The state, the rules, and the legal apparatus are called for in aid. Plato forms a generation of followers and he makes the best use he can of the medium of writing at the same time that he attacks mimetic copies of the world. Socrates perfects the structure of reasoning and the use of argument by claiming that no discussion should proceed in the absence of consensus. There must be agreement between speaker and interlocutor about the minimum points being proposed in order for a line of thought to unfold and make sense, otherwise steps may be taken by the speaker without the acquiescence of the interlocutor, thereby entirely losing their persuasive appeal. It is therefore more important to deepen knowledge within the bounds of consensus than to do it unilaterally.

In the same way that exceeding rhetorical eloquence may compromise an argument by overshadowing its content, outright use of power may lead to persuasion through domination and not reasoning. Finally, knowledge, likewise, by itself is worth nothing for it can remain dormant in the human soul without doing any good for man if it is not awakened by the maneuvers of rhetoric and power. But we may wish to wonder why some men like Socrates and Plato are the right ones to trigger off this quest for virtue, while others like Callicles and Lysias are wrong. If neither knowledge, nor power, nor rhetoric can be built as absolute grounds on which to decide right from wrong, and if virtue is in the souls of all men and not only a few, how is it that some are right and commendable and others not? The answer to this question is that rightness does not reside among a group of men to the exclusion of others, but on the procedure of argumentation and counterargumentation guided by consensus. A fuller discussion of consensus will appear in the forthcoming chapter.

The Socratic education is a combination of the maieutic method of questions and answers with the dialectic of destruction of weak arguments and replacement by ever stronger arguments. In the *Republic,* Socrates describes the method in detail. The teacher formulates a hypothesis or leads his pupil to do so, and then proceeds to unfold all the possible lines of reasoning stemming from that initial thought. The result is the bludgeoning of the hypothesis to its complete destruction. Another hypothesis is raised and then submitted to the same process. What the pupil learns is not the infallible hypothesis, but how to become more exacting and critical in his future formulations of hypotheses. This perfecting of reasoning necessarily entails a revitalization of power to persuade the interlocutors. Socrates' claim is that his dialectic also constitutes a more thorough surveillance against false arguments. The procedure is therefore not only destined to persuade others, but also to prevent the speaker from developing wrong beliefs. Maieutic and dialectic are consequently educational processes in both the senses of teaching and generating knowledge, while Socrates claims that the separation of these two senses is nefarious.[25]

If the coaching of an argument, that is, the rhetoric of its power basis, becomes divorced from its content, then it may become difficult to rescue the best argument from the hayloft of bad claims. Socrates feared that the art of debating could run amok, creating a tangle of chatter from which it would be impossible to rescue the truth. The best argument was always attached to truth, not the sensorially verifiable truth of our scientific and modernist world, but the virtuous truth of sincerity. However, in a jungle of ideological controversy, it seemed legitimate to fear that the best argument would come to be regarded as just one additional argument, and not the definitive one. The danger of this outcome was not the loss of definitive best arguments, which Socrates himself was not very keen in producing, but the emergence of a widespread belief that arguing was good, not for arriving at the truth, but for leading the speaker to a position of domination; consequently, the Sophist thesis that knowledge is power. The Sophists were certainly not only advocating, but decisively contributing to this argument chaos. Socrates found a good dam against this state of affairs in the unrelenting pursuit of consensus. The argument could only proceed in furthering knowledge. It is precisely for this reason that Socrates disavows any challenges to political institutions, because these can only produce disagreement and break down the consensual lattice, and in the absence of agreement, no matter how good a belief is, it becomes worthless.

In the *Protagoras* and in the *Apology*, Plato reveals the two fundamental strategies of Socrates' teaching: exhortation and examination. Socrates exhorts his interlocutors to expose their ideas and then examines them, persuading them of the weakness of their arguments, and exercising them in a more thorough form of reasoning. But this is only possible with those who are willing in mind and heart, while this willingness is founded on consensus. If the interlocutor is not ready to accept consensus at a certain level of the argument, it is incumbent on the speaker to lower the argument's claim and look for agreement. At the microscopic level of power in face-to-face interactions, it resides in the willingness to pursue the inquiry as a joint project, but at the macroscopic level of the polity it takes the form of an unbreakable obedience to rules and rulers, which preserves the wholeness of the social, the only locus where the best argument can prevail. A polity wrought by conflict stemming from disobedience and challenges cannot secure the minimum conditions for the appreciation of the best argument which begins to be regarded as just another ruse.

This educational/political/philosophical practice founded on consensus was faced with great difficulties in Socrates' Athens, where conflict loomed large and people struggled for domination, not understanding. Socrates tried to overcome those difficulties within the confines of an oral culture, drawing heavily and exclusively on the qualities of memory, wholeness, and immediacy, characteristic of verbal dialogues. Plato, on the contrary, turned to writing, but upheld the principles deriving from oral discourse. Literacy naturally allayed the problem of consensus by allowing the speaker/writer to create his interlocutors like a ventriloquist, and to compose his text as an argument against invisible debaters, assuming a certain degree of agreement. However, the authority of what was said did not spring any longer from the speaker's memory, but from the capacity of the text to store information. This wedge thrust between the speaker/writer and the said/written weakened the authority of knowledge (the content of the said or written), creating the impression that it was possible to persuade by using rhetoric or power (domination) alone, without recourse to knowledge. The power maneuvers of the written text are not as easily perceived as those of the speaker, because the key to the political games played by the text are concealed behind the depersonalization carried through by writing as opposed to oral discourse. These characteristics of the written text, added to its natural defenses against immediate challenges from interlocutors, created the impression that texts could persuade by the exclusive domination of its readers, either by the lures of style or the injunctions of authority founded on superordination of any kind. Knowledge was no longer the source of power, but only one of the multiple paths to it.

The rhetorical appeals of literacy were quite different from those of verbal discourse, and at the time so novel that it was difficult to gain a critical perspective over them. Plato's critique of poetry, for example, is blunt and includes the tragedies. He chooses verbal dialogues for his literary genre because of the helter-skelter character of the rhetoric of the text. As he wishes to persuade his interlocutors, he turns to the well-established context of speech, but does so employing the medium of writing. The fact that literacy clouds the issues of wholeness, immediacy, consensus, power, rhetoric, and knowledge present in communication may deceitfully lead us to conclude that orality, on the contrary, fully preserves them in meridian clarity. If that were the case an oral culture would always generate more awareness among its members than a literate one. The fact of the matter is that what is revealing about the juxtaposition of the two communication media is not the possible hierarchy that we can establish between them, but the different properties of our communicative habits illuminated by the contrast. Socrates chooses the oral medium and concludes that philosophy is incompatible with the crowds because, he reasons, "no polity of today is worthy of the philosophical nature."[26] He then turns to the perfecting of the argument in order to rekindle the fire of consciousness in the minds of a few individuals. He never seems to be very concerned with the political feasibility of his project. Plato prefers to write, creates the Academy, forays into politics, and trains followers. It is not necessary to identify Socrates' option with the context of orality and Plato's with literacy, but the different media undoubtedly backed the educational/political/ philosophical project of each thinker in its turn. Nevertheless, the Socratic-Platonic endeavor was one in its ethical foundation which by and large transcended questions of method. As Jaeger puts it, Socrates' basic attitude was "You can contradict me, you can't contradict *it* [the argument]."[27] After all, the dialectician's craftsmanship can ultimately be proven right or wrong by God alone, as is stated in the *Phaedrus*.[28]

9

CONSENSUS:

THERAPY OF THE SOUL

The Greeks did not develop a therapeutic discourse, not because of a lack of interest in doing so, but because they did not regard existential afflictions as something germinating in the soil of the individual self. Afflictions had social origin. They divided the realm of human discomfort into the physical—addressed by medicine—and the political—addressed by rhetoric, according to the Sophists, and by philosophy, according to Socrates. However, they developed several forms of therapeutic discourse aimed at turning minds or perfecting souls.

Physical Ailments and Seductive Types of *Logos*

Wrongdoing in ancient Greece was a moral rather than a psychological problem. It was a matter of virtue and justice. If the Greeks were to establish any links between existential afflictions and the psyche, this would have been done in their explanation of the mind. Bennett Simon undertook the research of this question, and found out that the links were tenuous. He studied the concept of the mind for the poets, the philosophers, and the physicians along four lines of research: (1) "the representation of the mind and of ordinary mental activity"; (2) "the representation of disturbance of the mind"; (3) "the treatment of disturbance of the mind"; and (4) "the relations between the craft of the practitioner (poet, philosopher, or doctor) and the theories of mind and mental disturbance."[1] The immediate motive of his essay is the puzzle of contemporary psychiatry in face of the problem of classification and treatment of schizophrenia. He shows how this concern was already present among the ancient Greeks who struggled with the ternary split of disease into medical, intrapsychic, and interpersonal factors, the three aspects being amalgamated in the phenomenal reality of disease as perceived by the physician. The undecidability of this tri-pronged classification has naturally led to the postulation of determinism of body, soul, and society in the explanation of disorganized behavior. The

Greeks preferred to separate strictly the physical from the sociopolitical problems, but never abandoned their understanding of causes as physical, psychic, and social jointly. As a consequence, the Greek cultural model of medicine and of politics was tinged with ambiguity. Twenty-five centuries went by before the concept of psyche became fully developed, something that only happened with Freud.

The medical model of the mind in the Hippocratic corpus can be derived from the book *On the Sacred Disease*. The treatise begins by warning its readers that epilepsy was considered sacred only by those who did not understand it, or by "the conjurors, purificators, mountebanks, and charlatans" in order to cover up their ignorance about the disease. It is a natural disease like all others and finds its seat in the brain. It occurs when the veins which carry air and blood to the brain become blocked by an excess of phlegm or other factors. It is also a hereditary disease. The symptoms of this illness—seizures, speechlessness, disorganization of thought, and other behavioral characteristics— are attributed to these temporary deprivations of the brain's vital elements, blood and air. The treatment is based on changes in the patients' diet and place of living.[2]

Although the brain is given such a central place in Hippocrates' medicine, it is often rivaled by the heart, and Simon writes that "the question of heart versus brain was not definitely settled in antiquity, and perhaps not even for many centuries later."[3] We do not need to know the current medical opinion on the matter to realize that the tension between heart and brain, emotion and reason, continues to be a central aporia in the Euro-American cultural heritage. In ancient Greece the question met with a palliative solution residing on a strict classification of physical and sociocultural problems and a division of the spheres of competence in dealing with them, medicine for the former, and rhetoric, poetry, tragedy, and philosophy competing for the latter.

When one looks at the richness of rhetorical resources developed by the Greeks from the height of the twentieth century, it is unavoidable to feel puzzled by the question of why they did not develop a therapy of the psyche. They got very close to it, but coming from rhetoric and philosophy which aimed at the problems of the polity, not of the individual, and not from medicine, the domain in which the individual was singled out by virtue of the limits of the body.

The great accomplishment of Hippocratic medicine was to establish the new art as a respectable scientific practice. Sickness was no longer regarded as an external disorder which befell the patient. Nor was it seen as a punishment against the species. The individual was singled out as having sole responsibility for the harmony between his body and soul, his individual life and that of the polity. The great threats against this harmony were *monarchia* (the predominance of one of the powers), and *ametria* (disorder among the powers). This did not imply that there should be absolute equality with all powers lined up at the same level, but that the hierarchy among powers should be flexible. Medicine became a *technē* ("knowing how"), and finally succeeded over magic with its claim to redress the flexible and harmonious hierarchy among powers.

As we discussed before, in chapter 6, the triumph of the medical model was so complete that its success became influential over other arts such as rhetoric. Moreover, medicine could not become entirely independent of other spheres of knowledge. Its notion of harmony depended on philosophy and the proselytizing of its practice depended on rhetoric. The physician, *iatros,* had to *see* the disease, for he was a *mantis,* a seer. However, this metaphor could not be taken too literally because diseases were not always available for the organ of vision, they had to be understood through reasoning. In the context of an oral culture, reasoning was basically dialogical and carried out through speech. Medicine attracted its coeval arts because of its political success at the same time that it depended on them for its foundation (a theory of harmony) and practice (a rhetoric of persuasion). Thus, the isolation of the physical—already faced with the cultural aporia which distinguished physical, intrapsychic, and social causes for ailments, although striving to single out the physical—was confronted with one further difficulty: it became ever more deeply intertwined with rhetoric and philosophy.

There were several types of discourse for the physician to choose from, such as supplication as in prayer *(euchē),* charming, which was largely employed by magicians *(epōdē),* and the beguiling speech *(thelktērios logos)* typical of lovers, poets, politicians, and all orators who used pleasant speech *(terpnos logos)* to persuade their interlocutors. Side-by-side with these rhetorics of persuasion, medicine was introducing a new one together with philosophy: the rhetoric of science based on unquestionable reasoning. The novelty of this new appeal to persuade could not stand on its own feet in the beginning because it lacked popularity. Consequently, the physicians as well as the philosophers had to resort to the other forms of rhetoric against which they were rebelling.

Consensus for What Purpose?

In his description of the Socratic dialogue, Jaeger writes that its purpose was "to reach an agreement which must be recognized as valid by everyone."[4] But how can a speaker obtain consensus if his interlocutor refuses to agree? And what is the nature of this consensus, is it instrumental, that is, a means to an end, does it constitute the very purpose of the debate, or is it both instrumental and purposive?

Socrates often prompts his interlocutors to answer his questions and then discusses their answers by formulating new questions, either expanding or shortening the subject. In the *Republic*, Thrasymachus reveals great irritation against Socrates, saying that he is constantly contriving to evade having to give answers himself, and is always ready to prod his interlocutor back into answering his own questions.[5] Toward the end of Book 1, Thrasymachus' irritation is such that despite answering Socrates, he refuses to acknowledge his opponent's argument, much like Callicles in the *Gorgias*. For Socrates, however, the position of questioner is not any more comfortable than that of respondent, and does not confer upon the inquirer any advantage over his adversary. Protagoras exchanges roles with Socrates and becomes the inquirer, so do Callicles, Polus, and Meno, but this turns out to be of no avail to Socrates' opponents. In the *Protagoras* and in the *Republic*, the possibility of having to judge to decide who is right is broached by his adversaries, but Socrates discards it because it would imply that the judge displayed a reason superior to that of the contenders. He defends himself from the tyranny of unilateral reasoning, embodied in the figure of the judge, by arguing that it was unlikely to find someone wiser than the great Protagoras, or the great Gorgias, thereby disarming his adversaries' suggestion with flattery. He claims that the best course to allow is that which has the discussants as referees and pleaders simultaneously. The presence of an arbiter would limit the range of consensus and replace genuine agreement by forced acceptance. For Socrates, the spontaneous acceptance of the argument is a sine qua non condition for the dialogue to proceed. What strikes some of his adversaries as irritating is his perseverance to draw them out to voice their agreement or disagreement with each step of reasoning. Socrates' obvious strategy as a questioner is not that of victor, but of someone who wishes to maintain a constant consensus throughout the debate. If a topic reveals itself as too controversial, Socrates will retract to more elementary assumptions lying along the way to the assertion of that topic, so that agreement can be reestablished.

It is intriguing that in spite of this unrelenting search for consensus, Socrates contends that the philosophers must know better than the crowds, that people must have differing opinions, and that society must be divided, if not by many chasms, at least by education which parts the crowds from the educated elite. Furthermore, not only is the philosopher's constituency fragmented, but even when he succeeds in seizing the minds of his few interlocutors, he may miss their hearts.[6] Finally, by proposing a state education as in the *Republic*, is Socrates not going against his own refusal to accept a referee? Is he not suggesting the establishment of an arbiter superior to all, and who could decide what people should learn?

In all debates Socrates never lets the lattice of consensus break down. As a matter of fact, for him it is more important to preserve the consensus than to forward novel knowledge. For that reason, sometimes, as in the *Euthyphro*, Socrates retracts from assertions of what is known to doubts that, although elementary, reveal themselves necessary to maintain the agreement with Euthyphro in their discussion of piety. This strategy for maintaining consensus is naturally a trait of classical culture in which the norm of politeness demands that even disagreement must tread the path of a certain verbal consensus. But Socrates' use of it does not merely illustrate his identification with his cultural context, because he lays special claims on consensus. Consensus becomes fundamental in the dialogues not in order for Socrates to persuade his interlocutors, but in order for the best argument to prevail.

Socrates' claim for the centrality of consensus is very much akin to that of psychotherapists of all persuasions, who acknowledge that the inability to establish a certain link with the patient renders psychotherapy impossible. The nature of this link is debatable as we saw in earlier chapters, from the psychoanalytic claim that it is transferential to the systemic view that it is communicative, passing through concepts such as "alliance," "joining," "empathy," and "rapport." Even in the more abrasive interventions in which therapists confront patients with unpleasant challenges, there is obviously a concern with the maintenance of consensus, for the therapist wants the patient to do or realize something, and in order for this to be effective, there must be agreement between the two interactants. This situation is quite different from debates characterized by conflict, in which the parties no longer pursue understanding, but argue merely to alienate the other, or to play out feelings of angst. The Socratic consensus and the therapeutic rapport are therefore stratagems destined to keep the argument flowing towards a possibility of understanding, and not maneuvers to win over the interlocutor. But the Socratic consensus is not merely instrument; it is purposive, too.

In our discussion of the *Protagoras*, it was seen that neither Socrates nor his opponents had a good definition of education. For Socrates education could not be the transmission of a body of knowledge. Since our knowledge of the world was steeped in deep controversy, to make positive assertions by default of the different opinions would not in any way help the pupil who was about the enter the disputation parlor. Assuming that there was a knowledge which was better than all others and couched in virtue, Socrates developed an education based on argumentation aiming at unravelling such knowledge. The art of arguing, however, was supposed to strike a balance between word and deed, capable of tapping the virtue that is lost in the human soul and bring it out to reform the polity. Education for Socrates was precisely this effort to link the impossible positive corpus of knowledge with the methods of critique, and to turn this into a search for that which was worthwhile. Thus it was not necessary to consider every opposing argument, because the criteria for the acceptance of an opinion were so stringent that most could not pass the test, turning the inquirer back to his search. The Socratic procedure in a way could never have an end. The Sophists on the contrary, by overlooking the question of content, rendered speech an empty shell. Their debates ended as soon as their adversaries were defeated. In a fable about Protagoras, it is told that his disciple Euatlus refused to pay for his education in rhetoric, because he had not won a single dispute. Protagoras claimed in turn that Euatlus had to pay in any case, because if Protagoras won the argument about payment, he should pay; if Protagoras lost, he should pay all the same because he was obtaining his first victory. From a Socratic point of view, a situation like this would be absurd since the issue of justice was entirely ignored, as if the obligation to pay were dependent upon the presentation of a good argument.

One of the reasons why Plato's dialogues are controversial, lies in the fact that if on one hand Socrates never arrives at a positive definition of the concepts he screens in his dialectic, on the other hand he is presented as forwarding prescriptions for the ideal state as in the *Republic*. Even considering that education is fundamentally his dialectic method of critique of self-assertive knowledge, the institutionalization of the method would inevitably emasculate the power of critical reflection. Simon writes: "The Academy was a meeting ground between the life of contemplation and the life of action," in other words, between philosophy and politics. He completes his portrayal of the Academy by saying that it was a good place "from which they [the philosophers] might foray into the world of Greek politics (and to which they might beat a hasty retreat)."[7] Is not this antinomy of the dialogues one of the best testimonies one can invoke in defense of Plato's method to convey Socrates' philosophy?

It seems that it was clear to Socrates that, in a polity ridden by power strifes, any philosophy of education willing to thrive would have to break through the tangle of power disputes and find its own place under the sun. Education therefore could not be apolitical because the claim of the right to educate involved a political standing. There were no educational institutions in the city-state, and the philosopher was struggling to establish one, in much the same way as the Christian a few centuries later tried and succeeded, and as would the Marxist and the psychotherapist. The essential tool of political practice was oratory, and consequently the educator and politician must also be a good orator.

The Sophists were all three, but still not good enough for Socrates. What did they lack? They espoused a certain humanism ("man is the measure of all things") based on the broadening of tolerance for meaning, so that one could get to the point of accepting that both A and not-A held true simultaneously, for there should be a higher value encompassing contradiction. The problem with this posture was that the humanistic acceptance of everything undermined the force of meaning by weakening the discriminating capacity of understanding. This consequence, however, exactly fitted the Sophist project of perfecting rhetorical skills to win arguments before the content of the discussion had been evaluated. The Socratic project was different in two crucially important aspects. First, it is true that it was highly argumentative, but the argument could only proceed on a track of consensus, which rendered the progression of the inquirer more difficult. For the Sophists, on the contrary, the escalation of differences did not matter as long as they won the discussion. Second, for Socrates man was intrinsically good and virtuous, and the virtuosity could be talked about in rational discourse. More than this, it could be expressed in rational discourse. The Sophists' humanism did not appeal to reason, only to tolerance, and as such revealed contempt for disagreement. In addition to being an educator, a politician, and an orator, the speaker should also be a philosopher, in the sense that his discourse could not be divorced from his moral interests as a human being, that is, a bearer of virtue. A philosophy thus defined is not unlike the conception of the therapeutic.

Communicative and Ideological Consensus

The heart of this theoretical practice, sharing qualities with what we understand today as education, politics, rhetoric, philosophy, and therapy, was the unflinching maintenance of consensus in the dialogues. But what is the nature of this consensus? Does consensus mean agreement with Socrates' ideas?

In order to better understand Socrates' strong claim for consensus we have to refine our notion of the concept, something that I will do by dividing it into five dimensions: (1) a linguistic dimension, (2) a cognitive-expressive dimension, (3) a speech dimension, (4) a power dimension and (5) a dimension of opinion or point of view. From a linguistic point of view the speakers in a conversation must, at least to begin with, speak the same language, a fact upon which we need not elaborate further. Second, the participants in a debate must agree upon the reality or truth of the subject matters under discussion. A therapist and his client, for example, cannot have cognitive consensus if one of them does not accept the existence of an entity such as "problems" while the other does. Notice that I am not talking about opinion, but really about a cognitive habit that leads some people to identify certain states of affairs as "problems." In the case of mere divergence of opinions, one party in the group may deny that there are such things as "family problems," or may think that problems are the creation of weak minds, but in order to have cognitive consensus there must be a basic agreement about the meaning of "problem," even if only to deny or requalify the concept. Expressive consensus relates to the intentions of the speakers. A similar illustration to that which we just established for cognitive consensus will help us here, too. Intention is not a matter of tactic or of unwilled actions such as slips of the tongue. Tactical communicative actions emphasizing the intentional dimension are those either conveying redundant messages in order to assert the intention–e.g., "I am saying that I do not smoke because I do not smoke, so that you understand that I do not smoke"—or concealing the intention—e.g., to say that I promise to take you to the movies when I have no intention of doing so. The dimension of expressive consensus is neither of these two. It is so deeply steeped in our ability to communicate, that breaching it would be equivalent to a speaker's uttering of a statement and immediately being astonished by it, as if he had no will or disposition to do it, either physically, emotionally, or intellectually.

Third, the interactants must share a repertoire of speaking skills which enable them to identify questions and answers, commands and obliging responses, constative assertions, reflective intimations; in short, the vast repertoire of communicative actions which, although encoded in language, are by and large expressions of interactive habits. The speaking skills include the knowledge of how and when to use the communicative actions. If this is the case, communicative actions are also social actions and the speaker's habits must include the capacity to recognize such actions.

Fourth, the power dimension refers to the countless social asymmetries found in the network of social interactions. They may be either institutionally established or produced in the course of the interaction itself. Institutionally established power asymmetries are those between judge and defendant, employer and employee, or mother and daughter, for example. The other types of asymmetry can be illustrated by a conversation between two peers who agree that the arguments of one are always going to be better than the arguments of the other. While the linguistic, cognitive-expressive, and speech dimensions of consensus can be indicated for different linguistic-cultural traditions without much ethnocentrism, the dimensions of power and opinion are extremely conditioned by the cultural context and may be sharply different from one tradition to the next. It is in the Euro-American cultural tradition stemming from the Greco-Roman civilization that we have become acquainted with attributing meaning to power relations in social hierarchies and even in microscopic social interactions. The dimension of power is not only constitutive of communicative actions, but it is also one of the objects of those actions, since in our heritage one of the meanings we assign to the transformation of the world is the alteration of power asymmetries.

The fifth dimension is opinion. It refers to agreement about the viewpoints, beliefs, or knowledge under discussion between the interactants. Differences of opinion do not challenge the communicative habitude, indeed they guarantee the flow of communication, because we communicate to sharpen, understand, or eliminate differences and not to harp on uniformity or dwell upon subject matters of mutual agreement and equal degree of conviction between ourselves and our interlocutors. In order to challenge the first three dimensions of consensus, we have to redeem their validity claims, otherwise we run into paradoxes of speaking without language, asserting without cognizance or intention, and talking without speech. These dimensions are rooted in our communicative habitude and without them we just cannot communicate. The same is not true of the dimensions of power and opinion. A power hierarchy can be contested with the critic standing outside of the relation of subordination, and an opinion can be challenged by a speaker who does not share the smallest bit of it. Power, however, is not as open to challenge as opinion. Under certain circumstances the critic has to heed the power asymmetry and challenge it from within. This can be illustrated with a student who is disputing the grading system by building his argument on his experience as a student who has taken a certain number of exams and earned grades within that system. These different planes on which the dimensions are cast indicate that there are at least two very different types of consensus, one fundamental for the communicative process itself, which we shall call *communicative con-*

sensus, and another necessary for certain actions, including a few communicative actions constituted by norms of social politeness, the *ideological consensus.* The first is formed by the linguistic, cognitive-expressive, and speech dimensions of our communicative habitude, as well as by many agreements with power asymmetries and a few cases of opinion consensus which are indispensable for the communicative process. Ideological consensus hinges on power and opinion and its breach does not hinder the pursuit of understanding.[8]

Socrates proceeds in the dialogues by prodding his interlocutors to fall into ideological consensus, that is, to agree with certain ideas and with the fact that their statement brings a certain power to the speaker, a power which furthermore is legitimized by the consensual acknowledgment of the interlocutor. He does not regard his debates as a clash of antagonistic opinions, but as a test in which he submits his companions' ideas to the scrutiny of his critique. The result is the expostulation of positive assertions as well as the realization of how precariously maintained they were. The effect is that next time they will be stricter in accepting an opinion from somebody else or in developing one of their own. The procedure to implement ideological consensus consists in building the argument progressively by formulating partial statements (partial hypotheses) aiming at the entertainment of the whole. These steps, however, move backwards as they meet with uninformed opposition or prove to be too complicated, forcing Socrates to backpedal. He retracts and starts over from an even finer and more hairsplitting argument, which turns out to be so bold that it cannot be opposed. It is easier for his adversaries to agree about minuscule propositions, but they never arrive at the whole, which would be a full-fledged definition of virtue. This is a fundamental goal of his dialectic because Socrates' wish to maintain consensus is stronger than his wish to forward knowledge. Is ideological consensus the final goal of Socratic dialogues? Is the insistence on the agreement of all about each step the stratagem to assure agreement about the final points, that is, the whole of the argument? This pursuit of consensus may seem a cruel ruse of Socrates to force his adversaries to ultimately agree with him.

In the *Crito,* Socrates discusses the issue of the best argument. He is in jail, waiting for the day of his execution which has been delayed for over a month. When the sentence was passed, a ritual season had begun which could not be tarnished by the impurity brought about by death, even to fulfill a decision of the state. A galley had been sent to the island of Delos where the rituals were performed, and Socrates' execution was stayed until the ship had returned to Athens. In the meantime Socrates' friends plot to get him out of jail and away from Athens, to another city where he could live peacefully for the rest of his days. Crito comes to visit him and tells the master of the plan. Socrates thanks him for his warm feelings, and proposes to discuss Crito's argument for his flight: "it has always been my nature never to accept advice from any of my friends unless reflection shows that it is the best course that reason offers."[9] Upon contrasting Crito's reasons to set him free with his intention of living an honorable and righteous life, Socrates concludes that the wrongdoing of one party is not a justification for the wrong-doing of the other. The disobeyance of the court order is wrongdoing. He knows his friend Crito is desolated by the possibility of losing his master, and consequently will be hardly willing to accept his argument that the execution should follow its course. Emotions have overtaken Crito's reason. He draws Crito into an intellectual agreement to over-come the emotional distress by saying, "Now be careful Crito, that in making these single admissions you do not end by admitting something contrary to your real beliefs."[10] Socrates keeps prompting Crito to respond to his questions, preventing his friend from falling completely into distress. The struggle is between the reasons of the mind and the reasons of the heart. Like many psychotherapists, Socrates believes that reason can tame the emotions, and thus he appeals to Crito's conscious-ness in the hope that his mind will sway his heart. He asks Crito to express any disagreements he may have so that these cannot thrive in a folding of emotions protected from the light of reason.[11] He says, "I know that there are and always will be few people who think like this, [that one should disobey the law in fulfillment of self-interest] and consequently between those who do think so and those who do not there can be no agreement in principle; they must always feel contempt when they observe one another's decision. I want even you to consider very carefully whether you share my views and agree with me, and whether we can proceed with our discussion from the established hypothesis that it is never right to do a wrong or return a wrong or defend oneself against injury by retaliation, or whether you disassociate yourself from any share in this view as a basis for discussion."[12] Here we find Socrates at his best as philosopher/therapist, smoothing over the ground of divergence, dangerously muddled by the powerful emotions, by appealing to rational consensus. In this dialogue, again, Socrates illustrates his fundamental attitude, the unity between words and deeds. Even when the state wrongly condemns him to death under the false accusation of corrupting the Athenian youth, he refuses to disobey the ordination because that would establish the dangerous precedent of breaking consensus in the name of self-interest. The lattice of consensus must be kept intact under all circumstances so that the best argument can be adequately redeemed.

The authority of critique does not thrive in a polity whose members ignore the opinions with which they disagree. Even when the philosopher's life is at stake, it is preferable for him to oblige the rulers by drinking hemlock than to escape from prison and deny the court's decision. His obedience to an unjust sentence preserves the moral authority from which he can launch his criticism against society.[13] Two interesting traits from classical culture stand out in Socrates' attitude. First, the individual is not yet the supreme power we have become acquainted with in the Western tradition. In ancient Greece, the basis of consciousness is not yet self-identity, it is still some form of collective consciousness. It was only after Freud that the individual self earned the status of ultimate bearer of consciousness. Second, while in our contemporary and modern ideology we tend to make no claims for the supremacy of one category of knowledge over all others, in classical culture the world was organized into well-ordered hierarchies, and consequently it was imperative to have a category or principle at the top. Thus Socrates regards the authority of criticism as absolute, while today there is a greater tendency to relativize the claims of any criticism. This does not mean that in our modern and postmodern world there are no claims for universal categories of knowledge, but only that they now meet with more skepticism than they did in ancient times.

From the illustration from the *Crito*, it becomes clear that Socrates' consensus does not oblige his adversaries to him alone, but obliges him equally to their opinions even when they are outright unjust and wrong, and the outcome of their mistake will cost him his life. But this is not the only consequence of Socrates' testimony of a coherence of word and deed. The other and far more important consequence is that argument cannot be elevated to the pinnacle of his cosmology. We have seen that knowledge cannot occupy this top position, because in dialogue after dialogue different systems of knowledge are put down. Rhetoric, likewise, cannot be hegemonic. Now we see that argument and dialectic cannot either because if on one hand they are the test for justificatory claims, on the other hand argument and dialectic by themselves have no virtue. Critique is not invincible; even when coupled with the best argument it may be defeated by a mightier power, rhetoric, or knowledge.[14]

Socrates' appeal for ideological consensus is not a strategy of conquest, it aims at protecting the contours of communicative consensus. It is a defensive strategy. He could have argued that since our communicative habitude depends on sharing language, cognition, expression, speech acts, and some normative principles such as power positions and certain opinions, consensus cannot be cut all the way to the bone. In that case it would always remain possible for us to reestablish the truth through undistorted communication. Socrates, however, is afraid that the acuteness of the strife amid ideological dissension may spread and contaminate communicative consensus. His proposal, then, is that of a therapist in uncommon times: struggle, in order to diminish divergence at the level of opinion, so that the argumental chaos of the polity dissipates, and thereby avoid the great danger of the erosion of communicative consensus.

In the *Republic*, Adimantus compares Socrates' method of question and answer to a game of draughts, played to confuse his opponents and to prove his points, which are consequently not couched in the best arguments.[15] Socrates agrees with him and temporarily relinquishes the method of question and answer, telling him a parable instead, for which he nonetheless requests Adimantus' agreement. The parable tells of a skipper, slightly deaf, and with impaired vision, who in addition does not have great knowledge of navigation. The crew wrangle with one another to take control of the helm, but since they are divided among themselves and the shipmaster is strong enough to remain in command, the situation becomes a standstill. The stalemate in the sailors' dispute derives from the fact that they all believe the art of sailing cannot be taught, and so each one claims to be entitled to steer the ship with his nautical knowledge. Soon a group approaches the skipper and manages to speak loudly in his ear, and with his alliance they put the others to death, poison the skipper, and take command. Then they go on a rampage, feasting and praising as master of navigation the man who managed to persuade the skipper. They do not know that the art of shipcraft resides in the knowledge of the time of the year, the seasons, the sky, the winds, the stars, and the seas. Socrates asks Adimantus, "with such goings on aboard ship do you not think that the real pilot would in very deed be called a stargazer, an idle babbler, a useless fellow, by the sailors in ships managed after this fashion?"[16]

The situation aboard that ship is like a polity which lost its communicative consensus. The shipmaster is partially blind and deaf. Notice that the power hierarchy is part of the communicative consensus, and that when the members of the polity do not share communicative premises and have a crooked power organization, a group can only prevail over the other through mutiny. The sailors on that ship do not believe that seamanship can be taught; that is, they do not believe in tradition. An incompetent skipper is replaced by an incompetent sailor, and this madness is in all likelihood bound to continue as long as the rebels do not settle around certain principles. The problem is not that the sailors and the ailing skipper have different opinions about the art of navigation; they ignore everything about the subject matter and furthermore are politically disorganized among themselves. The skipper stays in power by the use of force, he is toppled only when overcome by force, and his successors have to kill their adversaries in order to remain in power. What pits them against one another is a strife much deeper than ideological divergence. They do not share a common language, the skipper is deaf, and no one understands what the art of sailing is; they are not organized along a political hierarchy, for everyone wants to take the helm. The strife is lodged in the heart of their communicative actions which cannot be regarded as a habitude.

Socrates is afraid that Athens may end like that unfortunate ship. His proposal is not for ordinary times. Like the therapist's interventions, his discourse aims at an exceptional situation, only comparable to that of a psychopathological state. Under these circumstances the philosopher/therapist has to be careful and avoid clashes of opinions, otherwise, after having done away with ideological consensus, the contentiousness may begin to erode communicative consensus. Similar to the therapist who may not like a particular client, and may even disagree with his portrayal of reality, but has to maintain a certain consensus in order to be able to do therapy, Socrates in his philosophy has to pursue ideological consensus with its worst adversaries. The therapist and the philosopher, however, are always dealing with uncommon situations which challenge practical reason in everyday life. Consequently they develop an uncommon discourse, and practice a consensus of opinion which is unnecessary in ordinary relations, those which are not in crisis.

10 DIALECTIC AND

THE "GOOD" WITHIN

In the *Theaetetus*, after realizing that he does not know what knowledge is, Socrates undertakes his dialectic to unfold the concept in his conversation with Theaetetus. First he establishes the difference between "having" and "possessing" knowledge. In the first simile he employs, a man may have bought a coat, in which case he possesses it, but may not be wearing it about him, in which case he does not have it at that moment.[1] The second simile compares the acquisition of knowledge to the entrapping of birds. The birds would be "had" by their possessor, who could also choose to set them free again. Two relations of possession are then defined: having something but not having it at hand, and having something that can be freed. Then Socrates turns to arithmetic, and inquires whether the same could be said of numbers. Can the man who knows numbers have them and yet not have them available for use at a given moment? Could he let them go away like the birds and not have them anymore? Certainly not in the sense of the birds simile, and perhaps not in the case of the coat simile. The main conclusion to be drawn from this thought is that we either possess knowledge of matters or we do not. And if we do have knowledge, we cannot help but have it, we cannot rid ourselves of it. However, we may "possess" the knowledge of something without "having" it about us. The consequence of this line of reasoning is that it cannot be said that a man does not know what he knows, but only that he may make a false judgment about it.[2] He may need the number twelve, but mistakenly catches eleven instead. This does not mean, however, that he does not know it is twelve; he has just made a mistake in judgment and has got hold of eleven, believing that he was right. It follows that both true and false judgments do exist,"[3] but this should not cast doubt over knowledge itself, but only over judgment. The problem is that the holders of true and false judgments at times seem both equally convinced and persuasive and this undecidability of true and false at the level of appearance contaminates our trust in knowledge.

Socrates reveals his bemusement at how strange it is for a man to know something and next take it for something else. Theaetetus seizes the most accessible conclusion, and going back to the simile of the birds, suggests that there are birds standing for pieces of knowledge, and birds standing for ignorance; sometimes a man grabs at the former, on other occasions, at the latter.[4] But this reasoning, Socrates argues, brings us back to the vicious circle of considering ignorance and knowledge as qualities on the same footing, in which the two discussants found themselves before. If that were the case, it would be futile to talk about mistaken judgments, for we would know of what we know as well as of what we are ignorant, and that is self-contradictory. This passage tells us that the telling of true from false knowledge does not depend on the use of the best argument alone, but mainly on the speaker's ability to retrieve in his underlying base of knowledge the knowledge that is. By now, it should be clear from our discussion of Plato's dialogues that this process of recollection of subjacent knowledge does not take place in the bosom of reflective introspection; it arises in the course of dialogues in which the participants pursue the clarification of concepts. For Socrates, then, knowledge lies already buried in the human soul. The question is whether or not we can get hold of it.

In his search to find out what knowledge is, Socrates disavows the fragmentation of this quality into several components. The inquiry examines different virtues aiming at understanding what virtue is as a whole. This wholesome quality in the human soul could be called "knowledge" *(gnosis)*, or "virtue" *(aretē)*, as it sometimes is, or "temperance" *(sōphrosynē)*, or "wisdom" *(sophia)*, but at the moment we name it, either in the Greek cultural context or in ours, we fall prey to the limitations entailed by the mimetic representation of ideas. Socrates' philosophy develops by grappling with this problem. Naturally, it needs to lay hands on precise concepts, even if only to realize thereafter that exactness led us to miss the point. It is not a matter of hastening to conclude that misty concepts contain the answer to our quandaries. Of the entire array of concepts Socrates scrutinizes, the least well defined and most general is that of "goodness" *(agathon)*, and thus we shall take it as the pilot in our journey to bring into expression this wholesome quality of the human soul that allows man to tell right from wrong. At this point in our journey all that remains to be done is to see whether this wholesome quality is "in" the soul, or the soul itself, and whether it can be grasped or not.

The Greek word *agathon* conveys a sphere of meaning slightly different from the semantic field of our "good." This word in the European and American modern usage means right qualities in adequation to certain conditions. *Agathon*, in contrast, has an adjectival function corresponding to the noun *aretē*, and emphasizes the idea of excellence and of overcoming in the intersection of arts and virtues. *Agathon* is the faculty of realizing a virtue in full in the performance of an art. The virtue is an abstract quality that needs an art to be expressed, but the expression is always incomplete. As a consequence, its ethical implications are subject to cultural, historical, and linguistic conditions prevailing over the context in which the word is used.

Jaeger argues that Socrates lived in a city-state unmistakably foundering, and perhaps for that reason his philosophy looked for inspirational sources in an earlier period, "when the polis was the springhead of all the highest goods and values in life."[5] Under the pressure of the crumbling state, Socrates became a self-styled carrier of God's message, but as we shall see in a moment in our discussion of the *Parmenides,* God neither understood man nor had access to the *agathon* lying within his soul. This quality is different from the arts because a man may be skilled in those and still do evil. Unlike the Christian concept of virtue, in classical Greece this quality remained opaque to God because of his very omnipotence; God could not be humanized to the point of being credited with the knowledge of how to tell right from wrong.[6] Wrongdoing cannot take place in the face of knowledge. The human will always wills good, and if it lands in evil, it is because it lacks knowledge.[7] This propensity to do good is not a quality of things, it is not in the realm of ideas, otherwise it would be much easier to pin it down, it can only be in the soul. We must, however, bear in mind that Socrates' soul is not like the Christian, an ethereal quality defined as spirit, an abstract double of man's life. The Socratic soul is the wholesome quality, now *sophia,* now *agathon,* now *sōphrosynē,* now *gnosis.*

It is worthwhile to compare the Greek philosopher's quest for man's goodness to the pursuit of well-being in psychotherapy. Therapists of any persuasion would agree that they help their patients in their pursuit of well-being. Evidently, when we listen to these therapists talk to each other, we realize how little agreement there is about this underlying notion. Many will even claim that therapeutic discourse serves the interests of controlling people and suppressing freedom, but nobody will wrangle with the idea that the therapeutic discourse in itself is not evil. (Naturally, every candid statement such as this can always be followed by a sophistic and spirited denial.) We cannot simply cross our arms and accept that both Socratic dialogues and therapeutic discourse pursue "goodness," for we have to qualify what "goodness" is. Despite the fact that there are both good and evil, right and wrong, it is generally assumed that all of us always aim at the good and right, while the evil and wrong is a result of circumstances, misjudgments, or of difference of opinions. We do not have, for example, discursive traditions, such as therapy and philosophy going under the category of good, and science and politics filling slots in the roster of evil. Some may think so, but even they will have to admit that the politicians and scientists start off with good intentions. Is this attitude typical of the Western cultural heritage? Other cultural traditions harbor notions of black magic and witchcraft, but we cannot assess the value of their goals with the categories of our own milieu. They have to be evaluated with their own. What we can do is try to translate our goals of "goodness" into theirs and vice versa, but this ought to be done in a dialogue with them and not from within an allegedly neutral scientific discourse. In summary, I am saying that what is good in our cultural heritage is not clearly defined or agreed upon, but that we do have an unrelenting preoccupation with identifying our-selves as good; furthermore, that we cannot say anything else about the others outside our heritage, but we have to talk about these things with them; finally, that the good is not an object to be mimetically described, but a guiding star in the dialogical pursuits of its definition.

The mainstay of Socrates' assignment of *agathon* to the soul is his argument for its immortality, as developed, for example, in the *Phaedo*. In this dialogue, the hypothesis that we learn by recollection is intro-duced.[8] The things we learn are not merely objects exposed to opinions (*doxai*), but ideas endowed with qualities. If the ideas themselves are not deposited in the soul, at least the entity from which they originate is. In order for this hypothesis to hold true the soul must precede the body as well as outlive it. The soul is possessed with intelligence and identical to the absolute realities of beauty and goodness.[9] The binding of the soul to the body is tenuous and temporary, and nothing favors this fugacious link more than philosophy, that is, dialectic.

The theses that the absolute quality of wholesomeness is the immortal soul and that we learn by recollection find their most accomplished discussion in the *Meno*. In this dialogue, Socrates' interlocutor begins with the question of whether virtue can be taught or practiced.[10] As we have seen in all the other dialogues discussed so far, the subject matter of the discussion is replicated by the attitude of the philosopher in the interaction. The *Meno* is no exception to this rule, and while the possi-bility of teaching virtue is denied, the dialogue itself reveals a most virtuous Socrates. He says he does not know what virtue is, while Meno, who claims to know or at least to remember Gorgias' explanation, falls in the same trap of defining virtue by describing that which would be its component parts, a trap disarmed by Socrates so many times in the other dialogues. Socrates comments with good-humored irony, "I seem to be in good luck. I wanted one virtue and I find that you have a whole swarm of virtues to offer."[11] He insists that an answer to this question should single out a common quality shared by all virtues. He tries to make this issue more explicit to Meno and proceeds in a train of thought in which, by analogy with the definition of shape, he will show to Meno what a definition of virtue would look like. His interlocutor, however, is not a novice in the art of rhetoric and skillfully throws the question back to Socrates' field. Then they come to an agreement: Socrates will forward his definition of shape while Meno will forward his of virtue.[12] Socrates says that shape is that which goes with color. This, of course, is an unsatisfactory answer according to his own criteria, and is so intended to test the alertness of his opponent. Meno is alert and rebuffs the careless definition. Socrates then defines shape in terms of a combination of boundary, surface, and density, in what constitutes a wonderful example of precision that can by no means be matched by a definition of the abstract concept of virtue. Meno then asks for a definition of color, and the response comes as Socrates warns, à la Gorgias: "color is an affluence of shapes commensurate with sight and perceptible by it."[13] This definition naturally meets with the warmest approval of Meno, but it is fallacious since it never deals with what color is; it explains color, instead, in terms of shape, which is another quality, and perception, which is a function of color. Socrates tempts his adversary out onto thin ice in order to show him that he does not know how to choose his grounds. The tactic of proving one's point by first showing the absurdity of the other's is characteristic of classical culture. Today it seems to us irritating, an unnecessary sleight of sophistry. The difference is that the power asymmetries of the polity in the ancient Greek world were not veiled, as they are now, by an ideology of egalitarianism. In contemporary society the interactants in both superior and inferior positions in power structures tend to mask the asymmetries, and proceed as if the individuals in the full exercise of their individuality could step outside of the social structure and not only ignore but also alter the power constitution of the interactive setting. Evidently, power positions can be reversed, but not by ignoring them. In our cultural milieu we learn to recognize good fathers, teachers, and bosses whose goodness is not derived from fatherhood, pedagogy, and mastership, but from characteristics of the individuals' personalities. In ancient Greece, the good father was someone good in fatherhood. Substantive goodness was therefore identified with the arts and with the hierarchical constitution of society. It follows that it was natural for someone to proclaim his superiority once he occupied a superordinate position in relation to others. In our cultural context, the self of the individual is progressively regarded as detached from the sociocultural environment, in such a way that we think of ourselves more as entering and departing asymmetrical interactive settings, and we do not take either the blame nor assume the cause for change of the institutional organization of power. For that reason, it becomes unsavory for us to either critique or to praise power superiority. We believe that the power of the individual can counter institutional power, and although we have a utopian ideology of egalitarianism, we go along with the power asymmetries of our cultural setting. The Greeks were their society. Socrates begins to challenge this cultural state of affairs and undertakes what was probably the first step in the direction of creating a self independent of its cultural environment. However, the challenge does not spring from the individual Socrates, but from Socrates as spokesman for man's goodness.

Now comes the turn for Meno to define virtue, and he says that it consists of desiring and being able to acquire fine things.[14] Socrates proves this to be fallacious, because nobody desires evil things, and Meno, struggling to maintain his definitions, ends up by falling back into the fragmentation of virtue.[15] Indignant with his adversary's arguments, Meno's spite flares up, and he accuses Socrates of practicing magic and witchcraft.[16] He says that his lips are numb and that he has become speechless as if stung by a ray. Socrates, who in several passages remarks the use Meno makes of his handsomeness, harps on this topic again, arguing that the only reason for Meno to compare him to an ugly ray is to force him to compare the good looks of his adversary to something beautiful. Says Socrates: "But I am not going to oblige you,"[17] and explains that the perplexity he instills in others is the perplexity he himself feels. This, of course, is not true because he knows his definition of color was flawed, but since his opponent does not critique his definition, but chooses to launch a personal attack, Socrates no longer feels obliged to talk further about his definition and justifies instead his intention.

Here we find another trace of classical culture. A certain symmetry in the development of arguments is expected, and if one discussant raises physical qualities of his adversary as a simile to a point he is making, his opponent is expected to rejoin with a like simile. Socrates moves from the simile—his speech is like the numbness caused by sting rays—to the substance of the argument—perplexity with his definition of color. Instead of acknowledging that perplexity, Meno moves to a different plane in the discussion, that of personal attacks, while Socrates gives a vivid demonstration of virtuous behavior in warding off the provocation, justifying his withdrawal from following suit with the metaphor of physical predicates, and revealing that he himself is perplexed with his own definition of color; why should his adversary then be so defensive about acknowledging that feeling?

Meno, piqued in his hubris, touches a crucial point: he asks Socrates how he is going to search for something if he does not know what it is; because "even if you come right up against it, how will you know that what you have found is the thing you did not know?"[18] This gives Socrates a chance to introduce the subject matter that will dominate the conversation. He says that Meno's point is called the "trick argument" according to which "you cannot try to discover either what you know or what you do not know."[19] The fact, argues Socrates, is that the immortal soul once possessed the knowledge of virtue and so it can be recalled.[20] If you think you do not know something, this is not a reason for you to be complacent and not to search further for it, because in spite of your apparent ignorance, you may find yourself retrieving unexpected knowledge from your soul. Likewise, if you think you do know, this is not a good enough reason for you not to challenge your knowledge. After all, concludes Socrates, "searching and learning are in fact nothing but recollection."[21] Meno asks him for a lesson on the thesis that learning is recollection, but Socrates cunningly responds that that would be impossible without contradicting himself straightaway. But, of course, he can help Meno cull this knowledge out of his soul.

Socrates draws squares on the floor and quizzes one of the servants in the house as he reasons about the amplification of the figure and the ensuing increased numerical magnitudes. First the boy gives bold and incorrect answers. As Socrates proceeds, the boy begins to admit he does not know the answers. Socrates intimates to Meno, "At the beginning he did not know the side of the square of eight feet. Nor indeed does he know it now, but then he thought he knew it and answered boldly—as was appropriate he felt no perplexity. Now he does feel perplexed. Not only does he not know the answer; he doesn't even think he knows."[22] This is a good opportunity for Socrates to further respond to the accusation of being a sting ray, and indeed he does by asking Meno if "in perplexing him [the boy] and numbing him like the sting ray, have we done him any harm?"[23] Meno cannot help but agree with Socrates that they have not. With this demonstration Socrates illustrates his hermeneutics. Before you know anything you must become aware of the prejudices which make you believe you know it, but which in fact only lead you to misrepresent the subject matter.[24]

Now Socrates is ready to unfold the second part of his argument destined to show that one learns through recollection. He proceeds with his geometrical reasoning, but now leading the boy to provide the right answers. This makes it all the more obvious that the boy should have had that knowledge somewhere in his soul (today we would say, "In his unconscious"), for first he gave wrong answers to questions of a simpler kind than those he now correctly answers. Socrates then sums up the results of his demonstration: "So a man who does not know has in himself true opinions on a subject without having knowledge. . . . if the same questions are put to him on many occasions and in different ways, you can see that in the end he will have a knowledge on the subject as accurate as anybody's. . . . This knowledge will not come from teaching, but from questioning. He will recover it for himself."[25]

This notion of knowledge by recollection is typical of oral cultures, although Socrates undoubtedly is not merely voicing a cultural tendency, but grounding the notion on a philosophical bedrock with multiple ontological layers such as the immortality of the soul and the unquestionableness of truth.[26] Today, the thesis that we know by recollection would be regarded with skepticism because literacy gave us the belief that knowledge is in the texts. We learn by reading or by being told by those who read, and regard knowledge as something lying outside us, but available to being grasped if one so wills. In classical and oral culture, knowledge was literally *inside* man, for it was carried on through memory and not in texts. It is interesting, however, to observe that of all the major subcultural traditions of our heritage, only science came to rely absolutely upon texts by virtue of its dependence on the evidential truth of its referents. Philosophy, as long as it remains part of the academic and scientific establishment, emulates science, but a great part of classical philosophy and early Christianity were oral and assumed that knowledge and faith resided within man. The philosophy and Christianity of the age of literacy preserved a strong belief in the inwardness of the wholesome virtue; the philosopher develops his knowledge by thinking, that is, through self-reflection, more than by reading, while the faith is definitely a matter of personal judgment. Politics and psychotherapy appeal to the consciousness of persons and rely on oral persuasion. Science developed a belief in methodology, the assumption that by reading manuals one learns "what" and "how," and became indeed the only system of knowledge, power and rhetoric to assign virtue to the text. (The novel-reading fever did not break out with the advent of literacy, but with the triumph of science.) The prejudice against the notion that we know by recollection, because knowledge stems from the wholesome virtue residing inside man, is embodied in science, with its ancient roots chiefly in Aristotle's writings, and nowhere else does it appear as strongly as in science.

The question whether we know everything is not posed, because, although the objects of knowledge may eventually look separate and scattered, knowing is not a piecemeal activity. The knowledge recollected from the soul is holistic and underlies the knowledge that matters, *gnosis,* but not opinions, *doxai.* This bedrock of knowledge is always there in the soul, justifying our search for what we think we do not know, and it is based on this assumption that Socrates says that "one thing I am ready to fight for as long as I can, in *word and act*—that is, that we shall be better, braver, and more active men if we believe it right to look for what we don't know than if we believe there is no point in looking because what we don't know we can never discover."[27] With this declaration Socrates is ready to resume the inquiry into virtue. At this point Meno gives up his staunch claim to know the answers, and accepts Socrates' method of cross-examination of the subject in which Socrates presents hypotheses to his interlocutor to be agreed upon or refuted on the basis of sound argument.[28] The conversation, in summary, proceeds through the following arguments. First, can virtue be taught? Only if it is knowledge. But is virtue a form of knowledge? This remains unanswered as Socrates turns to the newly arrived Anytus and asks to whom should he go in order to learn virtue. Neither Meno nor Anytus seem to know at first. Socrates provokes them, would it not be the Sophists, those who claim to teach virtue? Anytus is dumbfounded, how could Socrates say such a thing, he who supposedly knows better than anybody that the Sophists' teachings are ruinous? Socrates pretends to be naive as he glibly enumerates the Sophists' deeds. But this is all a provocation aimed at Anytus in order to break down his defenses and enable him to speak from the heart.[29] Anytus, however, unsuspecting, adds criticisms to Socrates' recommendation of the Sophists. Socrates asks how he can know they are so bad if he has never had any experience with them. Anytus says he knows their kind, but he is only expressing the widespread prejudice against the Sophists, which although a true opinion does not count as knowledge since, after all, he does not know whether virtue can or cannot be taught. Socrates pushes towards a more substantial answer, and Anytus finally says that any fine gentleman could teach fine qualities.[30] Socrates asks if these gentlemen taught themselves these qualities, and Anytus says they "learned [them] from forebears who were gentlemen like themselves."[31] Socrates reviews concrete examples of good men in Athens who failed to teach virtue to their sons. One case after another shows that many arts can be taught—horseback riding, throwing the javelin, or wrestling—but not virtue.

Anytus thinks Socrates is attacking Athenian statesmen (he is reputed to be the man, who at Socrates' trial, proposed that the philosopher should be put to death) and warns him to mind his words.[32] Socrates, the skilled teacher/politician/philosopher/therapist, knows well how to steer away from trouble with someone who replaces the arguments he forwards by preconceived opinions, and swiftly turns to Meno in order to ease the tension and preserve the level of consensus. He says, "Anytus seems angry, Meno, and I am not surprised. He thinks I am slandering our statesmen, and moreover he believes himself to be one of them. He doesn't know what slander really is; if he ever finds out he will forgive me.

"However, tell me this yourself. Are there not similar fine characters in your country?"[33]

After Meno ponders that virtue at times seems to be teachable, at other times not, Socrates concludes that "if neither the Sophists nor those who display fine qualities themselves are teachers of virtue, I am sure no one else can be, and if there are no teachers, there can be no students either."[34] He proceeds: "And we have also agreed that the subject of which there were neither teachers nor students was not one which could be taught."[35] Socrates then establishes a parallel between true opinion and knowledge with the example of knowing how to get to a place and therefore being a good guide, and having the right opinion about how to get to a place, and all the same being a good guide.[36] Meno is puzzled at the similarities and differences between the two representations of reality and wonders why knowledge is more praised than true opinion. Socrates explains that true opinions are fleeting objects, but that once they are tethered by the works of reason, they become knowledge. He continues: "That process, my dear Meno, is recollection, as we agreed earlier. . . . That is why knowledge is something more valuable than right opinion. What distinguishes one from the other is the tether."[37]

In the conclusion of the argument, it still remains to be seen whether true opinion and knowledge are natural or acquired.[38] Socrates says that beholders of true opinion are like "prophets and tellers of oracles, who under divine inspiration utter many truths, but have no knowledge of what they are saying."[39] After all, man's virtue is of divine dispensation and that is what knowledge is.[40]

Summing up this part of the argument, Socrates claims that there is one all-encompassing quality in the human soul which it is our task to unravel. In some of the dialogues this quality seems to be virtue, in others knowledge, but it still remains for the philosopher to obtain a good grasp of it. This we will see Plato do in the *Parmenides*, but the grasping of the wholesome quality will not come from either Socrates' discourse, or from Parmenides', although it is the Eleatic philosopher who conducts the discussion; it emerges in the weaving of the conversation, which is a lesson in philosophy to the young Socrates, in the open-endedness of the system of knowledge forwarded, and in the variety of methetic possibilities linking the various parts of the argument.

Will this quality of the human soul emerge in the form of a mimetic picture? If not, how can we know that there is such an ultimate wholesome quality inside man? What kind of experience nourishes Socrates' belief in the existence of that quality if he knows that all that speakers can do is to present mimetic copies of utopias? Naturally, there is a nonutopian reality, but Socrates discards the importance of that kind of knowledge as trivial. A sight may be blurred, a sound indistinct, and so we sharpen our eyes and ears to perceive that object in what we consider a completely satisfactory manner. Perception, however, is not a model for intellectual knowledge, because virtue is not in the same category as the objects in the world exposed to the sensorium. Opinion is also not good enough, because as in the story of the three blind men and the elephant, it is a precarious kind of knowledge and cannot be defended on definite grounds; it is always vulnerable to confutation. The hallmark of ideological knowledge (that which is based on opinion) is the groping in the dark of blurred perceptions. The knowledge of virtue (and this is a pleonastic phrase in the context of Plato's dialogues since knowledge is virtue) has to germinate on totally different grounds. For Socrates the grounds are the dialectic exercised in dialogical situations. It consists in criticizing hypotheses by cross-examining the logic of their constitution until they become untenable, and once we do away with them we progress toward true knowledge. Socrates feels encouraged by the dialectic because it provides the speaker with something beyond rhetoric, outside the encroachments of power positions and independent of any mimetic knowledge of reality. The dialogues are an extensive testimony of this experience, particularly the *Sophist*, the *Statesman*, and the *Parmenides*.

There is no key dialogue in Plato's work, and different periods of scholarship have singled out varying dialogues as having outstanding importance in the Platonic corpus. The *Parmenides* bears witness to issues of contemporary relevance pertaining to the discussion of discourse, what it does to its subject matters, and how its users relate to it. Perhaps it is for that reason that it has been so little studied and only recently attracted the attention of Plato scholars.[41] It is one of the more complex dialogues, and although there have been no doubts about its authenticity, as there have about the *Letters*, for example, the *Parmenides* challenges the understanding of readers acquainted with the other dialogues. It stands away from them and yet strikes a puzzling continuity with them.

The dialogue is divided into three parts: Socrates' attack on Zeno's treatise on paradoxes, Parmenides' demolition of Socrates' ideas, and finally a lesson by Parmenides to Socrates about what the proper philosophical exercise should be. Socrates is young, perhaps in his twenties, while Parmenides is the old founder of the school of Elea, and is probably in his seventies. The references to Parmenides in the *Sophist*[42] and in the *Theaetetus*,[43] in addition to the *Parmenides* itself, show that the leader of the Eleatic school was held in high esteem by Plato, and that his visit to Athens in the 440s B.C. had great impact over the young Socrates. The philosophers of Elea strove to ground knowledge on the art of reasoning. They pursued the assertion of being as one and unchanging by arguing through paradoxes which dissolved notions of plurality, finitude, and limit. The paradox of the unchangeability of things entered the realm of untenable metaphysics, but the claim for the existence of an essential quality redeemable through discourse continued to reappear throughout the entire history of philosophy in arguments ever more powerfully posed.[44]

The narrative structure of the dialogue is peculiar. The conversation between Socrates, Parmenides, and Zeno is reported by Cephalus to a group of friends, repeating an account he heard from Antiphon, who in turn heard it from Pythodoros, who probably was present at the conversation which took place fifty years before. It is ironical that the most mimetic of the dialogues, that is, that one which is a fourfold copy of a real conversation (Plato's writing being the fourth recount), is also one of the most methetic, having the most disquieting impact over its readers. It fulfills, more than any other dialogue, the role of educating its readers by forcing them into a recursive spiral of critical reflections, illuminating the several steps of misunderstanding they can go through in reading the dialogue. It is not a piece to be enjoyed upon a first reading. It is a text in which Plato contradicts his earlier profession of faith against writing, that it is impossible to do philosophy by means of the written word, and leads his reader into the profoundest philosophical reflection. As will be argued in the following discussion, the *Parmenides* is first and foremost the glaring testimony of Socrates' education, showing how much the integration between methexis and mimesis branches off principles inherent in dialogue, and how mimetic pictures of reality which take that fact into consideration in earnest are puzzling.

The central theme of the dialogue is dialectic, something talked about, expressed in the turnings of the argument and in the attitude of the discussants. Dialectic submits mimetic representations of reality to a severe test and prods a methetic reorganization of categories of knowledge. However, in the aftermath of each exercise of critique, we see a new mimetic edifice rise from the ruins of the previous one. Dialectic leads us along the way to virtue, but since we cannot go straight to that essential quality in the heart of dialectic alone, we are in need of the ramparts constituted by these mimetic approximations. This journey calls for a temperate balance in which neither the critique is too demolishing nor the copy of reality too rigid. The paradox of the *Parmenides* resides in the fact that after criticizing Socrates' ideas, Parmenides somehow comes to agree with them. When the time comes for him to express his own ideas, what he presents is a puzzle, a collection of eight hypotheses built up through contradictory assertions, each hypothesis itself contradicting one or more of the others. These antinomies, however, are not built symmetrically, and consequently it cannot be said that paradox is the principle of construction of the *Parmenides*. This characteristic makes that dialogue an open-ended stimulation of possibilities. The reader turns the last page with the sense that a system of knowledge is worth only the moment of its formulation, an effect which is naturally intrinsic to oral discourse, but which the genius of Plato succeeds in capturing and conveying through writing. At the same time, the reader also develops the sense that it may be possible eventually to develop a system of knowledge which is perfect and final.

The dialogue—an elliptical text which I will summarize elliptically—begins with Socrates' critique of Zeno's treatise. The Athenian philosopher reasons that if things are many they must be alike and unlike. Yet this seems to be impossible, for like things must partake of some unlikeness with other things and vice-versa.[45] It then follows that it must be impossible for there to be plurality. In this argument Socrates is hinting at a separation between ideas and things destined to free the former from reification. If ideas can be conceived at this level of abstraction, then it becomes possible for all things to be one and simultaneously share unity and plurality.[46]

Parmenides begins his cross-examination of Socrates' proposition to separate ideas and things by inquiring what the nature of ideas is.[47] The turning point comes when Parmenides asks if there are ideas about things such as hair, mud, and dirt. Socrates first clings to his adamant separation between ideas and things, and calls these three items objects of perception. He soon realizes the difficult position in which he is and admits to being puzzled, accepting that there are ideas relating to these things. Parmenides' reaction is soft and kind, and constitutes a moderate critique. He says that Socrates is still young, "philosophy has not yet taken hold of you so firmly as I believe it will some day."[48] In the *Parmenides* we find the young and unripe Socrates advancing three arguments that he has often rebuked in the other dialogues. First, that the many cannot be one. Second, that the many can be one under special circumstances, when it is ordered in taxonomies, so that at one level of the taxonomy, my right side, for example, is different from my left side, and therefore I am split into this division, but at another level I am one, when in contrast to somebody else. Third, that in partaking of forms, things become those forms, in a way accruing to the fact that largeness or beauty, for example, make a thing be large or beautiful to the exclusion of all other possible outstanding characteristics. Parmenides razes these ideas to the ground, but with arguments quite different from those employed by Socrates in other dialogues. The teaching to be derived from this contrast is that arguments or rhetorical maneuvers cannot be fixed, as the Sophists thought, but must adapt to the peculiarities of each speaker in relation to his interlocutor, within each particular conversational situation.

The second attack on Socrates' ideas examines the participation of the plurality of things in one idea or in parts of it. Parmenides' argument here is sophistic, because while he claims that things earn their predicates from ideas, they cannot participate in the ideas.[49] Socrates tries to escape this besieging by thrusting forms into thoughts and thoughts into the mind.[50] Parmenides refutes this solution with the argument that if form and thought are blended, thought becomes form and vice versa, and the antagonism between wholeness and partition of forms continues to hold true. Socrates cannot help but agree. Ironically, Socrates is accepting an argument that he refuted in Zeno earlier, and that interestingly enough produces the same effect of his theory of ideas, that is, the reification of forms. Since ideas cannot stand by themselves, they lose their autonomy and join in the world of things. How much of "idea" and how much of "thing" do they become? Gadamer very aptly addresses this issue in his overall view of the *Parmenides*, pointing out that there can be "no collected whole of possible explications either for a single *eidos* [form] or for the totality of *eidē*."[51] If you wish to explain a single form on all its sides, you "have to mark it off from all other *eidē* as well."[52] Given that it is impossible to represent the whole of ideas or the whole of discourse in any particular discourse action, it follows that our knowledge is always limited to a certain horizon.[53]

Socrates struggles once again to move away from the corner into which Parmenides pushed him, and argues that perhaps the forms are "patterns fixed in the nature of things," and that it is these patterns which participate in the ideas.[54] Parmenides defeats this with an infinite regress type of argument, according to which, in order for the presence of the pattern in the idea and in the thing to be proven, a third idea is necessary, a meta-idea which establishes the link.[55] As can be seen in his lesson in philosophy, Parmenides leads Socrates through a progressive de-reification of ideas. From the bold statement that ideas are things, Socrates moves on to a more refined notion of ideas as thoughts; then he goes further on to identify ideas as patterns. He finally lands on the assertion that ideas are an autonomous whole opposed to things, which amazingly is his initial contention, now filtered through several refining arguments.

Toward the conclusion of his debate with Socrates, Parmenides shows that everything in the world is related, a master to a slave, and the slave to his master, one is not possible without the other.[56] This forms the network of reality identified by our knowledge.[57] If the forms are not part of this reality, then we do not know them, nor do we know what beauty and goodness are.[58] If, says Parmenides, "a man refuses to admit that forms of things exist or to distinguish a definite form in every case, he will have nothing on which to fix his thought, so long as he will not allow that each thing has a character which is always the same, and in so doing *he will completely destroy the significance of all discourse.*

"What are you going to do about philosophy, then? Where will you turn while the answers to these questions remain unknown?"[59]

Socrates answers that he does not know and asks Parmenides to advise him. In the course of his advice, the Eleatic philosopher says, "If you want to be thoroughly exercised, you must not merely make the supposition that such and such a thing *is* and then consider the consequences; you must also take the supposition that that same thing *is not.*"[60] Then, in a brief and revealing excursus, he shows the nature of the procedure. It looks so elusive that Socrates asks him to expatiate on the subject matter, which prompts Parmenides into the long formulation of the eight hypotheses about the one and the others and their relations to one another, to unity and multiplicity, and to time. If all things are related in the world, as Parmenides says, methexis is an exercise in reconstruction of states of affairs that are, before they are reconstructed. Is the result of this methetic organization of things a mimetic copy of reality? In other words, are the pictures of the world that we form with our intelligence, using our communicative habitude, copies of the *eidē* which we never succeed in grasping? The answer to these questions is "No," because otherwise how could we ever know that there are real forms and that our appropriation of reality is always a copy? This is a point made rather clear in the *Meno* and in the *Parmenides*, where Plato shows that the game between mimesis and methexis is not supposed to end in a tie, as the *Parmenides* may lead many readers to conclude. Parmenides' image of the man who refuses to admit the existence of forms marks the limits of possibilities for the practice of philosophy. The negation of forms of behavior would entail the same dilemma for the psychotherapist who, in the absence of a diagnostic and treatment plan, would be reduced to the role of an ad hoc communicator and be rendered unable to practice therapy. But Plato is not suggesting that we resume our exercises in forming opinions and that along the way of successive mimetic approximations we eventually grasp the essential form. Forms are not scattered in the world and subject to piecemeal retrieving. First, they constitute a whole. Second, this whole lies in the soul. The man who refuses their existence blocks off the way to his soul, that is, crushes the possibility of communication with others. Notice that in contrast to the Christian idea that we tap our souls upon self-reflection and introspection, in the Socratic rhetoric of reason, we do so in talking with others. Notice, furthermore, that the Freudian probing of the unconscious flows in two different channels, one closer to the guilt-ridden Christian introspection, the dreams, and the other closer to the pagan spirit of the Socratic dialogue, the psychoanalytic session. Insight for Freud derives from the combination of these two.

Parmenides warns Socrates that the man who denies the existence of forms destroys "the significance of all discourse," because discourse for this man becomes an erratic journey in which the meaning of the words lies in what they do to the interlocutor, satisfying the speaker's intentions. For Plato, the function of the word is to clasp this holistic *eidos*, and exhaust it in its being. But the word does not do this alone since the *eidos* is intrinsic to man, and more than in language, it is ground in the mill of the human soul. The vehicle between language and soul conveying forms back and forth is dialectic. But it cannot accomplish this function of go-between in the absence of communicative consensus. Insofar as ideological consensus is concerned, the dialectic sheds light upon opinionative preconceptions constituting mimetic copies of reality, which create in us the illusion that we know. But it also provides grounds for the recreation of systems of knowledge. Dialectic quells our craving for positive knowledge at the same time that it whets our appetite in a tantalizing performance. The puzzle of dialectic is the following: the moment we oppose dialogue and representation, a whirlpool is formed under our feet because one cannot live without the other; when, instead, we realize the complementariness between dialogue and representation, we completely trivialize their dialectic function, transforming the pair into the most banal representation.

What are some of the consequences of holding such a view of

matters? First, since discourse is obliged to mimetic pictures of reality, and since these in turn depend on discourse, neither function can have a telos of its own. But neither can they have a telos together or we would be forced to believe that we had finally arrived at the perfect knowledge, or alternatively, that such type of knowledge is impossible, that which would call our quest into question again. This is the puzzling conclusion of the *Parmenides*. However, the fact that this is not the last dialogue, that in fact there is not a final dialogue, indicates that the search must continue, and that it will eventually find its end, man's wholesome quality, that is, the ethical imperative of life.

For Plato, the soul of man is not *tabula rasa*, the desolate ground where the wranglings of uncertainty played havoc, and where new mimetic copies of illusion will rise. The soul of man is good, it is the ethical imperative of the absolute virtue, whatever name we decide to call it, whatever description we choose to impart to it. Socrates attacks the written text in the *Phaedrus* because it enters the soul as a spurious substance, and contrary to what the god Theuth says, it does not enhance memory, but dislodges it from its abode. Nonetheless, memory cannot be equated with the objects of knowledge, and although a text can rob those objects from memory and even numb memory by rendering it slack, it cannot disable it as the Egyptian king Thamous so much feared.[61] In times of transition, tradition seems shaken up and may indeed be completely abandoned or radically altered. Socrates' Athens was unquestionably experiencing one such historical period, and the projects for termination, preservation, or change were radical. Socrates wanted to preserve the Attic cultural heritage, and in his unsparing effort he often mixed the narrower goals of conservatism in his polity with the loftier philosophical aims. Instead of speaking for the preservation of the immediacy and wholesomeness of discourse, he spoke for the maintenance of oral discourse as opposed to written; instead of concerning himself with the fact that certain objects of memory could be lost, he developed the much greater fear that the faculty of memory could come to an end. But he conducted himself with moderation and exactness in the pursuit of the ethical foundation of man's life. Although he referred to this foundation with the word *agathon*, Socrates was aware of the simplification inevitably entailed by such linguistic enclosure, and did not allow his search for virtue to be disarmed or forestalled by such closure. This is the Socrates that Plato bequeathed to us and whose ideas twenty-five centuries later are astonishingly fresh to our senses and relevant to our lives today.

Conclusion

The dilemmas of Socrates' philosophy introduce cultural themes in the Western heritage that we have grappled with since the Greek philosophers and with which we have not yet come to grips. These themes can be summarized as follows. First, we have the problem of the mimetic copying of reality. Our pictures have systematically been imperfect and perishable. Should we keep trying to arrive at a perfect portrayal, or should we give up altogether on mimetic depicting? We saw that mimetic copying cannot be reduced to any particular medium —oral discourse, written text, or other—but can be carried out by all media. In addition, methexis has the capacity to overcome the limitations of mimesis, but it needs mimetic copies in order to unfold. However, if we assume that our mimetic copies of reality are mere fodder for our methetic exercises, then mimesis fails to accomplish its end, and such an incomplete representation of reality cannot properly fuel methexis. A balance between methexis and mimesis is necessary, but is also difficult to obtain. This creates the tension which constitutes one of the main dilemmas of our cultural heritage.

Second, this dilemma has a corollary in the skepticism about knowledge. The denial of knowledge in our heritage has always been self-defeating, either leading to more knowledge or to sterility. The dashing of knowledge has been equated with madness, to the complete dissolution of the communicative link binding us together. The importance of knowledge does not derive from the fact that it buttresses our security in the world by feeding our illusion that we have a complete representation of reality. It stems from the fact that our knowledge of the world constitutes the sinews linking our lives to the ethical moral bone, keeping us upright, and the thread of life flowing. Sophism in its several historical reoccurrences severed those sinews and invariably went limp.

Third, Socrates' philosophy arises as a project integrating different spheres of discourse into one, which searches for the wholesome quality. The hallmark of the rhetor, exemplified by Socrates' testimony, welds together the philosopher, the educator, the politician, and the therapist. This rhetor has to search for himself, but he has to do so in the company of others, helping and being helped. He has to be persuasive and aware of the power asymmetries surrounding him, and at the same time he cannot be selfish, but must keep in his mind the entire polity. Finally, he is not going to find a favorable environment, opposition will often be extreme, and he will find himself talking to those whose preconceptions prevent them from hearing what the philosopher actually says. Thus the rhetor must also be a healer in the sense that he must not only state the truth but also dissolve his audiences' resistances/ misconceptions.

Fourth, this pursuit of philosophy, furthering of education, practice of politics, and administering of healing cannot be carried out only by exhibiting the knowledge that the rhetor believes to be true, or by using a position of power superiority which smooths the way of persuasion, or through sophisticated rhetorical ruses which blunt the sight without awakening the mind. The task of the rhetor is to keep the thread of consensus flowing. The success in this endeavor does not depend so much on any outright effort, but on the knowledge that communicative consensus, which is based on the linguistic, cognitive-expressive, speech, and institutional power dimensions of consensus, is unbreakable; and that ideological consensus, which resides in flexible structures of power and on opinion, or point of view, can be broken without any consequences to the overall consensus that binds us together. This overall consensus is grounded on the ethical imperative which is in turn our communicative habitude.

Fifth and finally, man's wholesome quality, now virtue, now wisdom, now knowledge, now goodness, is the ethical imperative, that is, the communicative consensus. The dialectic is an expression of this faculty, and at the same time a means to bring it to fruition.

PART THREE

CONCLUSION

11 THERAPEUTIC DISCOURSE AND

SOCRATIC DIALOGUE

> *. . . in the power of self-reflection, knowledge and interest are one. . . . the unity of knowledge and interest proves itself in a dialectic that takes the historical traces of suppressed dialogue and reconstructs what has been suppressed.*
> Jürgen Habermas

> Japanese
> philosopher: *Now I am beginning to understand better where you smell the danger. The language of the dialogue constantly destroyed the possibility of saying what the dialogue was about.*

> Inquirer: *Because I now see still more clearly the danger that the language of the dialogue might constantly destroy the possibility of saying that of which we are speaking.*
> Martin Heidegger

Freud's reaction against religion was similar in nature to Socrates' reaction against the Sophist philosophers. Each, in his own time, rose against what appeared to be a soaring tide of belief in the power of rhetoric to persuade people to pursue a hollow goodness in life. In retrospect, we see that both the sophistic educational project and the religious sway over moral judgment were declining during the days of both Socrates and Freud, respectively, and probably one of the reasons for such a triumphant success of their ideas must be sought in the fact that they spoke out so vehemently against a state of affairs which they regarded as threatening, and yet which was in fact dying. Nowhere is this oppositional vocation more manifest than in the rhetoric of the Socratic and Freudian programs. The preceding order had committed excesses in the sphere of rhetoric, taking ideas for granted and overlooking the legitimacy of the knowledge it propounded. By sharpening their discursive abilities, the educational and religious preachers had enabled themselves to turn people's minds, assuming that their own purposes were the good ones. Socrates and Freud introduced a word of caution, warning that the preacher's blinding belief in what he preached was in itself evil, and could lead to catastrophe. As a consequence of this position, they could not reveal anything less than skepticism about their own ideas which, ironically, they had raised on one hand as an antidote to the rhetorical excesses and on the other hand as an alternative to the raging flows of those systems of belief that they opposed. This constraint led them to develop rather intriguing projects of knowledge, incomplete, open-ended, self-contradictory, yet deeply compelling.

The rhetoric of their programs also had to be restrained. The Socratic philosopher could not persuade his interlocutor outright, but had to help him draw the hidden knowledge out of his own soul. The process was enlightening for both rhetor and disciple. The therapist, by the same token, does not argue with his client, he shows, indicates, but does not exhort. Nevertheless, the philosopher did persuade his disciple, with the best argument, of an idea he believed legitimate, and the therapist equally persuades his patient of his view of matters, which he considers correct. The critics of Plato's philosophy and of Freud's therapy have persistently drawn on this point, wishing that the rhetors under attack either made explicit their rhetorical maneuvers, or abandoned the claim that they taught nothing. Socrates remained undaunted by his contemporary critics, and rebuffed with punctilious stoicism the accusations that he was "like a sting ray," or that he employed vicious arguments, to the embarrassment of his adversaries and to the delight of the readers of the dialogues. He is unquestionably the hero in those dramas, his heroism as well as the causes he espoused remain alive, even compelling to us. In many ways he is a character of Homeric Greece, in which truth is heroism. Therapists, in turn responding to the same challenge that they make explicit their rhetorical maneuvers or relinquish the claim that they do not persuade their interlocutors, became divided into two camps: those who subscribe to a system of knowledge describing conduct pathology, and those for whom every verbal transaction in everyday life or in therapy is a master of rhetoric. Psychoanalysis illustrates the former position while family therapy represents the latter, although in the recent times the proponents of an analysis of transference have turned their attention to rhetoric, while systemic therapists have tried to encompass communication within a system of knowledge.

Socrates carried out an unrelenting critique of written texts, of the old

Greek culture based on narratives of the past, and of the beatified extolling of history. Texts were unacceptable because they robbed knowledge from the interior of man's soul, that is, from memory, placing it on a sheet of paper. Furthermore, they concealed the speaker, thrusting a wedge between author and speech, which made the text look a great deal more truthful than it in fact was; no one was available to take responsibility for what the text said, and the statements could live on endlessly, without having to respond to criticism, keeping alive ideas that could be untruthful. Narratives, in the form of poems or tragedies, myths or tales, were equally unacceptable, because they invited a passive audience, as well as a prompt and uncritical acceptance of what was said. The knowledge conveyed in texts and narratives was consequently unreliable. Socrates chose oral discourse in dialogical situations as the medium within which to integrate knowledge with rhetoric. Nonetheless, Plato wrote the dialogues, and the Socrates whom we know is more a literary character than a historical figure, although so powerful that he has gained an enormous historical dimension. Socrates tells myths and tales in the dialogues, and as we saw in chapter 6, his opposition against the mimetic copy of reality does not target the medium of literacy or poetry, but a certain strategy to integrate knowledge and rhetoric within those media, the sophistic approach, which he regards as pernicious. He chose dialectic and dialogue because, in this context, knowledge could be restituted to the interior of man, and the habitude of its awakening could grow in real situations—not in the absence of one of the parties, momentarily represented by a text—and agreement could be obtained by means of the unavoidable magnetism of truth, instead of a tricky figure of speech.

In the time of Socrates, literacy had not taken hold of Greece; it was not a medium of communication posing a threat to oral culture. However oral Socrates' milieu was, in their efforts to resolve the tension between knowledge and rhetoric, Plato and Socrates summoned texts and narratives to their aid. Ironically, in the end, his testimony only survived to our day because of Plato's narration, bequeathing it to us in writing. The power of his textual narrative is such that we do not regard Plato only as a writer, the dialogues as a literary creation, and Socrates as a character in the dramas. Plato is the founder of Western philosophy and the *Dialogues* are one of our bibles for the project of integrating knowledge, power, and rhetoric, within the framework of argumentative reason.

The tension between knowledge and rhetoric resides in the difficulty of deciding what knowledge is, and what persuasion by argument is. Every system of knowledge exudes its rhetoric, and every rhetoric presupposes a system of knowledge, however unaware of it the rhetor is. Socrates tried to come to grips with this dilemma in the dialogues by making knowledge not the property of the philosopher, but the disciple's hidden treasure, by making rhetoric an art to persuade his interlocutors, not for the purpose of accepting what he said, but to continue to talk without foregoing dialectic. It is in this choice of dialogue that we find the most obvious resemblance between the Socratic and the therapeutic objects, but if dialogue was a difficult undertaking in Socrates' times, it has become even more so in ours.

Therapeutic discourse is also based on dialogue, but in contrast to the Socratic tête-à-tête, it takes place in the heart of a sociocultural tradition dominated by literacy, and if on one hand the transactions between patient and therapist are oral, on the other hand they are deeply informed by the constitution of therapy in texts. To begin with, the knowledge which the therapist brings into play does not entirely derive from his experience—it can be found in books—and although training in therapy is largely conducted through the practice of therapy itself, it depends on books and articles where the methods, theories, and principles are spelled out. The therapeutic knowledge is not something natural, to be realized in the person's potential during the flowing of the interaction. Even those therapists who seem to take the most radical position against preconceived knowledge, the systemic family therapists, who draw heavily on the intuitions they have in the here-and-now of the session, textualize their knowledge of human communications, trying to find principles and regularities in it. They claim, as we saw in chapters 3 and 4, that problems are definitions of a certain communicative setting, that the group of patients and therapists constitute one such setting, and that the therapist's task, therefore, is to avoid the perpetuation of the problem. The therapist's interventions, then, become noninterventions: he talks to avoid being sucked into the system; he uses his authority as a healer to relinquish his authority, freeing the patients from the belief that he will do something for them; he prescribes the symptoms which were originally brought in as diagnoses; he participates in the flow of communication as a strategy for not having a manipulative influence over his clients.

These caveats, on the whole, however spontaneous and forged in the heat of the here-and-now, once written down and organized into a comprehensive corpus of procedures, become textual guidelines for action. The therapist who employs them must be trained, he must rehearse, and even if he does this in the actual clinical practice, his verbal actions are clumsy in the beginning and specious in the end, and never have the freshness of a spontaneous conversation. The question hastens to mind: What is spontaneous conversation? Are not all verbal interactions inscribed within predefined cultural settings? Yes. But the spontaneous conversation in situations of everyday life springs from practical reason, and not from textual programs for action. The impatient reader may wonder at this point whether I am not claiming that practical reason is the limit of all knowledge, or the opening for the growth of knowledge, and whether practical knowledge may not equally be the object of cultural predefinitions. Attempts to describe the entire gamut of practical reason or to identify its rules and principles are obviously futile because we do not have complete control over all the things we say. In addition, our common sense is invariably colored by language and culture, but linguistic and anthropological descriptions, as well as grammar and cultural ethos do not replace or overlap with practical reason. There are two cultural inventions, however, which seem to allow us a fuller participation among language, culture, and practical reason. These are dialogue and self-reflection. Both are open-ended, the outcome of each can neither be foreclosed by projections nor by reconstructions, and both are also incompatible with one another, since dialogue "thematizes" interpersonal relations, while self-reflection "thematizes" thought contents. In a way, these two cultural habits perform the same function, that of arguing ideas and beliefs, but while one does it in a context of oral culture, through the participation of several speakers, the other carries it out in the context of literate culture, by allowing the thinker to take some distance from discourse.

Therapeutic discourse is oral in a very different sense from the Socratic dialogue, just as it was literary in ways very different from a therapy manual. In a literate culture, the texts are charts for action, reality is mapped out, and the actor's success depends on his studiousness. In oral ancient Greece, appearance, loquacity, and character played an important role. Socrates made the best use he could of his ugliness, and denounced the seductive appeal of Meno's handsome looks and Theaetetus' charm. A therapist may at times employ his innate gifts for therapeutic purposes, but within our literate heritage we learn to assume a degree of separation between our discursive behavior and our personal identities. Personalities are not absolute; a meek person can be trained as a forceful therapist, or a strong personality may learn how to restrain itself in the name of therapeutic success. These are accomplishments of self-reflection, which in turn became possible with the textualization of discourse. Despite this self-reflective character, the resolution of the therapeutic interaction has to be conducted through verbal actions and in dialogue. There are euphemistic ways for the therapist to say, "Wait, I do not know about that problem, I have to consult my book, or my supervisor, I need more time to think about it," but the relationship has to be brought to a conclusion on the interactive basis of turn-taking in conversation and of formulating adequate questions and satisfactory answers. Psychoanalysts naturally push the problem into the mechanics of the psyche. The analyst is himself analyzed, and although he may fail to be efficient as a therapist because of one of those numerous accidents of understanding plaguing communicative interactions, Freud provided us with a theory of symbols powerful enough to account for the majority of such mishaps. As a consequence, in order to be efficient, the therapist has to know, but he has to acquire such a knowledge. Family therapists are caught in an absolutely identical bind. Despite all the claims they make for rhetoric, despite their rejection of symbols accompanied by a profession of faith in the belief of communication as an open-ended process, they cannot help trying to describe and foreclose their dialogues as if they had complete control over them. In the end, family therapy favors a system of knowledge as much as psychoanalysis does, following the Freudian project, which leans more heavily upon the knowledge pillar of the epistemological edifice.

While the narrative mode of discourse was problematic for Socrates—who regarded himself as standing on the cusp of two eras, one dominated by poetry in epic narrative, the other involved with dialogical arguments—in a literate culture the narrative mode has become a relic preserved within texts and speech. Narratives are seen as speech actions, side-by-side with questions and answers, or as literary genres, together with poetry and satire. Freud paid a great deal of attention to narrative because he realized that it was the thread of narration which strung the symbols together, and thus he developed his method of deconstruction of the patient's narratives in order to reconstruct them, splicing them into the psychoanalytic narrative (see chapter 2). He also realized that the logic of narratives in speech was one thing, and the logic of narratives in dreams another. The latter provided us with a better access into the psyche than the former. The psychoanalytic narrative itself, with its mythical tales of Oedipus and Narcissus, was closer to the narrative language of dreams. Notice that, although Freud cast therapeutic discourse in a dialogical context, he preserved its narrative expression. (In the session of psychoanalysis transcribed in chapter 2, we find the patient acting as if it were a dialogue, while the analyst, by training, acts as a narrator and hearer of narratives, as a literary critic who edits the patient's narrative. The two family therapists whose sessions we transcribed in chapters 3 and 4 act no differently, and edit alike the stories their patients tell.) If therapeutic discourse is torn at one end between dialogue and text, it is equally rent at the other end between dialogue and narrative.

Power has been a hovering ghost, long tormenting the Western systems of knowledge and rhetoric. The attitude prevailing in classical and Christian culture, condemning the exercise of power as evil, has become deeply seated in the values of European and American societies. This prejudice against power created two interesting consequences. First, that the unacknowledged power, that is, the superiority exercised by means of a hidden hand, is more efficacious than overt power. Second, if power is assumed to be evil a priori, then it becomes more difficult to justify or legitimize any use of power. The Christian critique of power too readily equated hierarchy with domination, and in so doing eroded the very ground from which the exercise of power could be criticized. The consequence of the Christian radical criticism was certainly not the elimination of social asymmetries, but the obscuring of issues of domination by an exaggerated concern with power alone. In the Christian ideology, change had to bring about an elimination of power asymmetries, and since this was an impossible task within the categories of culture, which value difference and hierarchy as much as equality and harmony, the specific critique of domination became enfeebled.

This state of affairs led to the use of power as unabashed manipulation behind the scene, an issue which struck thinkers like Hobbes and Machiavelli, but the new identification of power with its terroristic use only contributed to a more indignant a priori critique addressed to the essence of asymmetry rather than to the actual use of power. The tide changed with Marx's critique of society. Marx posited that history was the product of conflict between social classes. He analyzed the ways in which power hierarchies changed over time within specific social formations. The proletariat, the revolutionary class, lacked power during a certain historical period, but in the following it would acquire power at the same time that it would put an end to domination. After Marx it became clear that power in itself was not evil but its exercise for the purpose of domination was. Thinkers such as Nietzsche, Freud, and Foucault harbored a fascination for the study of power, but refused to equate its positive exercise with any meaningful sociocultural spheres of life. Power became something immanent, as much a tantalizing reality as Socrates' knowledge embedded in the human soul was.

Freud was quite aware that he could not make power the central objective of the psychoanalytic project. Adler and Jung tried, the former by attributing all neurotic behavior to the inferiority complex, the latter by outlining a therapeutic strategy aiming at uplifting man's soul and lowering that of divinity, but both failed. Freud knew that if on one hand the complete denial of power, the power appeal of martyrdom (Socrates and Jesus), was no longer persuasive, on the other hand the outright claim for power was still shrouded in prejudice. The analyst's power, as foreseen by him, fell strictly within the canons of the Western cultural expectations and condemnations. Freud insightfully welded this ambivalence about power into his understanding of the psyche. In *Totem and Taboo*[1] he studies taboo as the source of a collective defense mechanism. He finds in the act of repression two permanent components: the anxiety triggered by fear and the love triggered by desire. At the level of individual behavior this tension between anxiety and love is exemplified through the case of little Hans. It is possible to treat him for his aggressive impulse towards his father, symbolized by his fear of being bitten by a horse, because this feeling is not hegemonic and shares Hans' heart with the feeling of love for his father.[2] The duality of emotions in collective symbols is exemplified by the ritual killing of an enemy, in which there is both hostility and admiration for the victim. The hostility is expressed in the act of killing, the admiration, in the grief ensuing from the act and in the purifying and expiatory rituals through which the killer goes.

The model of analyst carved in Freud's theory and clinical practice is rather ambiguous insofar as his power claims go. Freud's analyst is cut out in diametrical opposition to one of the first syndromes of psychopathology that he discovered, the hysterical type. Hysteria is characterized by hyperaction of a hallucinatory nature. The Freudian analyst is quiet, invisible (he sits behind the patient), speaks briefly in a low and subdued tone of voice; he is an impassive character whose emotions are not supposed to show in the course of treatment. The analyst naturally has an enormous amount of power over the analysand, but he cannot use it to cure him. He has to wait for the patient to "free associate" and learn by insight; he can facilitate this task, but cannot use persuasion. Moreover, insight is not generated at the surface of ideas and opinions, but in the depth of the psyche, where it pierces emotions (affects), bringing them out into facial expression. Freud makes sure that insight is grounded on emotions, otherwise it could result from rational agreement obtained through verbal negotiation. Everytime the psychoanalyst uses his power unawares, the interpretation backfires, triggering negative transference in the patient. Power is not the subject of Freudian psychoanalysis but, however veiled, its object.

Freud's power is the power of desire, the power of the will, and as such it precedes all structures of meaning. What is gained in the process of psychoanalysis that critical theorists and hermeneutic philosophers so well perceived is not the substantiation of the metapsychology, the triumph of one power position over another, or the proof that the rhetoric of insight is superior to other forms of persuasion, but a self-reflective consciousness experiencing itself as relatively independent from the content of knowledge, constellations of power asymmetries, and rhetorical strategies. It is a process very similar to that of the critique of ideology, as sponsored by the Frankfurt School in particular, and critical theory in general, in which the criticized ideology is not replaced by another. The critique is addressed not only to particular power quests but to the will-to-power itself. Unlike the Christian critique, however, the psychoanalytic does not exempt itself from self-criticism. As a consequence, it dismisses to a certain extent its dialogical vocation and comes to rely too heavily on self-reflection. Freud's project does not propose a world without neurosis, but a world which is at the same time neurotic and conscious. Consciousness naturally dispels neurosis, but the full development of consciousness is such a distant possibility that Freud prudently refrained from speculating that far. The psychoanalytic consciousness of the neurotic patient prevents him from indulging in utopia and only allays his disquietude insofar as understanding assuages the mind, but he remains basically a disenchanted being, who as the critic of society realizes its wrongs, may even try to act, but realizes that his most reliable undertaking resides in furthering his understanding.

Socrates sets out to discover what virtue, goodness, and knowledge are. By choosing dialogue as his mode of discourse, his quest becomes verbal and interactive, and not introspective and reflective: the knowledge to be gained is not the product of reflection but of debate. Naturally, Socrates does not join the debates as a candid equal of his adversaries. The superiority he feels himself invested with is associated with his stringent criteria to accept statements and not with any system of knowledge which he already has. Rhetoric for him is merely a useful tool. He employs rhetorical maneuvers identical to those of the Sophists, but in contrast to them, rhetoric for him has heuristic and not ontological value. Power, similarly, is a playful instrument, like a seesaw, alternating subordination and superordination. Unlike the Sophists he meets, such as Protagoras and Gorgias, who enjoy prestige in certain institutional circles and make the most of this advantage to forward their arguments, Socrates prefers to start off from an underdog position. The impact of his persuasive appeal comes in large measure from the contrasts he establishes between the boisterousness of his adversaries' untenable claims and the modesty of his inquisitiveness which proves them wrong. (This triumph of the true and modest over the false and boastful is a typical trait of classical culture which was appropriated by

Conclusion

Christianity in its radical critique of power.) Notice, however, that Socrates always triumphs over his adversaries in the dialogues (with the exception of the *Parmenides*), and consequently his claim for inferiority in power asymmetries can only be regarded as a strategy and not as a goal. Power is the object of his philosophical project (sometimes even its explicit project as in the *Republic*), but as in Freud, what is rendered explicit is knowledge. Power and rhetoric although ancillary to knowledge, are recognized as fundamental and fully employed by both the Socratic and Freudian epistemological programs.

In psychoanalysis, the therapist conducts himself as if all power tensions in interpersonal relationships could be resolved by a system of knowledge over which he, not the patient, has control. Evidently, the power disclaimer raised by his personal attitude is self-contradictory, just as Socrates' was, because clashes of interests are to be resolved within his system of knowledge, and not in negotiations and compromise with his interlocutor. Family therapists, unlike psychoanalysts, employ interpersonal power in their clinical strategies, exhorting the patients by all the means at their disposal to undertake certain courses of action, while avoiding others. The analysis of transference is naturally a step to remedying the contradictory power attitude of psychoanalysis. The analyst of transference relinquishes his power by accepting that certain experiences may fall outside the interpretive realm of competence of psychoanalytic theory. (In the analysis of transference, for example, the patient in chapter 2 would be assuaged by a therapist who would tell her that although her complaints against her boss were genuine, those complaints reminded the analyst that she could be experiencing similar feelings towards analysis and towards her therapist.) The therapist thus abdicates the right conferred upon him by psychoanalytic theory, accepting that certain statements made by the analysand may remain impenetrable to his analytical tools.

Every relation needs a sociocultural weld to keep the parties together within the institutionally defined framework. Socrates' debates, as we saw in chapters 7 and 8, were part of an Athenian tradition which brought to the sports centers young men in the pursuit of rhetorical skills, or politicians seeking followers. They contended with words as the wrestlers did with their bodies in the arena. Socrates, of course, did not regard these exchanges lightly, but he took advantage of the institutional context to try to turn the minds of those people, especially because the rulers of the city-state were recruited from their midst and he supposed that his disciples would make better rulers. Plato created the Academy and institutionalized the training of rhetors. Psychotherapeutic discourse is well established in cultural institutions, and continues to foray into hitherto inaccessible pockets of society through the omnipresent action of social agencies such as school districts, hospitals, guidance centers, police departments, and courts. Many patients choose the kind of therapy they want to have, while others soon realize what kind of service they are receiving, and enjoying its benefits, learn to appreciate its qualities. The conditions for a therapist to establish himself are similar to those applying to medical doctors, the support of an institution, or of a well-known sponsor, until the therapist develops a stable clientele. Today's therapist does not have to advocate his art, as the Sophist and the physicians had to do in ancient Greece, when their métiers were little known.

Before therapeutic discourse became institutionalized, existential problems were dealt with by the religious authority or by a relative or friend drawing on religious moral principles. The basis for this type of counseling was the same that underscores therapeutic discourse, that is, communicative consensus (linguistic, cognitive-expressive, speech practices, and institutionalized power hierarchies). Therapists do not seek ideological consensus with their patients through negotiation and compromise; the institution of the clinic is surrounded by the expectation that those who work for it have the expertise in the resolution of the problems. However, the subject matter dealt with by therapeutic discourse is of a very special nature; it is constituted by issues of ideological dissension. When the patient accepts the authority of the therapist without reservation, he accepts his view of matters, follows his advice and thereby feels better. Critical patients are treated for resistance by psychoanalysts, or bombarded with paradoxical messages by certain schools of family therapy, because the community of therapists is defined as endowed with authority over diagnosing, as well as over deciding what the cure should be.

Socrates, like our contemporary therapists, was presented by Plato as one invested with the authority to formulate questions and judge whether knowledge is tenable or untenable. However, Socrates did not act in accordance with a socially recognized institution; in order to keep his dialogical therapy going, he had to insure his adversaries' adherence to the dialogue. In the Athenian polity strewn with controversy, difficult interlocutors were to be avoided and unrewarding debates dropped (the goal of debating was victory). Socrates would not be an enticing contender, first because he did not regard the disputes as games, and second because the young rhetors in the *Gymnasium* were no match for his rhetorical skills. He had to lead his flock with the utmost care, restraining the awesomeness of his argument in order not to scare them away before they engaged in the debate, and wooing them to persevere once the discussion had started. His strategy to do this was the unrelenting maintenance of ideological consensus. Each new point in the discussion could only be undertaken once a previous issue had been agreed upon. For him it was more important to keep ideological consensus around the perplexity of ignorance than to advance knowledge in the absence of agreement. The dialogues are not chapters in a treatise of knowledge, but representations of different degrees of ignorance. The ideological consensus pursued by Socrates, however, should not violate the logic of reason; the only alternative to resistance or denial of a step in reasoning was retreat from that to a simpler level with the preservation of logical thinking. For Socrates it was rather clear that every time that reason broke down, rhetoric began. Having chosen dialogue in an oral context for his medium of expression, Socrates could only regard reason as a consensual welding binding together speaker and interlocutor. As a consequence, the art of dialogue was more important than the content of what was said.

Therapists often find themselves in a similar situation, pursuing ideological consensus with their patients by learning how they talk about the issues and by avoiding assertions that could create conflict with their interlocutors. Even those therapists who work with paradoxical messages, as well as other interventions which confront rather than coax the patients, gauge the level of acceptability of their statements before they make them. The maintenance of ideological consensus is important not only from the point of view of the survival of the institution, or of its establishment; it is important, as Socrates' testimony shows us, when it is carried on for the preservation of the thread of reason, because it prevents argument from running amok and losing credibility. Consequently, it is not enough to rely on the communicative consensus based on the common property of linguistic and communicative habitudes, nor to pursue ideological consensus to please and woo interlocutors. It is necessary to preserve the authority of argument, as Socrates' testimony and the therapists' experience show, through an ideological consensus seeking the continuity of reason, not the establishment of alliances or transient agreements.

The issue stirred up by Socrates' testimony and the therapists' experience is how to achieve this ideological consensus so minutely qualified. (The universality of the Socratic dialectic is not negligible and resurfaces, for example, in the procedures of the therapists from the Milan group who steer the session through questions, as the transcription in chapter 4 illustrates.) The issue resides in what I have been characterizing throughout this essay as one of the essential tensions of the Western cultural heritage: whether it is possible to achieve a unity of knowledge, power, and rhetoric, or whether, if this unity proves impossible, it is desirable to tear this trinity apart—a topic we will come back to in the following chapter.

This tantalizing puzzle finds expression in several ways within therapeutic discourse. In one instance, we can see that therapeutic discourse is kneaded into shape to fit the treatment of certain states of affairs, such as "schizophrenia" or "neurosis," "anorexia nervosa" or "family disorganization," which in turn are defined within a system of knowledge—Freudian psychopathology or characteristics of communicating systems, for example. Thinking along these lines, from a pragmatic and empirical point of view, one could argue that the question raised above is irrelevant, because after all, the therapists find a perfect balance among the categories of knowledge, power asymmetries, and rhetorical maneuvers that they need in order to conduct treatment. However, such an argument would be tantamount to claiming independence for therapeutic discourse in relation to the cultural setting within which it developed, thus denying the kinship between therapeutic discourse and its co-cultural sisters such as philosophical, political, religious, and literary discourses. By the same token, the insistence on this argument would entail that each sphere of discourse would stand on its own, accepting challenges exclusively from within and rebuffing questions from without. It remains for the defendants of this view to explain how their specialized spheres of discourse depart from the communicative consensus underlying our speaking habits. As long as such an explanation is not produced, we remain bound to the Socratic testimony according to which political, pedagogic, philosophical, or therapeutic discourse all belong to the genus of speech which permeates our everyday life.

After having discussed the issues of rhetoric and power in Socratic dialogue and in therapeutic discourse, we now turn to the question of knowledge. In the same way that we distinguished an institutionalized power relationship (that one based on the concrete uses of power) from the will-to-power, we must separate the system of knowledge informing the therapeutic approach from the knowledge of everyday life which both therapist and patient employ as a preliminary stance in their understanding of each other's discourses. Our practical knowledge is developed in dialogue as well as through self-reflection, but the course of its formation is composed by the unpredictable directions of our lives. A great deal of our knowledge of the world unfolds in this spontaneous way and is never submitted to any effort towards systematization. The knowledge thus unfolded may range from *how* to ride a bicycle to *how* to philosophize, but it does not exclude the metaknowledge of *what* it is to ride bicycles or to philosophize. Obviously, there are no hard and fast attitudes about these epistemological inclinations, because systematic knowledge may often become incorporated into practical knowledge. Our knowledge, for example, about dreams, unconscious emanations, and fantasies replacing thwarted desires was systematic at the time of Freud and may have become practical for many of us nowadays. The fact is that practical knowledge then becomes problematic because it can be regarded as a matter of degree in the effort to systematize practical knowledge, and not as a kind of knowledge qualitatively distinct. There is no reason for us to discuss the differences between practical and theoretical knowledge here. What I wish to emphasize is their inextricable association, a fact which although in no need of mention for some, requires emphatic statements for others—those who believe that practical and theoretical reason stem from different roots. The consequence of this discussion, which has relevance for my argument, is that those who believe in the autonomy of systematic knowledge from practical reason tend to transform dialogue and self-reflection into methods, thereby dissolving the open-ended characteristics of both practices.

Many therapists think about their knowledge as theoretical or scientific, depending on laboratory-like research and on experimentation. The approaches of the schools of therapy subscribing to such beliefs remain incomplete as long as they do not come to grips with the discrepancies parting them. These schools also do not regard themselves as ad hoc procedures for dealing with specific problems: family therapy for anorexia nervosa, psychoanalysis for neurosis, and psychiatry for schizophrenia, for example. Each claims to be therapy par excellence, to the exclusion of all rivals. In the clinical practice we find an ever-growing number of therapists presenting themselves as eclectics, combining bits and pieces of Freudian interpretation, the analysis of transference, ego therapy, the strategic and systemic interventions, etc. Nevertheless, the theory inventors in each subfield remain undaunted by such pragmatic ecumenicity. Furthermore, if the schools of therapy ever overcome their current fragmentation, then they will have to face the underlying problem of their cultural definition; that is, they will have to undertake in earnest the project for cultural reform intrinsic to a discourse which makes moral judgments about the ways in which people should lead their lives. As long as the schools of therapy continue divided among themselves, disagreeing with one another about the concept of therapy, they can proceed as subspecialties dealing with specific sets of practical problems in spite of their ambitious claims as systems of knowledge. One further advantage to be derived from the intellectual split is that no single school is forced to face the challenge of addressing the entire gamut of behavior: some develop expertise in dealing with children, others with alcoholics; some slant their approaches to fit narcissistic disturbances, others, communicative stalemates among members of a group. No one, however, has developed such a systematic and pervasive knowledge of the human conduct as Freudian psychoanalysis, including its multiple post-Freudian developments, and thus the metapsychology continues to be the best expression of a system of knowledge in therapeutic discourse. Nevertheless, the theory of psychotherapy is as incomplete as any other system of knowledge. Perhaps it became so successful in our cultural heritage because if on one hand it claimed to be self-sufficient, on the other hand it relied on one of the most fundamental procedures of practical reason, self-reflection. Socrates' philosophy, likewise, without making such a strong claim for a knowledge about how we should lead our lives, drew rather forcefully on another pillar of practical reason, dialogue.

The most interesting feature of the system of knowledge introduced with therapeutic discourse, as in Socrates' philosophy, however, is not its categorical cosmology; it is the mode of producing and reproducing knowledge. The development of therapeutic discourse has led from a separation between interpretive postures for understanding and argumentative postures for persuading to a welding of these hermeneutic and discursive strategies together, in such a way that the analyst of transference or the systemic therapist may combine in a single intervention their strategies for eliciting information and doing therapy. Luigi Boscolo, for example, isolates the components of the family that he believes should be rendered autonomous at the same time that he collects information. When he asks the epileptic girl about her personal life, he simultaneously inquires about the autonomy of her social life and establishes the independence of this subject matter as a relevant issue for discussion within that family (see chapter 4). This adjoining of understanding and explanation only becomes possible through the employment of innovating procedures in discourse. There are two ways for speakers in interactive situations to assess the state of affairs through observation and act upon it through participation: self-reflection and dialogical argument. In the first case the speaker ponders at the same time that he speaks, maneuvering in order for the gap between his interpretive and explanatory postures not to be widened to the point that his interlocutor can perceive the hiatus. In the second case he welds the process of reflection to the turn-taking intrinsic to dialogue. The situation is perfectly illustrated by the Socratic dialogue, in which both parties take turns in acting as interpreters and explainers, but always maintain the complementarity between the two roles. Family therapy has introduced clinical work with more than one therapist in the room, as well as the use of the one-way mirror behind which one or more supervisors observe the session. The enlargement of the therapeutic team allows the therapists to explore many communicative possibilities, including the different assignment of the roles of interpreter and explainer and the breaking of the session for the team to exchange viewpoints and tighten loopholes in their interpretive and explanatory procedures.

With the one-way mirror, part of the team is able to observe without the pressure of the consultation room itself. In that capacity, the consultant can dwell longer over each aspect of the situation, considering a variety of responses which do not have to be tested right away. In face-to-face interactions, the delayed response of an interlocutor who is notoriously protracting his assessment of the situation can indeed be irritating to the other party. The inflammatory element is the evidence that one's interlocutor is not wholeheartedly in the dialogue; while we know that the other makes assessments as much as we do, we like to experience dialogues as spontaneous situations in which the said reflects the totality of that which was thought. This aspect of dialogue evidently belongs to contexts of oral communication because in narrative or textual discourse the expectations about spontaneity must be of a rather different order: they are mediated by self-reflection. The facility with which multiple therapists and the use of the one-way mirror are accepted by patients, in general, attests to the demise of oral dialogue in a literate culture that may very well be witnessing the passing of writing, and its replacement by a variety of electronic media.

This organization of therapy combining dialogical and reflective inspirations puts the therapist at great advantage over his patients. While in face-to-face situations he relies on eloquence and articulation to bridge the gap between interpretation and explanation, with the use of the one-way mirror and the employment of one or more consultants, the therapist feels more secure, and can even allow a spontaneity in his discourse which otherwise would be difficult to attain. Notice that in psychoanalysis the therapist conquers this space to reflect and assess, by denying the need to respond promptly, and thereby gaining a well-protected distance over the patient. The analysis of transference is naturally a step towards narrowing that distance. The polarization between interpretive and explanatory postures, however, is not typical of ordinary conversational situations, but only of those circumstances in which there is a clash of opinions and the contenders have to try and persuade each other. In ordinary conversation, as Gadamer characterizes it, each speaker "gets inside the other to such an extent that he understands not a particular individual, but what he says."[3] Neverthe-less, patient and therapist have an easier time persuading each other than speaker and interlocutor in ordinary interactions because of the institutionally established character of the communicative setting which brings face-to-face complaintive patients eager to be heard and listening therapists eager to hear and advise. Ideological consensus is not imme-diately obtained, however, because the therapist tries to understand the person through *how* he says, and not just through *what* he says. (Socrates would naturally claim that the distinction is irrelevant, think-ing within the context of an oral culture in which speakers speak from their hearts.) The therapist keeps his interpretation withdrawn until he is sure it will be accepted by the patient and with the impact he wishes to have.

All in all, therapeutic discourse is so intricately woven that the sub-stantive meaning of the speech categories becomes less relevant than the performative or pragmatic deployment of those categories. In my opin-ion it was the realization of this fact which led Freud to abandon the seduction theory and to cast psychoanalysis as narrative deconstruction. The same element has been leading family therapists to regard commu-nication as a system over which some claim to be able to exercise com-plete control. This prominence of the performative situation over the content of that which is spoken is intrinsic to therapeutic discourse, but is not necessarily predominant in ordinary speech.

In conclusion, the Socratic dialogue modeled an ideal of dialogue which is open-ended, holistic, and immediate, that is, in which the reason of that which is stated springs from the counterpointing of conversation, but not from the exercise of self-reflection. This ideal of dialogue, however, has come to us through the writings of Plato, which make them closed as texts, historical products (therefore partial), and mediated procedures in which Socrates' art of reasoning is brought to the fore to the detriment of his interlocutors' reasoning. Dialogue remains by and large an unfulfilled goal of Western culture. Therapeutic discourse, in turn, developed self-reflection to its furthest, and in so doing disabled dialogue beyond the limitations already present in the Socratic ideal, but creating a speaker, the therapist, who maintains the right to edit the conversation in the name of therapy and cure. While Socrates tried to steer abreast from narrative and text, Freud made maximum use of narrative and writing, trying to braid these modes of discourse together with dialogue and, in addition, preserve the enor-mous reliance of his project on self-reflection. The Freudian project did not bury the *telos* of the Socratic ideal of dialogue, but revealed that this goal represented a much greater challenge than that envisioned in ancient Greece, because it had to integrate, at least now in the twentieth century, the three modes of discourse: dialogue, narrative, and text. It also rendered the project more difficult as a consequence of the importance Freud bestowed upon self-reflection, which neutralizes dialogue.

The Socratic dialogue finds its center of gravity in power and rhetoric transforming knowledge in its always approached but never attained goal. Therapeutic discourse, to the contrary, bases itself on a knowledge platform. (It is historically understandable why it does so since it epitomizes the values distilled by science, enlightenment, and modernity.) Furthermore, the objects of therapeutic discourse are power and rhetoric. Far apart as those two strategies of cultural criticism may be, they do not conceal the underlying common preoccupation with relating in a meaningful way knowledge, power, and rhetoric, so that the spoken conveys the truth underscored by power and with the best possible rhetoric. The permanence of such a concern within a cultural tradition over a span of twenty-five centuries can only attest to the centrality of the issue of fragmentation versus integration of the trinity constituted by knowledge, power, and rhetoric.

12 THE UNITY OR FRAGMENTATION

OF THE TRINITY

OF KNOWLEDGE, POWER,

AND RHETORIC

One of the dilemmas of the Western cultural heritage is undoubtedly whether to unify or to fragment the trinity constituted by knowledge, power, and rhetoric. This dilemma is nowhere represented better than in its earliest and latest manifestations: the onset of philosophy in the fifth century B.C. and the widespread acceptance of therapeutic discourse in the twentieth century. The unity of the trinity transpires in the fact that every system of knowledge which becomes socially and culturally pervasive entails a rhetoric of expression and generates a power claim. Likewise, every power claim is based on a certain knowledge of something opposed to other forms of knowledge, and chiefly to ignorance. Rhetoric is obviously a power strategy and the rhetor tries to persuade his interlocutor of something which is his knowledge. Nevertheless, it has been historically impossible to integrate completely knowledge with power and with rhetoric. The inventors and reinventors of culture have often attributed this bewildering state of affairs to the fallibility of all systems of knowledge, to the asymmetries of power hierarchies, or to the rhetorical effect of eclipsing knowledge and persuading by sleight of hand. Attempts to resolve the puzzle have consisted in the creation of new cultural constellations of knowledge, power, and rhetoric, such as the Platonic and Socratic, the Aristotelian, the Christian, the political, the scientific, and the therapeutic, to mention but a few of the numerous efforts in the history of Euro-American societies to create a hegemonic trinity from a subcultural sphere of discourse. But as the inventors and reinventors of culture realize the difficulties inherent in their project, from time to time they are led to procure alternative solutions consisting in the fragmentation of the trinity. This effort to fragment the trinity usually draws on a negative or nihilistic discourse, a discourse which struggles to overcome the paradox that every attack on power conjures power, every attack on rhetoric brings rhetoric forth, and every attack on knowledge needs a knowledge platform from which it can be launched. The pursuers of a nihilist strategy try to introduce an asymmetry into the trinity by attempting to suppress one or two of its elements. The fragmenting endeavor, however, is as frustrating as the integrative effort because if on one hand the trinity cannot be untied, on the other hand it also cannot be splintered.

Plato himself was already concerned with the unity of a trinity—that of thought, emotion, and language. He realized that the right thought which was capable of gaining minds could be rendered impotent if it did not equally gain hearts. The heart, however, is the domain of emotions which were conceptualized in rather different terms in classical culture. The contemporary discourse on emotions includes several elements which were absent in ancient Greece, such as the Christian love and guilt, self-love and romantic love, the Freudian desire bridled by anxiety, the association of pleasure and happiness to actions, and the venue to learn about emotions based on self-reflection. Of course, emotions in the present times are so much more complexly qualified that the link between thoughts and feelings has become a great deal more problematic in the world dominated by therapy than it was in Plato's world. Stephen Tyler discusses how this unity of the trinity became gradually shattered in the intellectual development of the Western heritage, beginning with the Aristotelian separation of logic and rhetoric, continuing with the scholastic use of rhetoric for rhetoric's sake, which was in a way a resumption of the sophistic project, and proceeding with the age of enlightenment, when an effort was developed in science to cast rhetoric off once and for all, grounding knowledge on the appeal to self-evidence. The last stroke came from the empiricist philosophers who separated reason and passion. Tyler concludes that "this separation of reason and passion destroyed the ethical basis of discourse."[1]

The issue of the ethical basis of discourse is raised in our times as urgently as ever. If it is true that our heritage oscillates between periods of descriptivism and periods of revisionism, we are definitely living in one of the latter. The contemporary debate on the matter can be characterized in two opposing viewpoints: that espoused by the modernists—who although accepting criticism of many beliefs which emerged during modernity wish to preserve continuity—and that of the postmodernists, who call for radical changes. The postmodernist revisionary inspiration, however, is not just a new claim for change, since the postmodernist thinkers do not want to replace one house of knowledge by another, but wish rather to adopt a permanent mode of skepticism which would be incorporated into systems of knowledge. If they are to succeed, critique will become part of the very process of developing and sustaining beliefs, of the act of building pictures of the world, that is, of the mimetic procedures in the description of reality. This project has been unfolded within different subcultures of our heritage such as therapeutic discourse, hermeneutic philosophy, and literary criticism. Therapists have been shifting the emphasis of the therapeutic dialogue from an a priori system of knowledge to the unpredictable flow of the communicative exchanges between clinician and patient. The analysis of transference and family therapy illustrate this tendency with eloquence. From hermeneutic philosophy we have learned that every assertion of positive knowledge is an answer to a question formulated within the parameters of certain cultural and historical horizons. As a consequence, the interlink between question and answer is more revealing than the meaning of positive knowledge out of context. Finally, literary criticism, particularly in its deconstructionist endeavor, has sharpened our critical understanding of aesthetics by shifting our attention from the object of art in itself to the fountainhead of representation which produces it.

From a historical perspective, if the modernist world was established by ousting the religious morality which held the Western culture together, the postmodernist world bursts forth crushing the techno-scientific mentality which claimed that existential problems had become a matter of science and politics, and could be resolved if only the appropriate methods were employed. The duel between modernity-cum-criticism and postmodernity is yet to be resolved, and expresses, in my opinion, a reawakening of the tantalizing dilemma of the unity versus fragmentation of the trinity. The advocates of reformed modernity would like to preserve some intellectual contributions of enlightenment, rearranging them in a constellation fitting our times. This proposal contains a rather revolutionary element in the denial that solutions to our cultural and social puzzles must come from innovating alternatives. The thinkers of postmodernity turn to a radical critique of representation of language and writing, speaking and thinking. Both groups of thinkers hope to further our capacity for self-reflection by reaching new horizons of criticism, but neither has come forth so far with any inclinations to pursue the ideal of dialogue.

The attack of postmodernity is aimed at the production and maintenance of knowledge, the question of authority, and the shortcoming of representation. It is worthwhile to reflect upon some issues of interpretation related to this topic. Understanding depends on three operations: *comprehension, acceptance, and appropriation.* In order to understand a

statement a person must be in command of the communicative consensus shared with the speaker. The interlocutor must speak the same
language as the speaker and share with him the cognitive-expressive
categories of knowledge, the conventions of the speech actions employed, and the normative background underlying the behavior of
speakers and hearers. This is the operation of comprehension. One may
comprehend the statement, "The contemporary trend towards conservatism in European and American governments reflects the loss of
primacy of Western societies in the world," and yet not accept it.
Acceptance depends on ideological consensus, an agreement about the
opinion being issued and about the right of the speaker to express the
opinion.

Comprehension and acceptance are circumscribed within cultural and
historical horizons, and since these are collectively shared, the community members experience the knowledge they comprehend and accept
as common property. They often raise universal validity claims to this
knowledge. We call the extremist manifestations of such claims "ethno-
centrism." The members of a knowledge community experience a loss of
cultural property when they encounter systems of knowledge different
from their own and somehow feel defied. The paradigmatic situation
occurs in the encounter of opposite ideologies, or of radically different
languages, cultural traditions, or historical periods falling outside the
horizons of comprehension and acceptance of the observers' community
of knowledge. The reason for this jingoism, I believe, resides in the fact
that understanding is not complete without appropriation. After having
comprehended an idea, and accepted it, the interpreter has the desire to
experience it as his own, but some ideas are more appealing to the
desideratum of ownership than others. The knowledge that 'the earth is
round," for example, is now completely unappealing as property
because it has entirely fallen into the domain of public ownership of
knowledge. For that reason, foreign languages and cultures have always
been treasure islands for the natives of all lands, from Herodotus to
contemporary anthropologists, because alien knowledge is always a
challenge insofar as it has not yet been appropriated.

Walter Benjamin muses about the ownership of ideas, arguing that
knowledge is the object of possession, but that truth cannot be so.
Knowledge is an appropriation of ideas, while truth is self-representation, and thereby dispenses with knowledge and with mimetic copies.
He makes an analogy with Plato's discussion of "beauty" in the *Symposium*. The beauty of a person surpasses his personhood insofar as it
lives on in the eyes of one who loves that person. Truth, likewise, is not
absolute in itself; it resides more remarkably in its seeker's search. Truth

is the enemy, simultaneously, of unity and of fragmentation; it breathes where "all essences exist in complete and immaculate independence, not only from phenomena, but, especially, from each other. Just as the harmony of the spheres depends on the orbits of stars which do not come into contact with each other, so the existence of the "mundus intelligibilis" depends on the unbridgeable distance between pure essences."[2]

The question of the appropriation of ideas is equally discussed by Heidegger, occupying a rather central position in his philosophy. In an imaginary dialogue with a Japanese philosopher,[3] Heidegger reveals how elusive is the sense of property over concepts of a different language and culture. The two discussants establish approximations of understanding about "Being" and "Metaphysics," about "Iki" and "Koto ba," and conclude in one instance after another that although each comes to what could be called a "full understanding" of the notion introduced by the other, the experience is somehow frustrating because the interpreter can never experience what the speaker does. "Iki" is close to "aesthetics," but in an utterly peculiar way: it addresses the essence of something which in the course of the dialogue is established as similar to that which the European word "aesthetics" refers to. However, it does so in such a singular way that Heidegger is led to wonder whether he understands at all the notion of "Iki." "Koto ba," similarly, takes the two discussants into perplexity. It is a possible gloss for "language," but the more Heidegger and the Japanese philosopher bridge the linguistic and cultural discrepancies, mapping out a whole world of difference, the more Heidegger's experience of appropriation over the notion seems alien to him. Refracting difference through languages and cultures has formidable heuristic effects because of the eloquence of the discrepancies. All one has to do is to try to translate one world into another and the difference spouts out. When, however, the subject matter is discourse within the same cultural heritage, the tool of translation ceases to be helpful, and difference can only be highlighted by means of critique. Nevertheless, the difficulty of appropriation within one's own discourse tradition is tantamount to that which one experiences along cross-cultural and crosslinguistic lines.

Underlying difference through translation or through critique is a function of appropriation and not of comprehension or of acceptance in the process of understanding. Knowledge can be publicly or privately (by individual or groups) owned, reappropriated, or destroyed. The activities involved in these relations between subjects and knowledge range from creation and authorship to repossession, and the leitmotiv of this enterprise resides in the Western preoccupation with the metaphysics of presence which is culturally expressed in several ways, including in the heroism attached to invention, ownership, and destruction. Public ideas gain sudden interest as soon as they can be challenged. Thus the demolishers may claim that "Jesus Christ never existed," that "Nazism is the best social philosophy for mankind," or that "Plato did not write the dialogues, but they were written by another man calling himself Plato," and if they succeed in this demolition of pillars of public knowledge, although they do not gain any new property, they find themselves rewarded by power for destroying property that was so public and so well established. As a consequence, the domain of public knowledge is never entirely safe, and for that reason it cannot be taken for granted as a haven of undisputed knowledge.

Privately owned knowledge, that which is identified with authorship, only becomes rewarding when it earns some degree of public recognition. The glamour of appropriation and of creation, as well as that of destruction, resides in the recognition by others, but this recognition, ironically, is the beginning of the transformation of private into public property. The world becomes more important than its creator, the estate outlives its buyer, and the demolisher disappears with the object of his destruction. Authority, appropriation, and demolition have a fugacious importance completely identified with the act characterizing each one, and largely divorced from the relation linking subject and knowledge. In the trade of each of these operations, rhetoric is what musters public recognition, while power performs the opposite function, that is, it preserves certain accomplishments from public dissemination. In this sense, rhetoric is an art of revelation, while power manipulation is an art of secrecy. The Western tradition has always revealed skepticism about the possibility of a system of knowledge becoming entirely publicly or privately owned. The corollary of such opposing utopias is that if one day all knowledge were made public property we would become rather uninteresting as "selves." On the contrary, if all knowledge were made private property, life with others would inevitably become unbearably complicated.

These levels of understanding (comprehension, acceptance, and appropriation) are grounded on will, but kneaded into different shapes according to the mode of discourse filtering them. Narrative and text naturally limit the property or authorship of storytellers and writers over that which they produce by congealing knowledge into forms of expression patterned and imbibed with impersonality. Still, nothing transforms knowledge into a more appealing object for appropriation than a text. Dialogue, in turn, establishes a more direct relation of property between speaker and knowledge in virtue of the immediacy, the wholeness and the open-endedness of the expressed knowledge. However, the ideal of dialogue does not aim at producing texts, consequently knowledge in dialogue is less appealing as an object for appropriation than in narratives and texts. If rhetoric and power are not decisive elements in the economy of appropriation of knowledge, neither are the modes of discourse—dialogue, narrative, and text. Knowledge becomes objectified by texts, criticized in dialogues, divulged through rhetoric, and preserved within power asymmetries, but none of these operations completely disclose the relationship entertained between the knowing subjects and their knowledge.

Different types of knowledge also determine different kinds of interest for creation, appropriation, and destruction. Common sense knowledge, for example, is unattractive for appropriation because it is refractory to copyright. Every time an attempt is made to describe common sense knowledge, transforming it into an object capable of being identified as the property of an author, it vanishes from practical reason and becomes a theory or a method. Common sense knowledge is consequently a better subject matter for the ideal of dialogue than any other form of knowledge, while theoretical knowledge is best for text.

The culture of literacy has to a large extent blurred the distinction between representation and action by pitching textual knowledge as a form of dialogue without coming to grips with the antidialogical nature of texts. Literacy compounded knowledge as representation, that is, the mimetic copy of reality, with knowledge as intention and action, the methetic intervention over reality. First, knowledge became identified with texts, and then with language itself, which led the analytic philosophers beginning with Frege, Russell, and Wittgenstein to examine the meaningful limits of language, as if beyond that threshold there was a mystery inaccessible to man's intelligence.[4] The consequence of the enclosure of knowledge within language was the weakening of the force of knowledge in the trinity, because if all that there was to knowledge lay in language, and if language could be completely explained by grammar, then philosophy was trivial and grammarians would be the true epistemologists. But there seems to be an ever-growing awareness, since the heyday of structuralism and of linguistics in the 1960s, that neither grammar nor linguistics have the last word about language, and that knowledge is not isomorphic to language. This train of thought indicates that, after all, knowledge may have an ethical foundation and we are justified in examining that claim again as it was formulated by Plato.

Another distinction blurred by literacy was that between a priori and a posteriori knowledge. The textualization of life created the impression that no sphere of action was left that we could penetrate before acquiring some textual knowledge about how to proceed within it. This, of course, is true of therapeutic discourse which grew in the age of enlightenment, side by side with science and politics. From the Freudian analyst to the systemic family therapist, clinicians have held hard and fast to the belief that the therapeutic dialogue can be anticipated in theory and accurately reconstructed in explanations—that is, the rational underlying explanations of therapy sessions. Naturally, Plato must have shared part of this belief, at least, when he proceeded to write the Socratic dialogues. But if in his time it was already difficult to achieve the ideal of dialogue because of the forcefully present past of epic narrative and of the fast growing prestige of the written text, nowadays, in order to pursue the ideal of dialogue, in addition to integrating narrative and text within our endeavor, we also have to resolve the incompatibilities extant between self-reflection and dialogue. Those family therapists who work in teams employing the one-way mirror and allowing the patient to speak to both parts of the team have undertaken a bold step towards integrating self-reflection into dialogue. The observers in the team are exposed to the patients' questioning in ways that the self-reflective mind of the solo therapist could never be. These daring steps, however, are like drops in the ocean of a soaring adherence to the injunctions of text to the exclusion of dialogue and narrative, as well as to the use of self-reflection as the ultimate rhetorical weapon to subdue one's interlocutor. Indeed, our world is one in which all forms of knowledge seem to have been covered by texts to such an extent that no interpretive action can claim to be innovating or original; every verbal action would have already been foreclosed by a text, and we would be living in a world at once preconstructed and reconstructed. The impression that the text overcomes the separation between a priori and a posteriori thereby rendering action more global is obviously false. Consequently, instead of moving forward, it seems more advisable to return to a classic distinction between a priori and a posteriori.

In Freudian parlance, the a priori knowledge finds its abode in the unconscious, and every reconstructive move may transform it into the conscious. Knowledge is not moral, because it stems from desires; it is filtered by mechanisms in the psyche and finally expressed through experience in meaningful ways. The moral assessment of expression would thus be futile, because that which can be acknowledged in action represents only the tip of the iceberg. In the Socratic ideal of dialogue, on the contrary, we find an absolute knowledge steeped in virtue and residing in the human soul. Its dialectic reconstruction is knowledge itself, while its moral foundation lies in man's essential goodness.

If the attempts at unifying or fragmenting the trinity of knowledge, power, and rhetoric are doomed to fail, judging from our historical experience, other angles of approach such as *modes of discourse, types of knowledge,* and *ways of thinking* remain largely unexplored. The glaringly unfulfilled promise of the Western heritage is the ideal of dialogue. Among the contemporary trinitarian constellations, the ideal of dialogue throbs in some uses of therapeutic, political, and religious discourse. Therapy is preferable for those who find that the way to emancipation crosses the territory of the individual rather than that of society or of the soul. But whatever the case may be, we can no longer realize the ideal of dialogue at the expense of other *modes of discourse* (whether literate, narrative, or perhaps electronic), *types of knowledge* (common sense, theoretical, or mystical), and *ways of thinking.* It would be unrealistic to suppose that we could abandon the mind's function of self-reflection in order to adapt our intellectual faculties to the vagaries of dialogue. This, however, is not an undertaking for therapeutic discourse alone, but calls for an effort of cultural proportions, although the therapeutic embodies the challenge better than any other discourse in our heritage.

NOTES

BIBLIOGRAPHY

INDEX

NOTES

Chapter 1

1　See Paul Ricoeur, "The Question of Proof in Freud's Psychoanalytic Writings," in *Hermeneutics and the Human Sciences* (1981); and Jürgen Habermas, "Self-Reflection as Science: Freud's Psychoanalytic Critique of Meaning," in *Knowledge and Human Interests* (1971).

2　The question of absolute versus relative spontaneity in discourse is a very complex matter that can be discussed, for example, within the theory of speech acts through the notions of convention and intention. For now we will have to leave it untouched, and refer the interested reader to the specialized literature on speech acts. For the purpose of our argument it will suffice to remember that there is more room for spontaneity in the application of psychoanalysis for those either outside its subcultural contours or those who experienced it in its earlier stages, such as Freud. Psychoanalysis started as a reconstructive reflection of interviews with patients. Under the sway of positive science, Freud transformed such a practice into a caricature of laboratory research, developing a theory of psychopathology and a metapsychology. Then he introduced the ambiguity according to which a therapy session was as much treatment as research. However, the discourse on which the reconstructive effort was applied was the ordinary discourse of everyday life, and in spite of all efforts to make psychoanalysis scientific—including the most recent by Adolf Grunbaum, *The Foundations of Psychoanalysis: A Philosophical Critique* (Berkeley: University of California Press, 1984)—the argument that therapeutic discourse is specialized, theoretical, and scientific remains largely unconvincing. Actually, it sounds bizarre in our times, just when scientists are awakening from the positivist dream that special languages would further knowledge and avoid the pitfalls and imprecisions of natural languages. If the complete success of psychoanalysis has been stayed by this incongruity between, on one hand, a conception of speech as divided into a theory and a practice and, on the other hand, an outward reliance on ordinary speech, its failures have illuminated the artificiality of the dichotomy between theory and practice.

3　See Philip Rieff, *The Triumph of the Therapeutic: Users of Faith after Freud* (1968).

4　See Erik Erikson, *Childhood and Society* (1963).

5　It is possible that every major rhetorical tradition begins with a paucity of means of persuasion, completely enthralled with its revolutionary message, and gradually develops its own bureaucracy and sees its foundations being challenged. See Max Weber's reflections about the rise of domination in *Economy and Society* (1978).

250

6   See David Rapaport, *The Structure of Psychoanalytic Theory: A Systematizing Attempt* (1960), and Philip Holzman, *Psychoanalysis and Psychopathology* (1970) for summaries of Freud's metapsychology.
7   See Ricoeur (1981), pp. 6–8.
8   See Sigmund Freud, *The Interpretation of Dreams* (1900), p. 387.
9   Ibid., pp. 387–401.
10 See Gananath Obeyesekere's discussion of the relationship between public/cultural and private/individual symbols in a healing cult in Sri Lanka, in *Medusa's Hair* (1981).
11 See S. Freud, *A Connection between a Symbol and a Symptom* (1916a), pp. 339–83.
12 S. Freud, *Introductory Lectures on Psychoanalysis* (1916b), p. 151.
13 See S. Freud, *The Future of an Illusion* (1927) and *Civilization and Its Discontents* (1930).
14 S. Freud, *On the History of the Psychoanalytic Movement* (1914a).
15 S. Freud (1900), p. 650.
16 Ibid., p. 651.
17 In *The Interpretation of Dreams*, Freud treated these components of the mind as organs or lenses in the metaphor of the telescope. Later on, in *Inhibitions, Symptoms and Anxiety* (1926), Freud referred to these categories as qualities of the ideas, and it is this later version that remained in the psychoanalytic tradition. In order to simplify matters I am grafting this later notion to the topography of the mind as presented in *The Interpretation of Dreams*.
18 S. Freud (1900), p. 583.
19 S. Freud, *Beyond the Pleasure Principle* (1920), p. 12.
20 S. Freud, *An Autobiographic Study* (1925), p. 42.
21 Cf. S. Freud, *Three Essays on the Theory of Sexuality* (1905), pp. 123–320, for the earlier formulation of the theory of drives in terms of sex and aggression, and S. Freud (1920), where Freud introduces the notion of self-preservation as a drive. Many psychological anthropologists, beginning with Geza Roheim, missed this point in Freud's writings and presented an explanation in which culture derived from repressive forces. Herbert Marcuse, looking for a positive aspect in Freud's theory, associated man's emancipatory struggle with Eros' plight against Thanatos. It is the modesty of Freud's treatment of ego drives and ego defenses compared to the exuberance of his analysis of repression that has led some to see the works of civilization as symptomatic symbols of suppressed drives. See H. Marcuse, *Eros and Civilization* (1961).
22 The psychology of the ego in psychoanalysis was developed only much later by Heinz Hartmann, *Ego Psychology and the Problem of Adaptation* (1958), and by Erik Erikson (1963). Ego psychology became the dominant force shaping psychoanalytically based forms of therapy in the United States, whereas Freud's theory of sexual and aggressive drives only found shelter among a few of his more orthodox followers.

23 The superego and the ego ideal have been troublesome and enticing concepts in Freudian metapsychology. Troublesome because precariously defined, and enticing because the superego is the seat of morality and, therefore, understanding it may be tantamount to unveiling the genesis of value judgment. The narcissism of the Oedipal stage becomes congealed in an ego ideal which thereon constantly spurs the ego toward perfection. This spurring is carried on by self-reproach which makes the ego feel guilty of its "failures." The mechanism in charge of evaluating the ego's accomplishments against the backdrop of the ego ideal is called the superego. In his later writings Freud dropped the distinction and referred to both functions, that of holding an ideal, and that of evaluating the attempts to fulfill it, as "superego." See James Strachey's "Introduction" in S. Freud, *The Ego and the Id* (1923), pp. 3–66. But it has remained inevitable to recognize that the two functions are entirely different. The ego ideal is further reinforced by the self-reproach that the ego, suffering from its primary Oedipal guilt, projects onto the father and other figures of external authority. The reproach is then experienced as real, coming from these eyes of surveillance lying outside of the ego. Wollheim, in a most interesting suggestion, regards the ego ideal as a preliminary stage of internalization, while the superego is the final stage. Self-reproach as ego ideal can still be perceived as an injunction over ego, but once it becomes superego it starts to be experienced as the ego's own criteria. See Richard Wollheim, *The Thread of Life* (1984), pp. 218ff.

24 Holzman (1970), p. 124.

25 See S. Freud (1923) and S. Freud (1926). With this turning in his theory, Freud was anticipating an epistemological shift which took place in all sciences of man and society in the forties and fifties, from functionalism to structuralism. Marx and Freud, like Socrates and Christ's apostles, forcefully argued that the object of their discourse was not a novelty to be instilled in their interlocutors, but something that was already in them, needing only to be brought to consciousness.

26 Habermas, *The Theory of Communicative Action* (1984), p. 87.

27 Cf. S. Freud (1923).

28 Cf. Winnicott, *Playing and Reality* (1971).

29 S. Freud (1923), p. 30.

30 Ibid., p. 40.

Chapter 2

1 Within the psychoanalytic movement, some of the proponents of such reforms are Donald P. Spence, *Narrative Truth and Historical Truth: Meaning and Interpretation in Psychoanalysis* (1982); Roy Schafer, *A New Language for Psychoanalysis* (1976); and Merton Gill, *Analysis of Transference* (1982).

2 See Roy Schafer, "Narration in the Psychoanalytic Dialogue" (1980).

3 S. Freud, "On Beginning the Treatment," in *Therapy and Technique* (1913a), p. 147.

4 See Wollheim's (1984) tour de force to combine Freud's metapsychology with the meaningfulness of experience.

5 Freud reports that in the beginning of the psychoanalytic movement, when he was still using the hypnotic method, he often found himself tired and bored of issuing commands such as "You are going to sleep! . . . Sleep!" and hear the patient remonstrate with him: "But, Doctor, I am not asleep." He would have to explain that he did not mean ordinary sleep but hypnotic sleep, and describe this state to the patient. See S. Freud, *Project for a Scientific Psychology* (1895), pp. 283–387.

6 See Rieff (1968) and Christopher Lasch, *The Culture of Narcissism* (1979).

7 See Gill (1982).

8 Rieff (1968), p. 32.

9 See Gill and Hoffman (1982).

10 Melanie Klein corroborates this outlook of analysis by casting man in a frame of original madness from which he can only free himself through psychoanalysis, or through other situations capable of hinting his insanity to his consciousness. See Hanna Segal, *Introduction to the Work of Melanie Klein* (1964).

11 See S. Freud, "Remembering, Repeating and Working Through," in *Further Recommendations on the Technique of Psychoanalysis II* (1914b), pp. 159–71.

12 Gill (1982), p. 102.

13 Anna Freud writes, "I will feel that somewhere we should leave room for the realization that analyst and patient are also two real people, of equal adult status, in a real personal relationship to each other." Farther ahead in this passage, however, she concludes in a cautioning tone that "these are technically subversive thoughts and ought to be 'handled with care.'" Anna Freud, *The Widening Scope of Indications for Psychoanalysis: Discussion.* The Writings of Anna Freud (1968), p. 373.

14 Gill (1982), p. 19.

15 Gill and Hoffman (1982), p. 56.

16 Ibid., p. 60.

17 Ibid., p. 65.

Chapter 3

1 Salvador Minuchin, *Families and Family Therapy* (1974), p. 55.

2 See Tullio Maranhão, "Family Therapy and Anthropology," in *Culture, Medicine, and Psychiatry* 8 (1984):255–79.

3 These concepts come from Minuchin (1974).

4 See Murray Bowen, *Family Therapy in Clinical Practice* (1978).

5 Hoffman writes: "It is not much help to rely on one's rational faculties when working structurally, any more than it is helpful to learn ballet by reading about it or watching it. Suffice it to say that to be a good structural therapist requires much experience, and extensive live supervision by a master." Lynn Hoffman, *Foundations of Family Therapy* (1981), p. 271.

6 See Minuchin, Rosman, and Baker, _Psychosomatic Families: Anorexia Nervosa in Context_ (1978), chapter 11; and Minuchin, "An Anorectic Family; Repatterning through Therapy," in _Family Kaleidoscope_ (1984), pp. 90–120.

7 Minuchin (1984), pp. 96–97.

8 Minuchin et al. (1978).

9 Minuchin (1984), p. 179.

10 Minuchin et al. (1978), p. 290.

11 See ibid., pp. 292–93.

12 Minuchin (1984), p. 100.

13 Minuchin et al. (1978), pp. 32–38.

14 Minuchin (1984), p. 112.

15 Ibid., p. 114.

16 Minuchin et al. (1978), p. 107.

17 Every text or narrative is an explanation. The meaningful is always self-explanatory. Yet the act of interpretation can be regarded as an appropriation of the explanation. Positivism in social sciences created the illusion that the explanatory and interpretive procedures were different from one another. Paul Ricoeur traces back the roots of the divorce between explanation and understanding, already in hermeneutics, to Dilthey's writings. See "What is a Text? Explanation and Understanding," in Ricoeur (1981), pp. 145–64. He takes the model of the written text as a point of departure to unfold his concept of meaning in the sciences of man, and writes: "It is in the very heart of reading that explanation and interpretation are indefinitely opposed and reconciled." We are invited to think about the decoding of meaning in any meaningful activity as an extension of the activity of the reader.

Chapter 4

1 See Lynn Hoffman (1981) and Bradford P. Keeney and Jeffrey M. Ross, _Mind in Therapy: Constructing Systemic Family Therapies_ (1985), for summary reviews of these different schools and discussion of their theoretical assumptions and clinical practices. There are several other groups including those of family therapists who try to integrate group therapy for the family with psychoanalytic techniques, as well as other therapeutic propositions and peculiar combinations of the four approaches distinguished here. However, it is the structuralists, the strategists, and the systemic therapists (of morphostasis and of morphogenesis) who occupy the center of the intellectual debate in family therapy. For a provocative suggestion toward the integration between psychoanalysis and family therapy, see Helm Stierlin, _Psychoanalysis and Family Therapy_ (1977). See also the groundbreaking work of Donald W. Winnicott, especially his _The Child, the Family, and the Outside World_ (1964). Finally, see also the interesting work of Howard F. Stein who has been marking off the territory of family therapy from the domains of cultural values and of psychoanalysis, espe-

cially, "Bowen 'Family Systems Theory': The Problem of Cultural Persistence, and the Differentiation of Self in One's Culture," *The Family* 8, 1
(1980):21–51.

2 Jay Haley's therapeutic approaches have picked and strung together a large
variety of clinical programs such as those designed by Bateson, Jackson,
Minuchin, and Erickson. The Haley who better fits my description here is
that one represented in *Problem Solving Therapy* (1977).

3 See G. Bateson, D. Jackson, J. Haley, and J. Weakland, "Toward a Theory of
Schizophrenia," *Behavioral Science* 1, no. 4 (1956).

4 See C. Sluzki, J. Beavin, A. Tarnopolsky, and E. Veron, "Transactional
Disqualification," *Archives of General Psychiatry* 3, no. 10 (1967):494–507;
and Gina Abeles, "The Double Bind: Paradox in Relationships" (1975).

5 Bateson, "Form, Substance, and Difference," in *Steps to an Ecology of Mind*
(1972), pp. 448-66.

6 See Humberto R. Maturana and F. J. Varela, *Autopoiesis and Cognition: the
Realization of the Living* (1980).

7 See Bruno Bettelheim, *Freud and Man's Soul* (1982), where the author shows
how the Freudian project is more a form of humanism than of scientism,
and how the earlier translations of Freud's books would have missed the
humanistic flavor of the German originals and put the text in the straitjacket of scientific parlance.

8 I base myself on the observation of videotapes and books of which I would
like to mention the following: Richard Fisch, John H. Weakland, and Lynn
Segal, *The Tactics of Change: Doing Therapy Briefly* (1982), for the MRI
approach; Haley (1977) for the strategic; and Hoffman (1981) and Keeney
and Ross (1985) for comparative discussions of the major schools in family
therapy.

9 See Fisch et al. (1982).

10 Haley (1977), p. 15.

11 Ibid., pp. 29–30.

12 Fisch et al. (1982), p. 93.

13 Ibid., p. 116.

14 Ibid.

15 Haley (1977), p. 15.

16 See Haley (1977) where those sequences are described in detail.

17 The question of power constituted the subject of a heated polemic among
family therapists. While Jay Haley regards power hierarchies as a mode of
family organization independent of the family's representations of their
reality, and therefore develops his therapy taking into consideration these
two spheres of power and representation separately, Gregory Bateson sees
power as just another metaphor in the system of representations. See
Haley, "Development of a Theory: A History of a Research Project," in
Carlos Sluzki and Donald Ransom, eds., *Double Bind: The Foundation of the
Communicational Approach to the Family* (1976), pp. 105–64, as well as
Bateson's comments on Haley's "History" in the same book, pp. 104–5.

Bradford Keeney, commenting on the controversy, argues that there is not an absolute incompatibility in treating power as actual hierarchy and as metaphor. He refers to the two as "political and semantic frames" for the development of therapeutic strategies and builds his comparative discussion of the different therapeutic approaches along the axis constituted by these two categories. See Keeney and Ross (1985).

18 Fisch et al. (198), p. 127.
19 Ibid.
20 The session is transcribed from Keeney and Ross (1985), pp. 221–50.
21 Ibid., p. 240.

Chapter 5

1 See Rieff (1968), p. 75.
2 See Max Weber's analysis of religions in terms of "inner world" and "other world" orientations, and of religious behavior as "world rejecting asceticism," "inner world asceticism," "world fleeing mystical contemplation," etc., in *The Sociology of Religion* (1964). An expression of this analytic dichotomy in practical reason can be found in the way Europeans and Americans classify cultures, including their own, in terms of distance and proximity of persons, "selves," and groups. The anthropological literature provides us with a conspicuous testimony to this outlook.
3 For a comparison between Freud and Nietzsche, see Paul Ricoeur, "Psychoanalysis and the Movement of Contemporary Culture," in *The Conflict of Interpretations* (1974), pp. 121-59. Foucault writes with sympathy about Nietzsche, stressing the importance of notions such as "genealogy," "atavism," and "heredity." For both thinkers the question of knowledge and power is the central one. Neither one of these two spheres can claim autonomy over the other, they are both fleeting; we must pursue their essences in our unending excavation. See Paul Rabinow, ed., *Foucault Reader* (1985). For Freud this also was the central question, but contrary to Nietzsche and Foucault, he did come forward with an explanation by creating an ontological basis for knowledge and power in the psyche.
4 Philip Rieff writes: "The distance between the Freudian freedom of choice and curative therapies of commitment may be bridged by the character of the analyst himself. One is inclined to believe that a cure cannot be achieved without an exemplary presence. And, indeed, the psychoanalysts maintain the collegial romance of such a presence in their common reverence for the founding father himself. Cure, when superadded to knowledge, would be the informed acceptance of an authority figure. When it is not exemplary, an authority figure has an uncertain therapeutic effect." See Rieff (1968), p. 102.
5 The anthropological literature on the subject is vast, and I refer the interested reader to three different and apt treatments of this subject: Roy Wagner, *The Invention of Culture* (1981); Clifford Geertz, *Works and Lives:*

The Anthropologist as Author (1986); and George E. Marcus and Michael M. J. Fischer, *Toward Anthropology as Cultural Criticism: An Experimental Moment in Ethnographic Writing* (1986).

6 It is interesting to note that the proponents of symbols as instruments, including both anthropologists and family therapists continue to use symbols in their writings as textually meaningful. Exceptions and noteworthy experimentations in this area are naturally found in the literature of fiction and in the writings of some literary critics such as Jacques Derrida. In anthropology there is intense experimentation in the writing of ethnographies. See Marcus and Fischer (1986) for a discussion of the issue, and Vincent Crapanzano, *Waiting: The Whites of South Africa* (1985), a nondescriptive ethnography whose discursive act endlessly resounds, particularly in the minds of those about whom it talks, until the problems it addresses can find their resolution.

Chapter 6

1 The contrast between literate and oral cultures underlies much of the contemporary debate about postmodernity. For an initial formulation of the issue, see Walter Ong's *Orality and Literacy* (1982). See also Jacques Derrida's *Writing and Difference* (1978) and Stephen A. Tyler's "Ethnography, Intertextuality and the End of Description" (1984) for a discussion of the issue in its consequences to writing ethnographies in anthropology. Postmodern criticism feeds itself in the critique of representation. Jacques Derrida directs his deconstructive strategies to the representation of language, either written or spoken. Jürgen Habermas takes a rather different approach in rearranging specific clusters of representation within the social sciences, philosophy, and dialectic materialism. The works of these two contemporary thinkers strike their readers as dialogical interventions rather than as prescriptive or descriptive texts. Derrida produces elliptical texts characterized by paralogisms which, instead of informing, provoke the reader. Habermas strikes his readers by unveiling ideas which had become covered by prejudice, rearranging pictures of the world system in different disciplines in the most challenging way. See J. Derrida, *Dissemination* (1981); J. F. Lyotard, *La Condition Postmoderne* (1979); and Habermas (1984).

2 See Derrida (1978).

3 See *Republic*, 506–9. The passages in the dialogue referred to are in Plato, *The Collected Dialogues* (1961).

4 See Friedrich Schleiermacher, *Introductions to the Dialogues of Plato* (1973); and Hans-Georg Gadamer, *Dialogue and Dialectic: Eight Hermeneutical Studies on Plato* (1980).

5 *Theaetetus*, 196e.

6 *Republic*, 597e.

7 Ibid., 598a.

8 Ibid., 598b.
9 Ibid., 602d.
10 Ibid., 398a.
11 Ibid., 393–94.
12 Plato's critique of mimetic art shares its fundamental intuition with Adorno's critique of the industry of mass communications. Both media numb consciousness, obliterating political action. See Theodor Adorno, "On the Fetish-Character in Music and the Regression of Listening," in *The Essential Frankfurt School Reader* (1978), pp. 270–99. Adorno and Benjamin also turned to art converting it into the most privileged object of their criticism. On one hand they thought that aesthetics could be emancipatory. Adorno singled out the essay as the genre par excellence for the writing of philosophy, while Benjamin became enthralled with Brecht's epic theater, which revolutionized art, harnessing it to emancipation. On the other hand both thinkers, like Plato, attempted to sharply separate the essence of knowledge from its form of representation, an effort which inevitably entails a stricter critique of the latter by drawing on the metaphor of content and receptacle, substance and purveyor, or being and form. This naturally is a central aporia in Western philosophy, and was a much-threshed issue in Plato's dialogues as well as in the writings of Benjamin and Adorno.
13 *Phaedrus*, 228d.
14 Ibid., 235a.
15 Ibid., 236e.
16 Ibid., 237a.
17 Ibid., 238d.
18 Ibid., 242d.
19 Ibid., 243b.
20 Ibid., 269d.
21 Ibid., 270e.
22 Ibid., 271b.
23 Ibid., 275a.
24 Ibid., see Derrida (1981).
25 *Gorgias*, 479b.
26 *Phaedrus*, 258d.
27 Ibid., 260c–d.
28 Ibid., 267a–b.
29 Ibid., 268c.
30 Ibid., 268d.

Chapter 7

1 See Werner Jaeger, *Paideia* (1965), and Gadamer (1980).
2 *Protagoras*, 315a.
3 Jaeger (1965), vol. 1, p. 300.

4 See Hermann Diels, ed., *Die Fragmente der Vorsocratiker* (1934).
5 Jaeger (1965), vol. 1, p. 5.
6 Ibid., p. 291.
7 See Marcel Detienne and Jean-Pierre Vernant, *Cunning and Intelligence in Greek Culture and Society* (1978).
8 See Jaeger (1965), vol. 1, p. 292.
9 The rise of anthropology in the nineteenth century, simultaneously in the United States and in England, illustrates the point with vivid colors. The cultures studied by anthropologists were those of the "others," different from "ours." They were patterned and expressively organized so that "we" could study them. "Our" culture in turn was fuzzy, in a constant process of change difficult to grasp and easily causing malaise. "Our" culture, after all, was the sole ground where anthropologists could stand, glance at the "others," and make sense of their existence. "Our" culture provided "us" with the ingredients necessary to make our picture of the world, as much as any other cultures did to their members, but claiming to be cleverer than the "others," we thought that our representations were not merely idiosyncratic congeries. We supposed they were "scientific" and took into account the "natives' point of view." This belief in the infallibility of ethnographic objectivity has subsided, but the resistance to study "our" own culture has remained intact, by and large underscored by the belief that it is unfathomable.
10 The distinction of rhetoric and ethics is a recurring theme in the Western heritage which Adorno and Benjamin addressed in their work in a compelling tour de force. Living in a time of reaction against scientism, they chose the aesthetic value, rather than scientific truth, as their objective. Benjamin, like Socrates, regarded the style and even the medium of production of the art object as a legitimate ground for the political battle of persuasion, while Adorno, from a more Platonic standing, claimed that aesthetic truth resided in the immanence of form to be captured in the moment of production of the art object. Benjamin, in turn, saw production and reception as inseparable. Naturally, neither one thought that art could transform the world, but they certainly believed that it occupied a central position, and that by moving it one could start a chain reaction in the entire world system. Bertold Brecht, who exercised a strong influence upon this Benjamin (Benjamin had a second, Janus face shaped after Jewish religious traditions), wrote: "I refuse to utilize my talent 'freely,' I utilize it as an educator, politician, organizer. There is no reproach against my literary persona-plagiarist, disturber of the peace, saboteur—which I would not claim as a complement for my unliterary, anonymous, yet systematic procedure." Quoted in Richard Wolin's *Walter Benjamin: An Aesthetic of Redemption* (1982), p. 146. Benjamin and Adorno somehow echoed the debate between the Sophists and Socrates. In ancient Greece Socrates did not succeed in making truth triumph over rhetoric, except in Plato's dia-

logues, and in recent times, Adorno does not seem to have vindicated an aesthetic of production of the object of art. Benjamin showed that the production and reception of the object of art were tantamount to aesthetic value; the Sophists likewise, and Socrates on their trail, showed that rhetoric could not be severed from truth. For a discussion of this question in Adorno's and Benjamin's writings, see R. Lane Kauffmann, *The Theory of the Essay: Lukács, Adorno, and Benjamin* (1981). See Andrew Arato and Eike Gebhardt, especially part 2, which contains Benjamin's article, "The Author as Producer," and Adorno's "On the Fetish-Character in Music and the Regression of Listening," both classics in the Frankfurt School. See also Wolin (1982) and Susan Buck-Morss, *The Origin of Negative Dialectic* (1977).

11 See *Gorgias*, 484c–85d.
12 The diagnostic of the times signalling a crisis of confidence stirred by the split between rhetoric and knowledge also seems to be a recurring theme in the Western tradition. In the present century it has emerged rather forcefully in social philosophy on the cusp of the Romantic and Modern eras, in Max Weber's writings, for example, and in the Frankfurt School's reaction against doctrinaire science and politics which many regard now as a precious epitaph for modernity.
13 See Diels (1934), p. 15.
14 Ibid.
15 Ibid.
16 See *The Medical Works of Hippocrates* (1950).
17 Jaeger (1965), vol. 1, p. 306, and vol. 2, pp. 32–34.
18 *Phaedrus*, 268c.
19 Ibid., 270b.
20 *Gorgias*, 475d.
21 Ibid., 448c.
22 Ibid., 450.
23 Ibid., 450d.
24 Ibid., 451d.
25 Ibid., 452d.
26 Ibid., 452e.
27 Ibid., 454b.
28 Ibid., 455a.
29 Ibid., 456b.
30 Ibid., 460d.
31 Ibid., 463d.
32 Ibid., 467c.
33 Ibid., 477–78.
34 Ibid., 481b.
35 Ibid., 464b, 465a, 501a.
36 Gadamer attaches great importance to the notion of "sensus communis"

throughout philosophy as a shelter against the imperialistic onslaught of method and science claiming hegemony over the faculty of knowing. See Hans-Georg Gadamer, *Truth and Method* (1975), p. 19ff.

37   Cf. *Protagoras*, 312b.
38   Ibid., 312c.
39   Ibid., 312d.
40   Cf. Jaeger (1965), vol. 2, p. 108.
41   *Protagoras*, 318e.
42   Ibid., 323d.
43   Ibid., 332e.
44   Ibid., 333c.
45   Ibid., 334d.
46   Ibid.
47   Ibid., 335a.
48   Ibid., 335b.
49   Ibid., 336b.
50   Ibid., 336d.
51   Ibid., 338c.
52   Ibid., 338d.
53   Ibid., 350d.
54   Ibid., 351a.
55   Ibid., 352d.
56   Ibid., 352b.
57   Ibid., 352c.
58   Ibid., 353a.
59   Ibid., 356c.
60   Ibid., 357d.
61   Ibid., 359b.

Chapter 8

1   The goal of Parmenides and the other thinkers of Elea such as Zeno and Melissus was to found all knowledge on pure reason.
2   Jaeger (1965), vol. 2, pp. 17–18.
3   See Mikhail Bakhtin, *Problems of Dostoevsky's Poetics* (1973), pp. 87–100.
4   Ibid., p. 88.
5   Ibid., p. 89.
6   Ibid., p. 91.
7   Gadamer (1980), p. 190.
8   Ibid.
9   Derrida shows the pitfalls of this separation present in de Saussure's project, responsible in great part for a science of linguistics describing languages as systems of signs with a relative autonomy from meaning. See Jacques Derrida, *Of Grammatology* (1974).
10   See *Theaetetus*, 201a–c, 186e–87a.

11 See *Republic,* 534 and ff.
12 *Theaetetus,* 170.
13 *Euthyphro,* 14b.
14 Ibid., 14c.
15 *Theaetetus,* 148e.
16 Ibid., 148e.
17 Ibid., 149a.
18 Ibid., 149d.
19 Ibid., 150d.
20 Gadamer discusses the triviality of historical objectivity, which like statistics pretends that facts speak for themselves above and beyond historical frames, as if these facts were not revealed as answers to certain questions, and these questions, in turn, were not bound to historical horizons. See Gadamer (1975), pp. 268ff.
21 "Seventh Letter," 326a–b.
22 Gadamer (1980), p. 201.
23 Ibid.
24 "Seventh Letter," 325ff.
25 The translator of Gadamer's studies, Christopher Smith, notes that there are three senses of dialectic mingling in the essays on Plato: first, the sense of maieutic, "the back-and-forth of discussion"; second, "the sophistic rhetorical skill of reducing a position or an assertion to an absurdity"; third, the philosophical operation of "collecting and of differentiating according to essence," which in our essay corresponds to methexis. Gadamer (1980) p. 1, n. 1. Gadamer also recognizes an "unwritten dialectic" in Plato expressed through the tension between word and deed and between unity and multiplicity, two aporias which Plato sets out to resolve.
26 *Republic,* 497b and 494a.
27 Jaeger (1965), vol. 2, p. 47.
28 *Phaedrus,* 266b.

Chapter 9

1 Bennett Simon, *Mind and Madness in Ancient Greece* (1978).
2 Ibid., p. 220.
3 Ibid., p. 224.
4 Jaeger (1965), vol. 2, p. 63.
5 *Republic,* 337e.
6 *Gorgias,* 513c.
7 Simon (1978), p. 188.
8 My descriptions of these five dimensions of consensus bear resemblance to Habermas' four validity claims constitutive of discourse. They are comprehensibility, truth, sincerity, and normative rightness. See Jürgen Habermas, *Communication and the Evolution of Society* (1979). While Habermas' discussion aims at the foundation of speech in terms of a communicative

competence, my own addresses the reflection about communication in the Western tradition in terms of a cultural habitude.

9   *Crito*, 46b.

10 *Crito*, 49a.

11 The strategy of making an interlocutor speak in order to expose and overcome emotions, which otherwise, benefiting from concealment, could grow into monstrous feelings and threaten reason, can be described through different portrayals and imputed to a variety of causes. Therapists of a classical Freudian persuasion regard this confessional talking as a vehicle for reason to penetrate the realm of emotions. Several revisionist schools of psychotherapy agree that speech is itself an exercise of the emotions and that by talking about loaded experiences the speaker gradually reduces their impact over his emotions. The two different views do not deny one another. According to the first, the "negative emotions" remain *within* the psyche, but can be dispelled by reason represented by speech. In the second case, speech/reason acts as a channel to draw the "negative emotions" out of the psyche. There are no substantive differences, in this regard, between Socrates and Freud, or between Freud and any revisions of psychotherapeutic discourse. A departure from this cultural outlook would consist, for example, in finding a metaphor different from container/content for the pair psyche/emotions, or in breaking away from the classification of emotions into negative and positive. Another line of cultural alternatives could part reason and speech, or blast the dichotomy between reason and emotion. By juxtaposing Socrates and Freud, and contrasting the metaphorical way of their thinking with fictional alternatives (they could also be concrete) we unravel the cultural context of the Western heritage.

12 *Crito*, 49d.

13 Socrates' claim for consensus around power asymmetry and divergence of opinion is similar to Habermas' contention that normative rightness must be redeemed together with the other three validity claims constitutive of speech (comprehensibility, truth, and sincerity) before challenges can be launched. This is a very interesting similarity because it reveals the long-standing view of the Western heritage according to which reason dwells in the willingness to tolerate every adversity (of injustice, of power domination, of wrong opinion) before it expresses itself to restore justice. The Greco-Roman and Euro-American cultural heritage has regarded acts of response that do not allow for that which they are in response to, to fully spell itself out as acts of terrorism and violence.

14 Argument in the dialogues is indeed not treated as sacred. The metaphors for argument are rather revealing of its secular character for Plato. An argument can be like a hunt, its subject matter being the prey. The discussants may find themselves hunting an argument. Arguments are like horses or other animals, they must be harnessed, yoked, let on the loose, or have their reins slackened. They volley, swarm, and fly away. The sea, the

winds, and the rivers are also built into similes. Thus, arguments can be like waves, a sea of words, calm or rough they blow indicating the course to be followed, and are winding like rivers and can be forded. Most interestingly, the speakers not only weave arguments and use them for different purposes, but can be affected by them in unexpected ways. The argument can do with us what it wills or even knock us out, which means that they do not always appeal to reason or unfold in a rational way.

15　*Republic*, 487b–d.

16　*Republic*, 489a.

Chapter 10

1　*Theaetetus*, 197a–c.

2　Ibid., 199a.

3　Ibid., 199c.

4　Ibid., 199e.

5　Werner Jaeger (1965), vol. 2, p. 70.

6　The discussion of Socrates' divine mission appears in *Apology*, 20d and ff.

7　See W. Jaeger (1965), vol. 2, pp. 68–69.

8　*Phaedo*, 76a.

9　Ibid., 76b and 76d–e.

10　*Meno*, 70a.

11　Ibid., 72a.

12　Ibid., 75b.

13　Ibid., 76d.

14　Ibid., 77b.

15　Ibid., 79b.

16　Ibid., 80a.

17　Ibid., 80c.

18　Ibid., 80d.

19　Ibid., 80e.

20　Ibid., 81c–d.

21　Ibid., 81d.

22　Ibid., 84a.

23　Ibid., 84b.

24　This hermeneutic caution is identical to Gadamer's discussion of the role of prejudices in knowledge formation. See Gadamer (1975), pp. 238 and ff.

25　*Meno*, 85c–d.

26　See Walter Ong (1982), pp. 31 and ff., for an exposition of the principle of learning by recollection in the context of oral cultures.

27　*Meno*, 86c.

28　Ibid., 91b.

29　Ibid., 91c–e.

30　Ibid., 92e.

31　Ibid., 93a.

32 Ibid., 94e.
33 Ibid., 95a.
34 Ibid., 96b.
35 Ibid., 96c.
36 Ibid., 97a–b.
37 Ibid., 98a.
38 Ibid., 98c–d.
39 Ibid., 99c.
40 Ibid., 100a.
41 See H. Sinaiko, *Love, Knowledge, and Discourse in Plato: Dialogue and dialectic in* Phaedrus, Republic, Parmenides (1979).
42 *Sophist*, 217c.
43 *Theaetetus*, 183b.
44 In the current times of intellectual skepticism about the existence of an essential quality grounding all knowledge, Jürgen Habermas stands out as one of the very few who cherishes that claim. He argues that the cacophony of the universe of discourse can be cleansed and the distortion of ideological discourse eliminated with the reestablishment of the claim for emancipation through the exercise of communicative actions. No matter how distorted communication has become, man's ability to recognize a question and an answer, a command and the adequate response to it precedes every social, cultural, and historical interest, and therefore can rise above ideological discourse and restore the quest for freedom and emancipation. He calls this ability "communicative competence" and discusses it in the light of the theory of speech acts as proposed by the British analytic philosophers of language. See Habermas (1984).
45 *Parmenides*, 127d–e.
46 Ibid., 29a–c.
47 Ibid., 130b–e.
48 Ibid., 130e.
49 Ibid., 131.
50 Ibid., 132b.
51 Gadamer (1980), p. 03.
52 Ibid.
53 See Gadamer's translator Christopher Smith's note 9, on p. 203. The limitedness of the horizons of truth of our knowledge at any historical moment is the cornerstone of Gadamer's hermeneutics. Hegel, one of Gadamer's points of reference, grounds truth on the idea of wholeness, therefore transcending historical moments; Plato, another point of reference for Gadamer, recognizes the tension between historical and universal truth and tries to resolve it. I believe that Gadamer is more attracted to Plato's struggle than to Hegel's solution.
54 *Parmenides*, 132d.
55 Ibid., 133a. The infinite regress in the relation between ideas and things is known in Plato's scholarship as "the third man argument."

56 *Parmenides,* 133e.
57 Ibid., 134a–b.
58 Ibid., 134c.
59 Ibid., 135b–c. Emphasis added.
60 Ibid., 136a.
61 *Phaedrus,* 274c–275a.

Chapter 11

1 S. Freud, *Totem and Taboo,* (1913b).
2 Jay Haley's treatment of his "Modern Little Hans" can be explained in the same terms of the duality or emotions proposed by Freud although, as a family therapist, he conducts the treatment dealing exclusively with the symptom (the fear of dogs), and not with the underlying meaning of symbols typical of psychoanalysis. See Haley (1977).
3 Gadamer (1975), p. 347.

Chapter 12

1 Stephen Tyler, *The Said and the Unsaid: Mind, Meaning and Culture* (1978), p. 167.
2 Walter Benjamin, *The Origin of the German Tragic Drama* (1977), p. 37.
3 See Martin Heidegger, *On the Way to Language* (1971), pp. 1–56.
4 Wittgenstein began his inquiry, in his *Tractatus,* with the assumption that all knowledge was encompassed within language, only to later realize that this was not the case, and that there were no limits to the games one could play with language. See L. Wittgenstein, *Tractatus Logico-Philosophicus* (1961), and *Philosophical Investigations* (1968).

BIBLIOGRAPHY

Abeles, Gina
1975   *The Double Bind: Paradox in Relationships.* Unpublished Ph.D.
                dissertation, Department of Psychology, Boston University.
                University Microfilms.
Adorno, Theodor
1978   "On the Fetish-Character in Music and the Regression of
                Listening." In *The Essential Frankfurt School Reader.* Edited and
                with introductions by Andrew Arato and Eike Gebhardt, 270–
                99. New York: Urizen Books.
Arato, Andrew, and Eike Gebhardt, eds.
1978   *The Essential Frankfurt Reader.* New York: Urizen Books.
Bakhtin, Mikhail
1973   *Problems of Dostoevsky's Poetics.* Translated by R. W. Rotsel.
                New York: Ardis.
Bateson, Gregory
1972   "Form, Substance, and Difference." In *Steps to an Ecology of
                Mind,* 448-66. New York: Ballantine Books.
Bateson, Gregory, D. Jackson, J. Haley, and J. Weakland
1956   "Toward a Theory of Schizophrenia." *Behavioral Science* 1,
                no. 4.
Benjamin, Walter
1977   *The Origin of the German Tragic Drama.* Translated by John
                Osborne. London: New Left Books.
Bettelheim, Bruno
1982   *Freud and Man's Soul.* New York: Vintage Books.
Bowen, Murray
1978   *Family Therapy in Clinical Practice.* New York: Jason Aronson.
Buck-Morss, Susan
1977   *The Origin of Negative Dialectic.* New York: Free Press.
Crapanzano, Vincent
1985   *Waiting: The Whites of South Africa.* New York: Random
                House.
Derrida, Jacques
1974   *Of Grammatology.* Translated by Gayaatri Chakravorty
                Spivak. Baltimore: The Johns Hopkins University Press.
1978   *Writing and Difference.* Translated by Alan Bates. Chicago:
                University of Chicago Press.
1981   *Dissemination.* Translated by Barbara Johnson. Chicago: Uni-
                versity of Chicago Press.

Bibliography

Detienne, Marcel, and Jean-Pierre Vernant
1978   *Cunning and Intelligence in Greek Culture and Society*. Atlantic Highlands, N.J.: Humanities Press.

Diels, Hermann, ed.
1934   *Die Fragmente der Vorsocratiker*. Revised by Walter Krauz, 1964. Zurich and Berlin.

Erikson, Erik
1963   *Childhood and Society*. New York: W. W. Norton.

Fisch, Richard, J. H. Weakland and L. Segal
1982   *The Tactics of Change: Doing Therapy Briefly*. New York: Jossey-Bass.

Freud, Anna
1968   *The Widening Scope of Indications for Psychoanalysis: Discussion*. The Writings of Anna Freud. New York: International Universities Press.

Freud, Sigmund
1895   *Project for a Scientific Psychology*. Standard Edition vol. 1. London: Hogarth Press, 1966.
1900   *The Interpretation of Dreams*. Translated and edited by James Strachey. S. E. vol. 5. New York: Avon Books, 1965.
1905   *Three Essays on the Theory of Sexuality*. S. E. vol. 7. London: Hogarth Press, 1953.
1913a   "On Beginning the Treatment," in *Therapy and Technique*. Translated by Philip Rieff. S. E. vol. 12. New York: Collier Books, 1963.
1913b   *Totem and Taboo*. Translated by James Strachey. S. E. vol. 13. New York: W. W. Norton, 1956.
1914a   *On the History of the Psychoanalytic Movement*. Translated by Joan Riviere. Edited by James Strachey. S. E. vol. 14. New York: W. W. Norton.
1914b   "Remembering, Repeating and Working Through," in *Further Recommendations on the Technique of Psychoanalysis II*. Translated and edited by James Strachey. S. E. vol. 12. London: Hogarth Press, 1958.
1916a   *A Connection between a Symbol and a Symptom*. Translated and edited by James Strachey. S. E. vol. 14. London: Hogarth Press, 1963.
1916b   *Introductory Lectures on Psychoanalysis*. Translated and edited by James Strachey. S. E. vol. 16. New York: W. W. Norton, 1966.
1920   *Beyond the Pleasure Principle*. Translated and edited by James Strachey. S. E. vol. 18. New York: W. W. Norton, 1961.
1923   *The Ego and the Id*. Translated and edited by James Strachey. S. E. vol. 19. W. W. Norton, 1960.
1925   *An Autobiographic Study*. Translated and edited by James Strachey. S. E. vol. 20. London: Hogarth Press, 1959.

1926   *Inhibitions, Symptoms and Anxiety*. Translated by Alix
                Strachey and edited by James Strachey. S. E. vol. 20. New
                York: W. W. Norton, 1959.
1927   *The Future of an Illusion*. Translated and edited by James
                Strachey. S. E. vol. 21. New York: W. W. Norton, 1961.
1930   *Civilization and Its Discontents*. Translated and edited by
                James Strachey. S. E. vol. 21. New York: W. W. Norton, 1961.
Gadamer, Hans-Georg
1975   *Truth and Method*. New York: Continuum.
1980   *Dialogue and Dialectic: Eight Hermeneutical Studies on Plato*.
                Translated by P. Christopher Smith. New Haven: Yale
                University Press.
Geertz, Clifford
1986   *Works and Lives: The Anthropologist as Author*. Stanford: Stan-
                ford University Press.
Gill, Merton M.
1982   *Analysis of Transference*, vol. 1: *Theory and Technique*. Psycho-
                logical Issues Monograph 53. New York: International Uni-
                versities Press.
Gill, Merton M., and Irwin Z. Hoffman
1982   *Analysis of Transference*, vol.2: *Studies of Nine Audio-Recorded
                Psychoanalytic Sessions*. Psychological Issues Monograph 54.
                New York: International Universities Press.
Grunbaum, Adolf
1984   *The Foundations of Psychoanalysis: A Philosophical Critique*.
                Berkeley: University of California Press.
Habermas, Jürgen
1971   *Knowledge and Human Interests*. Boston: Beacon Press.
1979   *Communication and the Evolution of Society*. Translated by
                Thomas McCarthy. Boston: Beacon Press.
1984   *The Theory of Communicative Action*. Translated by Thomas
                McCarthy. Vol. 1. Boston: Beacon Press.
Haley, Jay
1976   "Development of a Theory: A History of a Research Project."
                In Carlos Sluzki and Donald Ransom, eds., *Double Bind: The
                Foundation of the Communicational Approach to the Family*.
                New York: Grune and Stratton.
1977   *Problem Solving Therapy*. New York: Harper and Row.
Hartmann, Heinz
1958   *Ego Psychology and the Problem of Adaptation*. Translated by
                David Rapaport. New York: International Universities Press.
Heidegger, Martin
1971   *On the Way to Language*. Cambridge: Harper and Row.
Hippocrates
1950   *The Medical Works of Hippocrates*. Translated by John
                Chadwick and W. V. Mann. Oxford: Blackwell Scientific
                Publications.

270

Bibliography

Hoffman, Lynn
1981   *Foundations of Family Therapy*. New York: Basic Books.
Holzman, Philip
1970   *Psychoanalysis and Psychopathology*. New York: McGraw-Hill.
Jaeger, Werner
1965   *Paideia*, 3 volumes. Translated by Gilbert Highet. New York:
                      Oxford University Press.
Kauffmann, R. Lane
1981   *The Theory of the Essay: Lukács, Adorno and Benjamin*. Ph.D.
                      dissertation, University of California, San Diego.
Keeney, Bradford P., and Jeffrey M. Ross
1985   *Mind in Therapy: Constructing Systemic Family Therapies*. New
                      York: Basic Books.
Lasch, Christopher
1979   *The Culture of Narcissism*. New York: W. W. Norton.
Lyotard, Jean-François
1979   *La Condition Postmoderne*. Paris: Les Editions de Minuit.
Maranhão, Tullio
1984   "Family Therapy and Anthropology." *Culture, Medicine, and
                      Psychiatry* 8:255–79.
Marcus, George E., and Michael M. J. Fischer
1986   *Anthropology as Cultural Critique: An Experimental Moment in
                      the Human Sciences*. Chicago: University of Chicago Press.
Marcuse, Herbert
1961   *Eros and Civilization*. New York: Vintage Books.
Maturana, Humberto R., and F. J. Varela
1980   *Autopoiesis and Cognition: The Realization of the Living*. Boston:
                      Riedel.
Minuchin, Salvador
1974   *Families and Family Therapy*. Cambridge: Harvard University
                      Press.
1984   *Family Kaleidoscope*. Cambridge: Harvard University Press.
Minuchin, Salvador, B. Rosman, and L. Baker
1978   *Psychosomatic Families: Anorexia Nervosa in Context*. Cam-
                      bridge: Harvard University Press.
Obeyesekere, Gananath
1981   *Medusa's Hair*. Chicago: University of Chicago Press.
Ong, Walter
1982   *Orality and Literacy*. New York: Methuen.
Plato
1961   *The Collected Dialogues*. Edited by Edith Hamilton and Hunt-
                      ington Cairns. Bollingen Series 71. Princeton: Princeton
                      University Press.
Rabinow, Paul, ed.
1985   *Foucault Reader*. New York: Pantheon Books.

Rapaport, David
1960   *The Structure of Psychoanalytic Theory: A Systematizing Attempt.* Psychological Issues, Monograph 6. New York: International Universities Press.
Ricoeur, Paul
1974   *The Conflict of Interpretations.* Evanston: Northwestern University Press.
1981   *Hermeneutics and the Human Sciences.* Edited and translated by John B. Thompson. New York: Cambridge University Press.
Rieff, Philip
1968   *The Triumph of the Therapeutic: Uses of Faith after Freud.* New York: Harper and Row.
Schafer, Roy
1976   *A New Language for Psychoanalysis.* New Haven: Yale University Press.
1980   "Narration in the Psychoanalytic Dialogue." *Critical Inquiry* (Autumn):29–53.
Schleiermacher, Friedrich
1973   *Introductions to the Dialogues of Plato.* New York: Arno Press.
Segal, Hanna
1964   *Introduction to the Work of Melanie Klein.* New York: Basic Books.
Simon, Bennett
1978   *Mind and Madness in Ancient Greece.* Ithaca: Cornell University Press.
Sinaiko, Herman
1979   *Love, Knowledge, and Discourse in Plato: Dialogue and Dialectic* in Phaedrus, Republic, *and* Parmenides. Chicago: University of Chicago Press.
Sluzki, Carlos, and Donald Ransom, eds.
1976   *Double Bind: The Foundation of the Communicational Approach to the Family.* New York: Grune and Stratton.
Sluzki, Carlos, J. Beavin, A. Tarnopolsky, and E. Veron
1967   "Transactional Disqualification." *Archives of General Psychiatry* 3, no. 10:494–507.
Spence, Donald P.
1982   *Narrative Truth and Historical Truth: Meaning and Interpretation in Psychoanalysis.* New York: W. W. Norton.
Stein, Howard F.
1980   "Bowen 'Family Systems Theory': The Problem of Cultural Persistence, and the Differentiation of Self in One's Culture." *The Family* 8,1:21–51.
Stierlin, Helm
1977   *Psychoanalysis and Family Therapy.* New York: Jason Aronson.

Bibliography

Tyler, Stephen A.
1978   *The Said and the Unsaid: Mind, Meaning and Culture.* New
                York: Academic Press.
1984   "Ethnography, Intertextuality and the End of Description."
                Department of Anthropology, Rice University. Forthcoming
                in the *American Journal of Semiotics.*
Wagner, Roy
1981   *The Invention of Culture.* Chicago: University of Chicago
                Press.
Weber, Max
1964   *The Sociology of Religion.* Translated by Ephraim Fischoffs.
                Boston: Beacon Press.
1978   *Economy and Society,* 2 volumes. Edited by Guenther Roth and
                Claus Wittich. Berkeley: University of California Press.
Winnicott, Donald W.
1964   *The Child, the Family, and the Outside World.* Middlesex:
                Penguin Books.
1971   *Playing and Reality.* New York: Basic Books.
Wittgenstein, Ludwig
1961   *Tractatus Logico-Philosophicus.* Translated by D. F. Pears and
                B. F. McGuinnes. London: Routledge & Kegan Paul.
1968   *Philosophical Investigations.* Translated by G. E. M. Ans-
                combe. New York: Macmillan.
Wolin, Richard
1982   *Walter Benjamin: An Aesthetic of Redemption.* New York:
                Columbia University Press.
Wollheim, Richard
1984   *The Thread of Life.* Cambridge: Harvard University Press.

INDEX

COMPOSED BY POLEBRIDGE PRESS, BONNER, MONTANA
MANUFACTURED BY EDWARDS BROTHERS, INC., ANN ARBOR, MICHIGAN
TEXT AND DISPLAY LINES ARE SET IN PALATINO

Library of Congress Cataloging-in-Publication Data
Maranhão, Tullio.
Therapeutic discourse and Socratic dialogue.
(Rhetoric of the human sciences)
Bibliography: pp. 267–272.
Includes index.
1. Family psychotherapy. 2. Communication in
psychiatry. 3. Socrates—Contributions in psychotherapy.
4. Rhetoric and psychology. 5. Psychoanalysis and
culture. 6. Psychoanalysis and philosophy. I. Title.
II. Series (DNLM: 1. Family Therapy—methods.
2. Psychoanalysis—methods. WM 460 M311t]
RC488.5.M34   1986   616.89'156   84–40056
ISBN 0–299–10920–8